A Guide to Conversational Hindi

HINDI
FOR BEGINNERS

**Sunita Mathur Narain
and Madhumita Mehrotra**

TUTTLE Publishing

Tokyo | Rutland, Vermont | Singapore

ABOUT TUTTLE
"Books to Span the East and West"

Our core mission at Tuttle Publishing is to create books which bring people together one page at a time. Tuttle was founded in 1832 in the small New England town of Rutland, Vermont (USA). Our fundamental values remain as strong today as they were then—to publish best-in-class books informing the English-speaking world about the countries and peoples of Asia. The world has become a smaller place today and Asia's economic, cultural and political influence has expanded, yet the need for meaningful dialogue and information about this diverse region has never been greater. Since 1948, Tuttle has been a leader in publishing books on the cultures, arts, cuisines, languages and literatures of Asia. Our authors and photographers have won numerous awards and Tuttle has published thousands of books on subjects ranging from martial arts to paper crafts. We welcome you to explore the wealth of information available on Asia at **www.tuttlepublishing.com**.

Published by Tuttle Publishing, an imprint of Periplus Editions (HK) Ltd.

www.tuttlepublishing.com

Copyright © 2017 Periplus Editions (HK) Ltd.

ISBN 978-0-8048-4438-3

20 19 18 17   5 4 3 2 1   1703CM

Printed in China

Distributed by:

North America, Latin America & Europe
Tuttle Publishing
364 Innovation Drive
North Clarendon,
VT 05759-9436 U.S.A.
Tel: 1 (802) 773-8930
Fax: 1 (802) 773-6993
info@tuttlepublishing.com
www.tuttlepublishing.com

Asia-Pacific
Berkeley Books Pte. Ltd.
61 Tai Seng Avenue #02-12
Singapore 534167
Tel: (65) 6280-1330
Fax: (65) 6280-6290
inquiries@periplus.com.sg
www.periplus.com

Contents

सरस्वती नमस्तुभ्यम वरदे कामरूपिणी।
विद्यारंभम करिष्यामी सिद्धीर्भवतु मे सदा।।
(ऋषि अगस्त्य)

"Salutations to Devi Saraswati, the patron
of blessings and fulfiller of wishes
O Devi Saraswati, be my muse, bestow upon me the powers
of knowledge and wisdom as I am initiating my learning."

—Sage Agastya

Welcome

Namaskar! We welcome you to the world of Hindi and invite you to learn and experience the third-most spoken language of the world. Learning any language is challenging; we ourselves are no exception to this. So on behalf of fellow language learners we present this book as your step-by-step guide in acquiring the skills to accurately communicate as well as understand the cultural aspects that come with learning the language.

Acknowledgments

We would like to express our gratitude to Devi Saraswati, who has given us the intellect and powered our pen to write this book; our fathers, the late Dr. Lalit Behari Lal Mathur and Mr. K. K. Sarkar; and our mothers, Mrs. Sarla Mathur and Mrs Bani Sarkar, who gave us their blessing, and the will, and the desire to learn and grow, and ultimately empower others.

We would especially like to thank our family members Beena Mathur, Devanshu Mehrotra, Hina Mathur Shehzad, Khurram Shehzad, Madhvi Mathur and Prerna Mathur, who have provided us with the current language trends in India. We would also like to acknowledge and thank our dear friend Carmen Ibarra, (Sunita's) neighbor Renata Rios, son Sameer Mathur Narain, and daughters Rakhi Mathur Narain and Nikita Majumdar for becoming our alpha field testers and translators, and of course our dearest husbands Rishi Mathur Narain and Rajeev Mehrotra for their continued support and encouragement.

We would also like to thank Dr. Roshan Bharti, who helped us by lending his voice in the conversations.

Introduction

The idea of this book came from our belief in the importance of maintaining our students' Hindi language skills; not only in reading and writing but also in the communicative competence they have acquired in a year's time period. It's possible they may have forgotten some of the concepts after finishing their Basic Hindi Course—we want to solidify its presence. We also feel that there are a growing number of heritage language speakers from different parts of the world—as well as the new generation of Indians born and brought up outside of India—who need to learn and keep their mother tongue, the Indian culture, customs, norms and behaviors that are part and parcel of being Indian. Hence, this book *Hindi for Beginners.*

This book is designed for self-study, aimed at people who travel extensively, work and/or live in India, take some private lessons, but who may not have time for a proper classroom course. *Hindi for Beginners* will cover all the basics, starting with meeting and greeting others, getting around, dining etc. We have also provided lessons on how to behave appropriately and respectfully, upon meeting or dealing with someone in India.

The simple and effective introduction to Hindi pronunciation teaches you the basics of its sound system. Keep listening to the audio recordings of these sounds, until you are able to master the various sounds. Once you are able to pronounce or speak the Hindi words, you will be able to converse with other Hindi speakers and survive in India.

Keeping those facets in mind, those who have no linguistic background will appreciate that the grammar section in each lesson is purposefully kept simple yet detailed. Each new concept is clearly explained with many examples, thus making it ideal for anyone who wants a thorough review. The exercises aim to reinforce sentence patterns and vocabulary learned, as well as test your understanding of listening comprehension. Dialogues are kept very conversational, practical and colloquial. It is the sort of language book that would not intimidate someone who's not sure if they're "a language person."

All the Hindi words in this book are given in Devanagari script and Romanized text, followed by English transliterations, thus enabling learners to read and understand Hindi easily. The book includes natural dialogues, clear grammar notes and vocabulary building exercises. Useful notes on culture, cuisine, and geography make understanding the language easier. An extensive English-Hindi glossary at the end of the book is included for quick reference.

The Answer Key gives suggested answers to the exercises. You should try doing the exercises first, before referring to the Answer Key.

The recordings in the audio disc teach proper pronunciation, as well as show how natural dialogues are carried out. Practice as you listen to the audios—constant practice will help tremendously in your journey to speaking and sounding like a native speaker.

Learning a language is not easy; however, perseverance and determination pays off! Take every opportunity to listen, read, speak and write it—and you'll be surprised how much easier the journey towards mastering the language becomes as time passes.

Good luck and enjoy each moment of learning Hindi!

Pronunciation Guide 🎧 00-01

The following Hindi sounds and their approximate sounds in English are listed below, first by Hindi vowels and then by consonants.

Vowels

Hindi Vowels	IPA symbols	Pronunciation (used in this book)	Similar Sounds in English
अ	a	(uh)	inherent vowel is present in all Hindi consonants as in _bus_, _cup_, and _up_
आ ा	ā	(aa)	the long /ā/, similar to _art_, _ark_, _cart_, and _smart_
इ ि	i	(i)	the short /i/, similar to _ink_, _link_, _ring_, and _Hindi_
ई ी	ī	(ee)	the long /ī/, similar to _eat_, _meek_, _geek_, and _leak_
उ ु	u	(ü)	the short /u/, similar to _book_, _cook_, _shook_ and _look_
ऊ ू	ū	(oo)	the long /ū/, similar to _root_, _hoot_, _loot_ and _boot_
ऋ ृ	ṛ	(ri)	the /ṛ/, similar to _rig_, _rim_, _bridge_ and _Chris_
ए े	e	(ay)	the /e/, similar to _ate_, _ace_, _aim_ and _gate_
ऐ ै	æ	(ai)	the /æ/, similar to _ambulance_, _ant_, _egg_ and _brag_
ओ ो	o	(o)	the short /o/, similar to _four_, _more_, _core_ and _sore_
औ ौ	au	(aw/au)	the long /o/, similar to _aura_, _awe_, _caught_, and _bought_
अं ॐ ं	an	(o/ė)	a dot over a consonant/vowel indicates a nasal sound above that vowel/consonant, similar to the nasal sound in _ring_, _bank_, _monk_, and _sang_. It represents the half **n** sound when placed between two consonants. The consonant and the nasal sound are always pronounced together to produce the nasal effect.
अ:	aḥ	Uh-huh	When a semicolon (:) is placed after a consonant it adds a _huh_ sound to the consonant. Hindi words with such a semicolon are generally seen in words derived from the Sanskrit language. There is no equivalent sound as _uh-huh_ in English.

Consonants 00-02

Hindi Consonants	IPA symbols	Pronunciation symbols (used in this book)	Similar Sounds in English
क	ka	(k-uh)	unaspirated /ka/, similar to ca*k*e, ba*k*e, and bar*k*
ख	kha	(kh-uh)	aspirated /kha/, similar to *k*eys, *c*ane, *c*ar, and *c*at
ग	ga	(g-uh)	unaspirated /ga/, similar to *g*old, *g*oose, *g*ame and *g*ate
ङ	ṅa	(ung-uh)	nasal /ṅa/, similar to /ng/ sounds in ba*ng*, sa*ng* and ga*ng*
च	ca	(ch-uh)	unaspirated /cha/, similar to the sounds in cat*ch*, mat*ch*, *ch*icken, *ch*at
छ	cha	(Ch-uh)	palatal aspirated, the closest sound is the "choo" in aa-choo the sneezing sound
ज	ja	(j-uh)	unaspirated /ja/, similar to *J*anuary, *j*ug and *j*oke
ञ	ña	(ny-uh)	nasal /ña/, similar to /ny/ sound in new
ड	ḍa	(D-uh)	unaspirated /ḍa/, similar to *d*octor, *d*og, and ba*d*
त	ta	(t-uh)	unaspirated /ta/, similar to ta*c*o, ta*m*ale in Spanish or Italian mol*t*o with a softer /ta/sound that is less explosive
थ	tha	(th-uh)	voiceless /tha/, similar to ma*th*, ba*th*, and Ca*th*y
द	da	(d-uh)	voiced /da/, similar to *th*ough, *th*en and *th*em
न	na	(n-uh)	the /na/ sound, similar to *n*eck, *n*ow, and *n*ever
प	pa	(p-uh)	unaspirated /pa/, similar to a*pp*lication, a*pp*le and a*pp*ointment
फ	pha	(ph-uh)	aspirated /pha/, similar to *p*ant, *p*ocket and *p*a*p*er
फ़	fa	(f-uh)	aspirated /fa/, similar to *f*an, *f*ix and *f*old
ब	ba	(b-uh)	unaspirated /ba/, similar to Sin*b*ad, flat*b*ed, *b*aby and *b*ag
भ	bha	(bh-uh)	aspirated /bha/, similar to a*bh*or
म	ma	(m-uh)	the nasal /ma/, similar to *m*an, *m*ango and *m*oon
य	ya	(y-uh)	the semi-vowel /ya/, similar to *y*es, *y*ale and Ma*y*a
र	ra	(r-uh)	the semi-vowel /ra/, similar to *r*ed, *r*ace and *r*oll
ल	la	(l-uh)	the semi-vowel /la/, similar to *l*amp, *l*ight and *l*ate

Hindi Consonants	IPA symbols	Pronunciation symbols (used in this book)	Similar Sounds in English
व	va/wa	(v-uh)	the semi-vowels /va/ and /wa/, similar to _van_, _walk_ and _vase_. There is no distinction in "v" and "w" in Hindi
श	śa	(sh-uh)	the /śa/ similar to _shy_, _shame_ and _shoo_
ष	ṣa	(Sh-uh)	the /ṣa/ sound, similar to _kosher_, _bash_ and _smash_
स	sa	(suh)	the/sa/sound, similar to _Sam_ and _song_
ह	ha	(huh)	the /ha/sound, similar to _hand and hope_

Sounds Unique to Hindi

These are the unique Hindi sounds:

Hindi Consonants	IPA symbols	Pronunciation symbols (used in this book)	
घ	gha	(Gh-uh)	velar aspirated
ध	dha	(dh-uh)	dental aspirated
झ	jha	(jh-uh)	palatal aspirated
ट	ṭa	(T-uh)	retroflex unaspirated
ठ	ṭha	(Th-uh)	retretroflex aspirated
ढ	ḍha	(Dh-uh)	retretroflex aspirated
ड़	ṛa	(rD-uh)	retroflex unaspirated flap
ढ़	ṛha	(rDh-uh)	retroflex aspirated flap
ण	ṇa	(rN-uh)	retroflex unaspirated flap
क्ष	kṣ	(ksh-uh)	special conjunct of क् + ष
त्र	tr	(tr-uh)	special conjunct of त् + र
ज्ञ	jñ	(gy-uh)	special conjunct of ज् + अ

Loan Sounds from Arabic, Persian and English Languages

These Hindi sounds are based on sounds from Arabic, Persian and English words:

Hindi Sounds	Pronunciation symbols	Details
क़	(q)	the /q/ is used in the words such as _quila_

ख़	(kha)	the /kha/ is used in the words such as *khaleefa*
ग़	(gha)	no equivalent
ज़	(za)	the /za/ is used in the words such as *zink*
फ़	(fa)	the /fa/ is used in the words such as *fan*

The Hindi Alphabet

Hindi is a phonetic language, which means it is spoken the same way as it is written. In Hindi there are no silent sounds or hidden letters. The Hindi language is made up of 13 vowels and 33 consonants.

Vowels in Hindi are divided into two categories: independent vowels and dependent vowels.

Independent Vowels   स्वर

The independent form of a vowel in Hindi is used when the vowel occurs alone, at the beginning of a word, or after another vowel or a consonant.

अ	आ	इ	ई	उ	ऊ	ऋ
a	ā	i	ī	u	ū	r̥
(uh)	(aa)	(i)	(ee)	(ü)	(oo)	(ri)
short	long	short	long	short	long	short

ए	ऐ	ओ	औ	अँ/अं	अ:
e	æ	o	au/aw	aṅ	uh-h
(ay)	(ai)	(o)	(au/aw)	(un/um/ung)	(aḥ)
short	long	short	long	nasal	

Dependent Vowels   मात्रा

A dependent vowel known as **matra** in Hindi is used to make a syllable. It is used to indicate that a vowel is attached to a consonant. Following are the 13 **matras** that are placed at various positions—before, after or under a consonant.

	ा	ि	ी	ु	ू	ृ
	ā	i	ī	u	ū	
	(aa)	(i)	(ee)	(ü)	(oo)	(ri)
	long	short	long	short	long	short

े	ै	ो	ौ	ँ/ं	:
e	æ	o	au/aw	aṅ	uh-h
(ay)	(ai)	(o)	(au)	(un/um/ung)	(aḥ)
short	long	short	long	nasal	

Consonant and Dependent Vowel Combined

Hindi independent vowel	Sound	Dependent vowel symbols with consonants	Position as a dependent vowel	Pronounced as
अ	uh	कृ + अ = क (kuh)	Present in all consonants	*but, cut*
आ	aa	क + ा = का (kaa)	ā sound follows a consonant	*star, bar*
इ	i	क + ि = कि (ki)	Precedes a consonant	*it, kit*
ई	ee	क + ी = की (kee)	Follows a consonant	*meat, seat*
उ	ü	क + ु = कु (kü)	Placed under or to the side of a consonant	*put, foot* *rupee*
		र + ु = रु (rü)		
ऊ	oo	क + ू = कू (koo)	Placed under or to the side of a consonant	*fool, toot* *root*
		र + ू = रू (roo)		
ऋ	ri	क + ृ = कृ (kri)	Placed under a consonant	*grip, grit*
ए	ay	क + े = के (kay)	Placed above a consonant	*gate, bate*
ऐ	ai	क + ै = कै (kai)	Placed above a consonant	*sat, rat*
ओ	o	क + ो = को (ko)	Placed to the right of a consonant	*goat, boat*
औ	au/aw	क + ौ = कौ (kau/kaw)	Placed to the right of a consonant	*caught, bought*
अं	un, um, ung	क + ं/ँ = कं/कँ (kṅ)	Placed above a consonant/ dependent vowel as a nasal symbol	*blunt, stunt*

NOTES The dependant vowel ु is used differently with the consonant र. The long sound is written as रू, and the short sound as रु. Along with a dot, the ँ *chandrabindu* (the crescent moon with a dot) is also used with a consonant using the long ा and ु vowels representing the nasal vowel.

The ऑ (au/aw) vowel

When we use English words such as *doctor, college,* and *chocolate,* Hindi uses the crescent moon sign ऑ as a dependent vowel on top of the "long ā" vowel for these words: Dawk-Tor डॉक्टर *doctor,* caw-lay-ge कॉलेज *college,* chawk-late चॉकलेट *chocolate.*

Below is a table indicating how sounds for Hindi consonants and vowels are made.

Consonants & Vowels	Pronunciation	Category
अ आ क् ख् ग् घ् ङ् ह्	At the back of the oral cavity and the tongue	Guttural/ Velar
इ ई च् छ् ज् झ् ञ् य् श	Tongue touches the palate	Palatal
ऋ ट् ठ् ड् ढ् ण् ड़् ढ़् र् ष्	Tip of the tongue curls back against the roof of the mouth	Retroflex or Cerebral
त् थ् द् ध् न् ल् स्	Tongue touches the upper teeth	Dental
उ ऊ प् फ् ब् भ् म्	Produced using both lips	Bilabial
ए ऐ	Produced near the throat with the tongue touching the roof of the mouth	(Palato-Guttural)
ओ औ	Produced near the throat by the rounding of the lips	(Labio-Guttural)

Consonants व्यंजन (with pronunciation) 🎧 00-05

	unaspirated		aspirated				nasal
Velar	क (k-uh)	ग (g-uh)	ख (kh-uh)	घ (gh-uh)			ङ (ung)
Palatal	च (ch-uh)	ज (j-uh)	छ (Ch-uh)	झ (jh-uh)			ञ (ny-uh)
Retroflex	ट (T-uh)	ड (D-uh)	ठ (Th-uh)	ड़ (rD-uh)	ढ (Dh-uh)	ढ़ (rh-uh)	ण (rN-uh)
Dental	त (t-uh)	द (d-uh)	थ (th-uh)	ध (dh-uh)			न (n-uh)
Labial	प (p-uh)	ब (b-uh)	फ (ph-uh)	भ (bh-uh)			म (m-uh)
Semi Vowels	य (y-uh)	ल (l-uh)	र (r-uh)	व (v-uh/w-uh)			
Sibilants	श (sh-uh)	स (s-uh)	ष (Sh-uh)				
Fricative	ह (h-uh)						
Conjunct	क्ष (ksh-uh)	त्र (tr-uh)	ज्ञ (gy-uh)				

The first vowel अ is inherent/present in all the consonants, without which a sound is incomplete. Every consonant is considered to be complete only when the vowel अ is added to it, for example:

क् + अ = क   ख् + अ = ख   ग् + अ = ग   घ् + अ = घ
k + uh = kuh   kh + uh = kh-uh   g + uh = guh   gh + uh = ghuh

An incomplete or half consonant is written with a *halant* (्): क्, ख्, ग्, घ्. In words ending in the inherent अ, the vowel is not pronounced separately. It is implied within a consonant. English sounds such as *bus* and *cut* in Hindi are written without explicitly showing the inherent अ vowel, such as बस and कट. The sound is not written with the ü vowel in Hindi: बुस and कुट. Therefore make sure you do not pronounce it that way. Often English speakers pronounce words such as *Ram* राम as *Rama* रामा; *Ashok* अशोक as *Ashoka* अशोका; and *Ved* वेद as *Veda* वेदा, adding the **aa** आ vowel to the last consonant. These Hindi words do not end in a dependent vowel **aa**; the **a** अ is simply inherent in the last consonant. Therefore, when pronouncing words that do not end in the dependent long **aa** आ vowel, make sure you do not add another vowel sound to it unless it is written.

🎧 00-06 **Consonants with *Matra* (Dependent Vowels):**
The Hindi Syllabary Chart with Pronunciation Used in this book

क	का	कि	की	कु	कू	के	कै	को	कौ	कं
(k-uh)	(kaa)	(ki)	(kee)	(kü)	(koo)	(kay)	(kai)	(ko)	(kaw)	(kun/m)
ख	खा	खि	खी	खु	खू	खे	खै	खो	खौ	खं
(kh-uh)	(khaa)	(khi)	(khee)	(khü)	(khoo)	(khay)	(khai)	(kho)	(khaw)	(khun/m)
ग	गा	गि	गी	गु	गू	गे	गै	गो	गौ	गं
(g-uh)	(gaa)	(gi)	(gee)	(gü)	(goo)	(gay)	(gai)	(go)	(gaw)	(gun/m)
घ	घा	घि	घी	घु	घू	घे	घै	घो	घौ	घं
(gh-uh)	(ghaa)	(ghi)	(ghee)	(ghü)	(ghoo)	(ghay)	(ghai)	(gho)	(ghaw)	(ghun/m)
च	चा	चि	ची	चु	चू	चे	चै	चो	चौ	चं
(ch-uh)	(chaa)	(chi)	(chee)	(chü)	(choo)	(chay)	(chai)	(cho)	(chaw)	(chun/m)
छ	छा	छि	छी	छु	छू	छे	छै	छो	छौ	छं
(Ch-uh)	(Chaa)	(Chi)	(Chee)	(Chü)	(Choo)	(Chay)	(Chai)	(Cho)	(Chaw)	(Chun/m)
ज	जा	जि	जी	जु	जू	जे	जै	जो	जौ	जं
(j-uh)	(jaa)	(ji)	(jee)	(jü)	(joo)	(jay)	(jai)	(jo)	(jaw)	(jun/m)
झ	झा	झि	झी	झु	झू	झे	झै	झो	झौ	झं
(jh-uh)	(jhaa)	(jhi)	(jhee)	(jhü)	(jhoo)	(jhay)	(jhai)	(jho)	(jhaw)	(jhun/m)
ट	टा	टि	टी	टु	टू	टे	टै	टो	टौ	टं
(T-uh)	(Taa)	(Ti)	(Tee)	(Tü)	(Too)	(Tay)	(Tai)	(Toe)	(Taw)	(Tun/m)
ठ	ठा	ठि	ठी	ठु	ठू	ठे	ठै	ठो	ठौ	ठं
(Th-uh)	(Thaa)	(Thi)	(Thee)	(Thü)	(Thoo)	(Thay)	(Thai)	(Tho)	(Thaw)	(Thun/m)
ड	डा	डि	डी	डु	डू	डे	डै	डो	डौ	डं
(D-uh)	(Daa)	(Di)	(Dee)	(Dü)	(Doo)	(Day)	(Dai)	(Dough)	(Daw)	(Dun/m)
ढ	ढा	ढि	ढी	ढु	ढू	ढे	ढै	ढो	ढौ	ढं
(Dh-uh)	(Dhaa)	(Dhi)	(Dhee)	(Dhü)	(Dhoo)	(Dhay)	(Dhai)	(Dho)	(Dhaw)	(Dhun/m)
त	ता	ति	ती	तु	तू	ते	तै	तो	तौ	तं
(t-uh)	(taa)	(ti)	(tee)	(tü)	(too)	(tay)	(tai)	(toe)	(taw)	(tun/m)

The Hindi Syllabary Chart for Pronunciation

थ (th-uh)	था (thaa)	थि (thi)	थी (thee)	थु (thü)	थू (thoo)	थे (thay)	थै (thai)	थो (tho)	थौ (thaw)	थं (hun/m)
द (d-uh)	दा (daa)	दि (di)	दी (dee)	दु (dü)	दू (doo)	दे (day)	दै (dai)	दो (do, though)	दौ (daw)	दं (dun/m)
ध (dh-uh)	धा (dhaa)	धि (dhi)	धी (dhee)	धु (dhü)	धू (dhoo)	धे (dhay)	धै (dhai)	धो (dho)	धौ (dhaw)	धं (dhun/m)
न (n-uh)	ना (naa)	नि (ni)	नी (nee)	नु (nü)	नू (noo)	ने (nay)	नै (nai)	नो (no)	नौ (naw)	नं (nun/m)
प (p-uh)	पा (paa)	पि (pi)	पी (pee)	पु (pü)	पू (poo)	पे (pay)	पै (pai)	पो (po)	पौ (paw)	पं (pun/m)
फ (ph-uh)	फा (phaa)	फि (phi)	फी (phee)	फु (phü)	फू (phoo)	फे (phay)	फै (phai)	फो (pho)	फौ (phaw)	फं (phun/m)
ब (b-uh)	बा (baa)	बि (bi)	बी (bee)	बु (bü)	बू (boo)	बे (bay)	बै (bai)	बो (bo)	बौ (baw)	बं (bun/m)
भ (bh-uh)	भा (bhaa)	भि (bhi)	भी (bhee)	भु (bhü)	भू (bhoo)	भे (bhay)	भै (bhai)	भो (bho)	भौ (bhaw)	भं (bhun/m)
म (m-uh)	मा (maa)	मि (mi)	मी (mee)	मु (mü)	मू (moo)	मे (may)	मै (mai)	मो (mo)	मौ (maw)	मं (mun/m)
य (y-uh)	या (yaa)	यि (yi)	यी (yee)	यु (yü)	यू (yoo)	ये (yay)	यै (yai)	यो (yo)	यौ (yaw)	यं (yun/m)
र (r-uh)	रा (raa)	रि (ri)	री (ree)	रु (rü)	रू (roo)	रे (ray)	रै (rai)	रो (ro)	रौ (raw)	रं (run/m)
ल (l-uh)	ला (laa)	लि (li)	ली (lee)	लु (lü)	लू (loo)	ले (lay)	लै (lai)	लो (lo)	लौ (law)	लं (lun/m)
व (v-uh)	वा (vaa)	वि (vi)	वी (vee)	वु (vü)	वू (voo)	वे (vay)	वै (vai)	वो (vo)	वौ (vaw)	वं (vun/m)
श (sh-uh)	शा (shaa)	शि (shi)	शी (shee)	शु (shü)	शू (shoo)	शे (shay)	शै (shai)	शो (sho)	शौ (shaw)	शं (shun/m)
ष (Sh-uh)	षा (Shaa)	षि (Shi)	षी (Shee)	षु (Shü)	षू (Shoo)	षे (Shay)	षै (Shai)	षो (Sho)	षौ (Shaw)	षं (Shun/m)
स (s-uh)	सा (saa)	सि (si)	सी (see)	सु (sü)	सू (soo)	से (say)	सै (sai)	सो (so)	सौ (saw)	सं (sun/m)

ह (h-uh)	हा (haa)	हि (hi)	ही (hee)	हु (hü)	हू (hoo)	हे (hay)	है (hai)	हो (ho)	हौ (haw)	हं (hun/m)
क्ष (ksh-uh)	क्षा (kshaa)	क्षि (kshi)	क्षी (kshee)	क्षु (kshü)	क्षू (kshoo)	क्षे (kshay)	क्षै (kshai)	क्षो (ksho)	क्षौ (kshaw)	क्षं (kshun/m)
त्र (tr-uh)	त्रा (traa)	त्रि (tri)	त्री (tree)	त्रु (trü)	त्रू (troo)	त्रे (tray)	त्रै (trai)	त्रो (tro)	त्रौ (traw)	त्रं (trun/m)
ज्ञ (gy-uh)	ज्ञा (gyaa)	ज्ञि (gyi)	ज्ञी (gyee)	ज्ञु (gyü)	ज्ञू (gyoo)	ज्ञे (gyay)	ज्ञै (gyai)	ज्ञो (gyo)	ज्ञौ (gyaw)	ज्ञं (gyun/m)

Nasal Consonants and Conjuncts

1. In every category of Hindi consonants, the last consonant is a nasal consonant, which is depicted by a dot over a consonant in modern Hindi script.
2. You will also sometimes see a crescent moon with a dot over a consonant; this is called a ***chandrabindu***. When a vowel is pronounced both with the mouth and the nose, then the ***chandrabindu*** is generally used in writing such as **funs-naa फँसना**, **maan माँ**, and **hunsaa-naa हँसाना**.
3. The consonants ङ, ण, न, and म can be used both independent and dependent.
4. A nasal conjunct is placed between two consonants. Sometimes you will see it in the half **na न** form and sometimes a dot is used to indicate nasalization.

Examples of Nasal Conjuncts

With a dot/ *chandrabindu*	With an independent consonant	English meaning
कंघा (kung-ghaa)	कङघा (kung-ghaa)	comb
कंधा (kun-dhaa)	कन्धा (kun-dhaa)	shoulder
मंदिर (mun-dir)	मन्दिर (mun-dir)	temple
बंदर (bun-der)	बन्दर (bun-der)	monkey
पाँव (paȧv)		feet
गाँव (gaȧv)		village

Let's practice combining these consonants and vowels into words and then reading them out loud. Make sure you recognize and pronounce the words correctly because a change in a consonant or a vowel in a word can change the entire meaning of the word. You can also transcribe the words as they are pronounced.

Vowels: अ आ ा इ ि ई ी उ ु ऊ ू ऋ ृ ए े

ओ ो औ ौ

ॉ (English "au" sound)   ँ ं (vowel nasalization)

Consonants:

क क़ ख ख़ ग ग़ घ   nasal ङ

च छ ज ज़ झ   nasal ञ

ट ठ ड ड़ ढ ढ़   nasal ण

त थ द ध   nasal न

प फ फ़ ब भ   nasal म

य र ल व

श ष स ह

क्ष श्र ऌ ज्ञ   (special conjuncts)

- **Two-letter words without a dependent vowel (*matra*)**   [🎧 00-07]

A अ   अख अग अछ अट अठ अड अड़

(ukh ug uhCh uhT uhTh uhD uhrD)

अंक अंख अंग अंघ अंच अंछ अंज

(uhnk uhnkh uhng uhngh uhnch uhnCh uhnj)

(inherent **a**—no *matra*)

कट गज घट चख जग झड़ टच

(cut g-uhj gh-uhT ch-uHkh jug Jh-urDh T-uhch)

कंठ खंद गंद घंट कंद चंट तंग

(kuh-unTh kh-und guh-und Gh-unT kuh-und chuh-unt tuh-ung)

- **Three-letter words without a dependent vowel (*matra*)**

कटक खटक गटक घटक चटक छटक जकड़

(CuT-Tuck kh-Tuck guh-Tuck gh-Tuck ch-Tuck Chuh-Tuck juh-kuhrD)

- **Four-letter words without a dependent vowel (*matra*)**

अचकन कचकच चकचक खचखच गदगद चकमक झटपट टमटम डगमग ढमढम

(Uhch-kuh-un kuhch-kuhch chuck-chuck khuhch-khuhch guhd-guhd chuck-muck Jh-uT-puh-T Tuh-um Tuh-um Dug-mug Dhuh-um Dhuh-um)

- **Conjunct words without a *matra* (dependent vowel)**

चक्क कच्च खच्च गच्च थक्क फक्क

(Chuh-ukk kuh-uchch khuh-uchch guh-uchch thuh-ukk phuh-ukk)

- **Two-and-three-letter words beginning with independent vowel आ**

Aa आ   आक आख आग आज आट आठ

(Aa आ aak aakh aag aaj aaT aaTh)

आँख आंग आतंक आढ़त आगाज़

(aan-kh aa-ng aa-t-unk aa-rDh-ut aagh-aaz)

- **Two-letter words with long ा *matra* (dependent vowel)**

(ाा) काका खाका गंगा चाचा छाछ जागा झाग

(kaa-kaa khaa-kaa g-ung-gaa chaa-chaa Chaa-Chuh jaa-gaa Jhaa-g)

खाँचा चाँटा जाँघ झाँका कंचा टांड काँटा

(khaȧ-chaa chaȧ-Taa jaȧ-ghuh jhaȧ-kaa k-un-chaa Taȧ-Duh kaȧ-Taa)

- **Three-letter words with long ा *matra* (dependent vowel)**

काग़ज़ मकान गागर चादर मचान अच्छा जाजम

(Kaa-guh-uz muck-aan gaa-ger chaa-der much-aan uch-Chaa jaa-jum)

- **Conjunct words with long ा *matra* (dependent vowel)**

धक्का कच्चा मग्गा छज्जा कत्था गट्ठा अध्धा दद्दा गड्डा बच्चा

(Dh-uk-kaa kuh-uch-chaa muh-ug-gaa Ch-uj-jaa kuh-uth-thaa guh-uT-Thaa Uh-dh-dhaa Duh-ud-daa guh-uDh-Dhaa buh-uch-chaa)

- **Two-letter words beginning with independent short vowel**

I इ इक इत इद इध इट इंक इंच

(ik it id idh iT ink inch)

- **Two-letter words with short ि *matra* (dependent vowel)**

(ि) टिक डिग तिल पिक फ्रिग बिल मिग

(Tick Dig til pick fig bill mig)

ताकि बाक़ि चिंता ज़िंक लिंक सिंक

(Taa-ki baa-ki chin-taa zink link sink)

- **Three-letter words with short ि *matra* (dependent vowel)**

(ि) खिसक खिंचाव त्रिकाल गिनती निकलना मिस्त्री किसका

(khi-suck khin-chaav tri-kaal gin-tee nick-ul-naa mis-tree kis-kaa)

- **Two-letter words beginning and ending with independent long vowel ई**

E ई ईख ईद कई मई गई मलाई सगाई

(Ee-kh Eed kuh-uee muh-ee guh-ee m-ul-aa-ee suh-ug-aa-ee)

- **Two-letter words with long ी *matra* (dependent vowel)**

(ी) खीरा लगी फटी गयी नीली क़ीमत खींचना

(khee-raa luh-gee fuh-Tee guh-yee nee-lee kee-muh-ut kheen-ch-naa)

- **Conjunct words with long ी *matra* (dependent vowel)**

(ी) मक्खी बच्ची कच्ची खट्टी बत्ती लम्बी मम्मी

(muck-khee bug-ghee kuh-uch-chee khuhT-Tee buh-ut-tee luh-umb-bee mummy)

• **Words with independent short vowel उ**

Ü उ   उदार उपला उबलना उफनना उमंग बउआ पउआ

       (üdaar üplaa üb-ul-naa ü-phun-naa üm-ung buh-ü-aa puh-ü-aa)

• **Words with short ु *matra* (dependent vowel)**

(ु)   मुट्ठी युक्ति मरु खुशी गुलाब टुनटुन ठुमका

       (müTh-Thee yük-tee muh-rü khü-shee ghü-laab Tün-Tün Thüm-kaa)

• **Words with independent long vowel ऊ**

OO ऊ   ऊन ऊँट ऊँघ ऊँच ऊँची ऊर्जा ऊपर

       (oon oonT oon-gh oon-chaa oon-chee oor-jaa oo-per)

• **Words with long ू *matra* (dependent vowel)**

(ू)   कूक खूब गूलर घूमना चूहा गुड्डू झाड़ू

       (koo-k khoo-b goo-ler ghoom-naa choo-haa güd-doo jhaa-rDoo)

• **Words with independent short vowel ए**

A   ए एक एढ़ी एतराज़ गए लिए किए दिए

       (ayk ay-rDhi ayt-raaz guh-yay li-yay ki-yay di-yay)

• **Words with short े *matra* (dependent vowel)**

(े)   केला खेत गेम घेरा मज़े झेलम मुझे

       (kay-laa khay-t game ghay-raa muz-ay jhay-lum müjh-ay)

• **Words with independent long vowel ऐ**

Ai ऐ   ऐब ऐग ऐनक ऐश ऐसा ऐसे ऐसी

       (aib egg ai-nuk aish aisaa ai-say ai-see)

• **Words with long ै *matra* (dependent vowel)**

(ै)   कैसा कैसी कैसे ख़ैर ग़ैर चैरी तैयारी

       (kai-saa kai-see kai-say khair ghair cherry tai-yaree)

• **Words with independent short vowel ओ**

O ओ   ओक ओखली ओम खाओ जाओ बनाओ

       (oak oak-hlee om khaao jaao bun-aao)

• **Words with short ो *matra* (dependent vowel)**

(ो)   कोयल खोल गोली घोलना चोरी छोड़ना जोड़ी

       (Ko-yal khol go-lee ghol-naa cho-ree ChorD-naa jo-rDee)

• **Words with independent long vowel औ**

Au औ   और औरत औसत औटाना औक़ात औघड़

       (awr awe-rut awe-sut awe-Taa-naa awe-qaat awe-gh-urD)

• **Words with long ौ** *matra* **(dependent vowel)**

(ौ) कौन पौन गौना बौना नौ फ़ौरन

      (kaw-n pawn gaw-naa baw-naa naw faw-run)

(The Hindi ौ (au) matra is found only in the words that are of Hindi origin. For English words having this sound the matra ॉ is used to distinguish these words from those of Hindi origin.)

Au ऑ

(These are English loanwords that carry **o** as a vowel following the first consonant in words such as *college, gossip, chocolate, Jon, Tom, doctor, pop.*)

(ॉ) कॉलेज गॉसिप चॉकलेट जॉन टॉम डॉक्टर पॉप

      (caw-lay-ge gaw-sip chawk-late jaw-n Taw-m dawk-Tor Paw-p)

Special Conjunct Consonants are used mainly in Sanskrit words.

Special Conjuncts 🎧 00-08

1st	2nd	Conjunct	Words	Sounds	English meanings
क्	ष	क्ष (ksh-uh)	शिक्षक क्षत्रिय, भिक्षा	(shick-shuck, ksh-uh-triy-uh, bhik-shaa)	teacher, warrior, alms
ज्	अ	ज्ञ (gy-uh)	ज्ञान विज्ञान, संज्ञा	(gy-aan, vig-yaan, sung-yaan)	knowledge science, noun
त्	त	त्त (tt-uh)	कुत्ता मुक्ता	(küt-taa, mük-taa)	dog, freedom
त्	र	त्र (tr-uh)	त्रिशूल सत्रह	(tri-shool, sut-ruh)	trident, seventeen
द्	म	द्म (u-dm)	पद्म पद्मा	(p-udm, p-ud-maa)	lotus
द्	य	द्य (dy-uh)	विद्या द्युति	(vid-yaa, dyü-tee)	education, luster
द्	ध	द्ध (ud-dh)	बुद्धि सिद्ध	(büdh-dhee, sidh-dhee)	intellect, proven
द्	व	द्व (dw-uh)	द्वार विद्वान	(dwaa-r, vid-waan)	door, scholar
श्	च	श्च (ushch-uh)	निश्चित पश्चिम	(nish-chit, p-ush-chim)	definite, west
श्	र	श्र (shr-uh)	मिश्री श्रम, मिश्रित	(mish-ree, shr-um, mish-rit)	crystal sugar, labor, mixed
श्	व	श्व (ushv-uh)	अश्व विश्व, श्वास	(ush-wuh, vish-wuh, sh-waas)	horse, world, breath
ह्	म	ह्म (hm-uh)	ब्रह्म ब्राह्मण, ब्रह्मा	(Bruh-hum, braah-mun, bruh-maa)	god, a priest, Brahma (God)

Regular Conjuncts  00-09

Conjunct letters are comprised of a double consonant or a half and a full consonant:

क, फ, फ़	क् + क = क्क मक्का (muk-kaa)	क् + ख = क्ख मक्खी (m-ukh-khee)	फ़् + त = फ़्त कोफ़्ता (kofe-taa)	
ग, म, प, व, च, घ, न, ध, ल, त, स, श, ष	ग् + ग = ग्ग मग्गा (muh-ug-gaa) घ् + न= घ्न विघ्न (vi-ghn) स् + स= स्स रस्सी (r-uh-us-see)	म् + म = म्म गुम्मा (gü-üm-maa) प् + प = प्प कुप्पी (kü-up-pee) श् + त = श्त गश्ती (g-ush-tee) ष् + ठ = ष्ठ कोष्ठ (kosh-Th)	न् + न = न्न चुन्नी (chün-nee) ल् + ल = ल्ल गुल्लक (gül-luck) व् + व = व्व कव्वाली (k-uw-waa-lee)	च् + च = च्च कच्ची (k-uch-chee) ज् + ज = ज्ज सज्जा (suhj-jaa) त् + थ = त्थ कत्था (k-uth-thaa)
द, ट, ठ, ड, ढ	द् + द = द्द गद्दा (guh-ud-daa)	ट् + ट = ट्ट खट्टा (kh-uT-Taa)	ठ् + ठ = ठ्ठ गठ्ठर (guh-uTh-Ther)	ड् + ड = ड्ड गुड्डा (gü-üD-Daa) ड् + ढ = ड्ढ गड्ढा (guh-uDh-Dhaa)
र When precedes a consonant/ vowel	र् + म = र्म कर्म (kuh-erm)	र् + फ़ = र्फ़ बर्फ़ (buh-erf)	र् + म + ी = र्मी गर्मी (guh-er-mee)	र् + व + े = र्वे सर्वे (sur-vey)
र When follows a consonant without inherent अ	क् + र = क्र क्रम (crum)	भ् + र = भ्र भ्रम (bhr-um)	ग् + र = ग्र ग्रह (gre-eh)	व् + र = व्र व्रत (vruh-ut)
ऋ When precedes a consonant	ग् + ऋ = गृ गृह (gri-h)	म् + ऋ = मृ मृग (mri-g)	व् + ऋ = वृ वृन्द (vri-nd)	त् + ऋ = तृ तृप्त (tript) ह् + ऋ = हृ हृदय (hri-duh-yuh)

Remember to pronounce the short **u** sound of English as an inherent अ in Hindi when it comes in the beginning or middle of an English word as mentioned above: us, up, bus, and cup. Pronounce it as the short **oo** of English as in _put, foot,_ and _book_ in places where the dependent ु appears underneath a consonant. The English speaker often gets confused while reading or writing Hindi words using both these vowels.

Abbreviations used in this book

adj.	adjective	*fem.*	feminine
adv.	adverb	*masc.*	masculine
caus.	causative	*obj.*	object
cpp.	compound postposition	*pl.*	plural
comp. v.	compound verb	*sing.*	singular
conj. v.	conjunct verb	*subj.*	subject
conj.	conjunct	*v.i.*	verb-intransitive
conj. v.i.	conjunct verb-intransitive	*v.t.*	verb-transitive
conj. v.t.	conjunct verb-transitive		

Definitions of Grammar Terms

Causative Verb—This is a linguistic term used to express that an intermediary agent has caused an action to be performed or a condition to come into being.

Compound Verb—A compound verb in Hindi is a unique feature in which two verbs are combined: the root of the main verb carries the meaning, and the second verb serves as the auxiliary or an intensifier. The auxiliary verb in the compound verbal form loses its meaning; however, it adds various shades of meaning to a sentence such as completion of an action, suggestion, polite request, capability, advice, and uncertainty.

Conjugation—The manner in which a verb changes its form to indicate number, tense, or a person. In other words, a subject–verb agreement based on gender, number, and tense.

Conjunct Verb—A conjunct verb is made up of a noun or an adjective, and the verbs करना /ker-naa/ (to do) or होना /ho-naa/ (to be), and लगना /lug-naa/ (to feel).

Direct Case—The direct case is also known as the nominative case, where a subject directly agrees with a verb in required tense. In this case a subject is never blocked by any postposition. The present and past habitual tenses, present and past progressive tenses, the future tense, and modal verbs use a subject in the direct case.

Imperatives—Imperatives in Hindi are used to give commands, orders, instructions, directions, and suggestions.

Oblique Case—In an oblique case, a noun, a pronoun, or a verb is always followed by a postposition that blocks it to agree with the verb.

Oblique Singular—When a singular marked masculine noun, a pronoun, or a verb is followed by a postposition, it is called the oblique singular. In this form, the marked singular noun, pronoun, and verb changes its form and looks like a marked masculine plural noun: कमरा-कमरे में /kum-raa/kum-ray may/ (in the room), जूता-जूते पर /joo-taa/joo-tay per/ (on the shoe), मैं को-मुझे /main ko/müjhay/ (to me), वह से-उससे /veh say/üs say/ (from him/her), and रहना-रहने के लिए /reh-naa/reh-nay kay li-yay/ (to live).

Oblique Plural—When a marked or unmarked plural masculine or feminine noun is followed by a postposition, it is called the oblique plural. In this form, the marked or unmarked plural nouns change their form and altogether take a different shape: कमरे-कमरों के सामने /kum-ray/kum-ro kay saam-nay/([*masc.*] in front of the rooms), जूते-जूतों के नीचे /joo-tay/joo-tȯ kay nee-chay/ ([*masc.*] under the shoes), and लड़कियाँ-लड़कियों के पास /lerD-ki-yaa/lerD-ki-yo kay paas/ ([*fem.*] next to girls), मेज़ें-मेज़ों के ऊपर /may-zein/may-zȯ kay ooper ([*fem.*] above the tables).

Postposition—A postposition functions similar to English prepositions. A Hindi postposition always follows a noun, a pronoun, or a verb. There are two types of postpositions: simple and compound. Simple postpositions are में /mein/ (in), से /*say*/ (from), पर /per/(on), तक /tuk/ (till), का /kaa/ (of [*masc.*]), की /kee/ (of [*fem.*]), के /kay/ (of [*masc. pl.*]), and को /ko/ (to), whereas a compound postposition is made up of के or की and the words for location or association: के लिए /kay li-yay/ (for X), के आगे /kay aa-gay/ (ahead of X), के पीछे /kay pee-chay/ (behind X), के नीचे /kay nee-chay/ (under X), की तरफ़ /kee ter-uf/ (towards X), and की बग़ल में /kee bug-ul may/ (next to X).

Intransitive Verbs—An intransitive verb is a verb that does not require a direct object for the action. It is an action word expressing activity such as आना /aa-naa/ (to come), जाना /jaa-naa/ (to go), पहुँचना /puh-hün-ch-naa/ (to reach), नहाना /nuh-haa-naa/ (to bathe), बैठना /baiTh-naa/ (to sit), उठना /üTh-naa/ (to wake up), रोना /ro-naa/ (to cry), and हँसना /huns-naa/ (to laugh).

Transitive Verbs—A transitive verb is an action verb that takes a direct object, and the verb agrees with the direct object in number, gender and tense. Examples of transitive verbs are खाना /khaa-naa/ (to eat), पीना /pee-naa/ (to drink), करना /ker-naa/ (to do), देना /day-naa/ (to give), लेना /lay-naa/ (to take), पढ़ना /perDh-naa/ (to read), and लिखना /likh-naa/ (to X).

*Read the full dialogue on page 57.

1

Personal Information

1.1 Addressing Others दूसरों को सम्बोधित करना

Objective

By the end of this lesson, you will learn how to address people properly, according to their age and status.

> 📖 **Culture Note**
>
> Addressing people properly, politely, and according to their age and status is the most important cultural practice in Indian society. As a learner of Hindi, you must remember to use the correct pronoun while addressing someone; the wrong usage may create problems.

Grammar: Basic Sentence Structure and Possessive Pronouns

Basic Sentence Structure

A Hindi sentence has the following pattern: subject + object + verb. Contrast this against a typical English sentence:

English structure			vs	Hindi structure		
I	am	John		I	John	am
Subject +	Verb +	Object		Subject +	Object +	Verb

Practice 1  01-01

Listen to the audio and repeat after each sentence. Through this exercise you will be able to practice and understand basic Hindi sentence structure.

मैं सैरा हूँ। (main Sai-raa hoo)　　　　　　I am Sara.
तुम कौन हो? (tüm kawn ho?)　　　　　　Who are you? *(informal)*

आप कैसे हैं? (aap kai-say hain?)	How are you? *(polite)*
तू कहाँ से है? (too kuh-haa say hai?)	Where are you from? *(intimate—with a person younger in age)*
आप लोग कहाँ से हैं? (aap low-g kuh-haa say hain?)	Where are you *(people)* from? *(plural)*
हम अमरीकन हैं। (hum um-ree-kun hain.)	We are Americans. *(plural)*
यह मैट है। (yeh Matt hai.)	This is Matt. *(singular & closer in proximity)*
वह सूज़न है। (veh Susan hai.)	That is Susan. *(singular & distant in proximity)*
ये मेरे पिता जी हैं। (ye may-ray pi-taa-jee hain.)	This is my father. *(respectful)*
ये बच्चे हैं। (yay b-uch-chay hain.)	These are children. *(plural)*
वे कौन हैं? (vay kawn hain?)	Who are they? *(pl.)*/Who is he/she? *(for an older male/female)*

NOTE Pronouns such as तुम (tüm), तू (too) and आप (aap) are used mainly to ask questions, give suggestions, or issue commands. *Who* (कौन kawn), *how* (कैसे kai-say), and *from where* (कहाँ से kuh-haa say) are question words frequently used in introductions. It is better to use the polite/respectful form आप if you are conversing with strangers in India.

Practice 2

Now, fill in the blanks and read out loud the basic Hindi sentence structure. Insert names, nationality, or question words in the blank spaces.

मैं _____ हूँ
(main.. hoo)
I am ...

हम _____ हैं
(hum... hain)
We are ...

तुम _____ हो/ तू_____ है
(tüm ho/ too hai)
You are ... *(informal/intimate)*

आप _____ हैं
(aap hain)
You are ... *(honorific/respect)*

आप लोग _____ हैं
(aap low-g...... hain)
you people are ... *(honorific/respectful and plural)*

हम लोग _____ हैं
(hum low-g ....hain)
we people are ...

यह _____ है
(yeh hai)
he, she, it, this is...
(closer /singular)

वह _____ है
(veh hai)
he, she, it, that is..
(distant & singular)

ये _____ हैं
(yay hain)
he, she, it, this is/these are ...
(closer, honorific, plural)

वे _____ हैं
(vay hain)
he, she, it, that is/those are ...
(distant, honorific, plural)

Practice 3

Translate the following sentences into Hindi, using the correct structure:

1. I am John.   _____.

2. Who are you?   _____.

3. Where are you from?   _____.

4. How are you?   _____.

5. Where are you (people) from?   _____.

6. We are Americans.   _____.

7. This is Mat.   _____.

8. That is Susan.   _____.

9. This is Father.   _____.

10. These are children.   _____.

11. Who are they?   _____.

Introducing Possessive Pronouns

Since Hindi is a gender-oriented language, the pronouns are modified according to the genders of the nouns they precede, thus functioning as adjectives.

NOTE All ā ा-ending pronouns are used with masculine nouns; ī ी-ending pronouns are used with feminine nouns; and e े -ending pronouns are used with plural masculine nouns.

My

मेरा my *(masc. sg.)*	मेरी my	मेरे my
(may-raa)	(may-ree)	(may-ray)
	(fem. sing./pl. and honorific)	*(masc. pl. and honorific)*
मेरा भाई my brother	मेरी बहन my sister	मेरे पिताजी my father
(may-raa bha-ee)	(may-ree beh-hen)	(may-ray pi-taa-jee)

Our

This word can be used for multiple people, or used by a single individual from the Indian state of Utter Pradesh and Bihar, where "we/our" is commonly used for "I/ my."

हमारा our *(masc. sing.)*	हमारी our *(fem. sing./pl.)*	हमारे our *(masc. pl.)*
(hum-aa-raa)	(hum-aa-ree)	(hum-aa-ray)
हमारा परिवार our family	हमारी माताजी our mother	हमारे पिताजी our father
(hum-aa-raa pur-i-waar)	(hum-aa-ree maa-taa-jee)	(hum-aa-ray pi-taa-jee)

Your

This informal form is used with a person who is younger in age, or a friend.

तुम्हारा your *(masc. sing.)*	तुम्हारी your *(fem. sing./pl.)*	तुम्हारे your *(masc. pl.)*
(tüm-haa-raa)	(tüm-haa-ree)	(tüm-haa-ray)
तुम्हारा भाई your brother	तुम्हारी बहनें your sisters	तुम्हारे पति your husband
(tüm-haa-raa bhaa-ee)	(tüm-haa-ree beh-nė)	(tüm-haa-ray puh-uti)

Your

This polite/formal form is used to address a person who is older in age or unknown to the speaker.

आप का your *(masc. sing.)*	आप की your *(fem. sing./pl.)*	आप के your *(masc. pl.)*
(aap-kaa)	(aap-kee)	(aap-kay)
आप का घर your house	आप की पत्नि your wife	आप के पति your husband
(aap-kaa gher)	(aap-kee puh-utni)	(aap-kay puh-uti)

His, her, its, of this, of that

This form of possessive pronoun is used to show the relationship with a person or a possession of an object, such as "Martha's son" or "her son."

इसका *(masc. sing.)*	इसकी *(fem. sing./pl.)*	इसके *(masc. pl.)*	⇒	used with someone physically close to the speaker
(is-kaa)	(is-kee)	(is-kay)		
उसका *(masc. sing.)*	उसकी *(fem. sing./pl.)*	उसके *(masc. pl.)*	⇒	used with someone far away from the speaker
(üs-kaa)	(üs-kee)	(üs-kay)		

His, her, their, of these, of those

This form of possessive pronoun is used to show respect to a person due to age or position.

इनका *(masc. sg.)* (in-kaa)	इनकी *(fem. sg./pl.)* (in-kee)	इनके *(masc. pl.)* (in-kay) ➠	used with someone physically close to the speaker
उनका *(masc. sg.)* (ün-kaa)	उनकी *(fem. sg./pl.)* (ün-kee)	उनके *(masc. pl.)* (ün-kay) ➠	used with someone far away from the speaker

Practice 1

Read the examples below and practice using the highlighted pronouns.

My name is Michelle.
मेरा नाम मिशैल है।
(May-raa naam Mischelle hai.)

His name is Jordan.
उसका नाम जॉर्डन है। (Üs-kaa naam Jordan hai.)
(far away from the speaker)

Her name is Sara.
इसका नाम सैरा है। (Is-kaa naam Seraa hai.)
(physically close to the speaker)

NOTE In the sentences above, the gender for the word नाम (name) is masculine; therefore, the possessive pronoun or adjective that precedes it is masculine as well.

Practice 2

Translate the phrases below (the receiver is physically close to the speaker). Remember the noun gender in each sentence. Choose from इसका, इसकी, or इसके for pronouns his/her, and choose from बेटी (daughter), बेटा (son), or बच्चे (children) for nouns.

1. his daughter   _____
4. her son   _____

2. his son   _____
5. his children   _____

3. her daughter   _____
6. her children   _____

Practice 3

Translate the words below (the receiver is far away from the speaker is a third person/honorific/plural). Choose from उनका, उनकी, or उनके.

1. his daughter   _____
2. his son   _____

3. her daughter   _____

4. her son   _____

5. his children   _____

6. her children   _____

7. their child   _____

8. their children   _____

Practice 4

Follow the examples above and create your own sentences, stating the names of your family members. Fill in the blanks with the appropriate pronouns and the names.

1. _____ माँ का नाम _____ है। *(fem.)*

2. _____ बहन का नाम _____ है। *(fem.)*

3. _____ पिताजी का नाम _____ है। *(masc. pl.)*

4. _____ भाई का नाम _____ है। *(masc. pl.)*

5. _____ पति का नाम _____ है। *(masc. pl.)*

Practice 5

Practice other possessive pronouns in the same way and introduce your family and friends.

my मेरा, मेरी, मेरे	(may-raa, may-ree, may-ray)
your *(formal)* आपका, आपकी, आपके	(aap-kaa, aap-kee, aap-kay)
your *(informal)* तुम्हारा, तुम्हारी, तुम्हारे	(tüm-haa-raa, tüm-haa-ree, tüm-haa- ray)
your *(intimate)* तेरा, तेरी, तेरे	(tay-raa, tay-ree, tay-ray)
our हमारा, हमारी, हमारे	(hum-aa-raa, hum-aa-ree, hum-aa-ray)
his, her, its *(sing., physically close)* इसका, इसकी, इसके	(is-kaa, is-kee, is-kay)
his, her, its *(sing., far away)* उसका, उसकी, उसके	(üs-kaa, üs-kee, üs-kay)
his, her, their *(pl., honorific [sing.], physically close)* इनका, इनकी, इनके	(in-kaa, in-kee, in-kay)
his, her, their *(pl., honorific [sing.]) far away)* उनका, उनकी, उनके	(ün-kaa, ün-kee, ün-kay)

Grammar: Postpositions

You will see that in addition to the basic sentence structure "I am ...," we add a postposition **se** से (from) and **maẏ** में (in) to practice answering and inquiring about someone's whereabouts.

From and *in* in English are known as prepositions since they are positioned before a noun. In Hindi, में maẏ (in), बाहर baa-her (out), and ऊपर oo-per (on) are positioned AFTER a noun and are thus called postpositions.

There are two forms of postpositions: simple and compound. They play a very important role in Hindi sentence structure as they are considered to be the backbone of Hindi. The placement of these postpositions determines the cases in Hindi.

Sentence Structure

Subject + place + sè से *(from)* + auxiliary verb *(according to the subject)*
आप कहाँ से हैं? Where are you from?
(Aap kuh-haȧ say hain?)

मैं भारत से हूँ। I am from India. (Literally, "I India
(main Bhaa-rut say hoȯ.) from is.")

Practice 1
Read the sample sentences.

Question: **Where are you from?**
1. आप कहाँ से हैं? (Aap kuh-haȧ say hain?)
2. तुम कहाँ से हो? (tüm kuh-haȧ say ho?)
3. यह कहाँ से है? (Yeh kuh-haȧ say hai?)
4. वह कहाँ से हैं? (Veh kuh-haȧ say hain?)
5. ये कहाँ से हैं? (Yay kuh-haȧ say hain?)
6. वे कहाँ से हैं? (Vay kuh-haȧ say hain?)
7. आप लोग कहाँ से हैं?
   (Aap low-g kuh-haȧ say hain?)
8. अमरीका में कहाँ से हैं?
   (Um-ree-kaa maẏ kuh-haȧ say hain?)

Answer: **I am from...**
मैं भारत से हूँ। (Main Bhaa-rut say hoȯ.)
मैं नेपाल से हूँ। (Main Nepal say hoȯ.)
यह चीन से है। (Yeh cheen say hai.)
वह अमरीका से है। (Veh Um-ree-kaa say hai.)
ये रूस से हैं। (Yay roos say hain.)
वे मलेशिया से हैं। (Vay Malasia say hain.)
हम लोग जापान से हैं।
(Hum low-g Japan say hain.)
अमरीका में टैक्सस से हूँ।
(Um-ree-kaa maẏ Texas say hoȯ.)

Practice 2 🎧 [01-02]

Listen to each sentence below and repeat it in order to practice the Hindi postpositions से *and* में. *Compare the placement of Hindi postpositions with that of English prepositions in the sentences below.*

मैं जॉन हूँ। मैं अमरीका से हूँ। I am John. I am <u>from America</u>.
(Main John hoȯ. Main Um-ree-kaa say hoȯ.)

मैं कियोको हूँ। मैं जापान से हूँ। I am Kiyoko. I am <u>from</u> <u>Japan</u>.
(Maiṅ Kiyoko hoȯ. Maiṅ Japan say hoȯ.)

मैं नाइजल हूँ। मैं अफ्रीका से हूँ। I am Nigel. I am <u>from</u> <u>Africa</u>.
(Maiṅ Naigel hoȯ. Maiṅ Uf-ree-kaa say hoȯ.)

मैं मोनीक़ हूँ। मैं फ्राँस से हूँ। I am Monique. I am <u>from</u> <u>France</u>.
(Maiṅ Monique hoȯ. Maiṅ France say hoȯ.)

आप कौन हैं? आप कहाँ से हैं? Who are you? Where are <u>you</u> <u>from</u>?
(Aap kawn haiṅ. Aap kuh-haȯ say haiṅ?)

तुम कौन हो? तुम कहाँ से हो? Who are you? Where are <u>you</u> <u>from</u>?
(tüm kawn ho. tüm kuh-haȯ say ho?)

अमरीका में, तुम कहाँ से हो? Where <u>in</u> <u>America</u> are you from?
(Um-ree-kaa maẏ tüm kuh-haȯ say ho?)

<u>अमरीका</u> में, मैं न्यूयॉर्क से हूँ। <u>In</u> <u>America</u>, I am <u>from</u> <u>New</u> <u>York</u>.
(Um-ree-kaa maẏ maiṅ New York say hoȯ.)

Practice 3

Use the table of possessive pronouns below to practice addressing others and asking questions.

I	मैं (maiṅ)	हूँ (hoȯ)
you *(honorific, formal, sing.)*	आप (aap)	हैं (haiṅ)
you people *(honorific, formal, pl.)*	आप लोग (aap low-g)	हैं (haiṅ)
you *(informal, familiar, sing.)*	तुम (tüm)	हो (ho)
you people *(informal, familiar, pl.)*	तुम लोग (tüm low-g)	हो (ho)
you *(very informal, sing.)*	तू (too)	है (hai)
he, she, it, this *(sing., physically close)*	यह (yeh)	है (hai)
he, she, it, that *(sing., far away)*	वह (veh)	है (hai)
he, she, it, they, these *(pl., honorific, physically close)*	ये (yay)	हैं (haiṅ)
he, she, it, they, those *(pl., honorific, far away)*	वे (vay)	हैं (haiṅ)

1.2 Introducing Oneself अपना परिचय

Objectives

After completing this lesson, you will be able to:

1. Introduce yourself and state where you're from, your age, and your educational background.
2. Introduce your family members and their ages, educational backgrounds, and professions.
3. Use pronouns such as मैं-हूँ and possessive pronouns such as मेरा, मेरे, मेरी.

> 📖 **Culture Note**
>
> People in India are very friendly toward any guests, local or foreign. It is a custom to show utmost hospitality toward a guest, with the belief that "a guest is like a God" अतिथि देवो भव: and so Indians show no formality in greeting them. They feed them and treat them like family members, hence the very reason why they ask personal questions such as marriage, children, and family: questions that indicate that you are a family member. Don't be offended when they ask these questions. They mean no harm; they are just very inquisitive.

Preview the important words before listening to Practice 1. Try to read the words and pronounce them. If you are not comfortable reading the words, then simply listen to them.

Vocabulary 01-03

Nouns

नाम	(naam)	*masc.*	name
साल	(saal)	*masc.*	year
विद्यार्थी	(vid-yaar-thee)	*masc./fem.*	student (for both male and female)
भारत	(bhaa-rut)	*masc.*	India
घर	(gh-er)	*masc.*	home
परिवार	(perr-iwaar)	*masc.*	family
पिता जी	(pit-aa-jee)	*masc.*	father
माता जी	(maa-taa jee)	*fem.*	mother
बहन	(beh-hen)	*fem.*	sister
भाई	(bhaa-ee)	*masc.*	brother
गृहिणी	(gri-hi-nee)	*fem.*	housewife
शिक्षक	(shick-shuck)	*masc.*	male teacher

Adjectives

मेरा	(may-raa)	*masc.*	my
मेरे	(may-ray)	*masc. pl./honorific*	my

मेरी	(may-re)	*fem. sing./pl./honorific*	my
बड़ा	(berD-aa)	*masc.*	older/big
छोटी	(Cho-Tee)	*fem. sing./pl./honorific*	younger/small
छोटा सा	(Cho-Taa saa)	*masc.*	very small, rather small
एक	(ayk)		one, a
बीस	(bees)		twenty
दसवीं	(dus-veė)	*fem.*	tenth
बीस साल का/ की/के	(bees saal) (kee/kaa/kay)	*masc./fem./pl.*	twenty years old

Other Parts of Speech

है	(hai)	*aux. v.*	is
मैं	(maiṅ)	*pron.*	I
हूँ	(hoṅ)	*aux. v.*	am
की	(kee)	*postposition (fem.)*	of (apostrophe)
का	(kaa)	*postposition (masc.)*	of (apostrophe)
में	(maẏ)	*postposition.*	in
से	(say)	*postposition*	from

NOTE Use the postposition का for the age of a male, की for the age of a female, and के for the age of older male members.

Practice 1 01-04

Listen to the audio in which a native speaker will introduce herself. Repeat what the speaker says. Listen as often as you like for the pronunciation.

मेरा परिचय
मेरा नाम नीना है। मैं बीस साल की हूँ। मैं एक विद्यार्थी हूँ। मैं बी.ए फ़र्स्ट इयर में हूँ। मैं भारत से हूँ। भारत में मेरा घर लखनऊ में है। मेरा परिवार छोटा सा है। मेरे परिवार में मेरे पिता जी, मेरी माता जी, मेरा एक बड़ा भाई और एक छोटी बहन है। मेरे पिता जी एक शिक्षक हैं, मेरी माँ गृहिणी हैं। मेरा बड़ा भाई एक इंजीनियर है और मेरी छोटी बहन दसवीं कक्षा में है।

Romanization

May-raa naam Neenaa hai. Main bees saal kee hoṅ. Main ayk vid-yaar-thee hoṅ. Main B.A. first year may hoṅ. Main Bhaa-rut say hoṅ. Bhaa-rut maẏ may-raa gh-er Lucknow maẏ hai. May-raa peri-waar Cho-Taa saa hai. May-ray peri-waar maẏ may-ray pi-taa-jee, may-ree maa-taa-jee, may-raa ayk berDaa bhaa-ee aur ayk Cho-Tee beh-hen hai. May-ray pi-taa-jee ayk shick-shuck haiṅ, may-ree maȧ gri-hini haiṅ. May-raa berDaa bha-ee ayk in-jee-near hai aur may-ree Choti beh-hen dus-veė kuck-shaa mein hai.

Translation

My name is Neena. I am twenty years old. I am a student. I am in my first year at university. I am from India. In India, my home is in Lucknow. My family is very small. My family consists of my father, my mother, an older brother, a younger sister and myself. My father is a teacher, my mother a housewife. My older brother is an engineer. My younger sister is in the tenth grade.

Practice 2

Listen one more time and fill in the missing words from the monologue. This monologue will help you practice the Hindi vocabulary used in this introduction and in the list earlier.

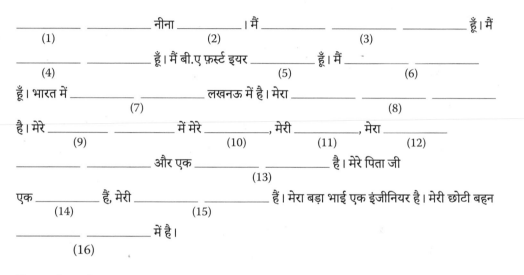

_____ _____ नीना _____ । मैं _____ _____ _____ हूँ। मैं
   (1)   (2)   (3)

_____ _____ हूँ। मैं बी.ए फ़र्स्ट इयर _____ हूँ। मैं _____ _____
   (4)   (5)   (6)

हूँ। भारत में _____ _____ लखनऊ में है। मेरा _____ _____ _____
                     (7)   (8)

है। मेरे _____ _____ में मेरे _____, मेरी _____, मेरा _____
       (9)   (10)   (11)   (12)

_____ _____ और एक _____ _____ है। मेरे पिता जी
                                 (13)

एक _____ हैं, मेरी _____ _____ हैं। मेरा बड़ा भाई एक इंजीनियर है। मेरी छोटी बहन
   (14)   (15)

_____ _____ में है।
   (16)

Practice 3

Replace the information with that of your own and then translate the sentences into Hindi. Use the sentences in the recording as reference.

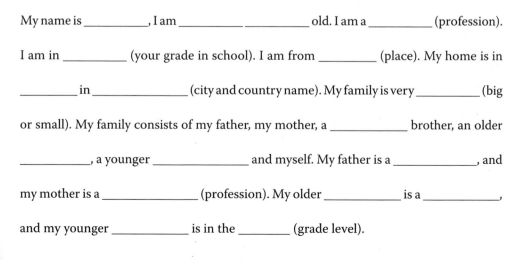

My name is _____, I am _____ _____ old. I am a _____ (profession).

I am in _____ (your grade in school). I am from _____ (place). My home is in

_____ in _____ (city and country name). My family is very _____ (big

or small). My family consists of my father, my mother, a _____ brother, an older

_____, a younger _____ and myself. My father is a _____, and

my mother is a _____ (profession). My older _____ is a _____,

and my younger _____ is in the _____ (grade level).

1.3 Greetings अभिवादन

Objectives

By the end of this lesson, you will be able to:

1. Ask *what, from, where, who and how many* questions in Hindi.
2. Introduce people to each other.
3. Greet others upon meeting.
4. Exchange pleasantries.

Vocabulary and Phrases 🎧 01-05

नमस्ते/ नमस्कार	(num-us-tay, num-us-kaar)	hello/goodbye
जी	(jee)	sir/madam (an honorific way of addressing people)
आपका नाम क्या है?	(aap-kaa naam kyaa hai)	What is your name?
मेरा नाम...... है।	(may-raa naam ... hai)	My name is… .
आप से मिलकर ख़ुशी हुयी।	(aap-say mil-ker khü-shee hü-ee)	Nice to meet you
मुझे भी	(mü-Jhay bhee)	(to) me too
फिर मिलेंगे	(phir mil-aẏ-gay)	We'll meet again.
आप क्या करते हैं?	(aap kyaa ker-tay haiṅ)	What do you do? (to be used when asking an older or unknown male about his profession)
आप क्या करतीं हैं?	(aap kyaa ker-teė haiṅ)	What do you do? (to be used when asking an older or unknown female about her profession)
आप कहाँ से हैं?	(aap kuh-haȧ say haiṅ)	Where are you from?
आपके परिवार में कौन-कौन है?	(aap-kay per-i-waar maẏ kawn-kawn hai)	Who are the members of your family?

Nouns and Pronouns

पति	(puh-uti)	*masc.*	husband
बच्चे	(buh-uch-chay)	*masc. pl.*	children
बेटा	(bay-Taa)	*masc.*	son
बेटी	(bay-Tee)	*fem.*	daughter
काम	(kaam)	*masc.*	work
वक़ील	(waq-eel)	*masc./fem.*	lawyer
चिकित्सक	(chik-it-suk)	*masc./fem.*	doctor
आप	(aap)	*formal*	you

Adjectives

आपका	(aap-kaa)	*masc. sing.*	your
आपके	(aap-kay)	used with masculine plural nouns or if a noun is followed by a postposition such as **mein** or **se** (oblique)	your
शादी-शुदा	(shaa-dee-shü-daa)	*masc./fem.*	married
दो	(though)		two

Question Words

कितने	(kit-nay)	*masc. pl.*	how many/how much
क्या	(kyaa)		what
कौन-कौन	(kawn-kawn)		who all
कहाँ से	(kuh-haà say)		from where/where from

Conversation Practice

Practice 1

Listen to the conversation and repeat the question part of the conversation to get used to hearing and asking questions.

ललित	: जी नमस्ते, आपका नाम क्या है?	(Jee num-us-tay, aap-kaa naam kyaa hai?)
सुमन	: जी मेरा नाम सुमन है।	(Jee may-raa naam Suman hai.)
ललित	: सुमन जी आप कहाँ से हैं?	(Suman jee aap kuh-haà say hain?)
सुमन	: मैं भारत से हूँ।	(Main Bhaa-rut say hoò)
ललित	: भारत में कहाँ से हैं?	(Bhaa-rut maỳ kuh-haà say?)
सुमन	: भारत में कानपुर से।	(Bhaa-rut maỳ Kaan-pür say.)
ललित	: क्या आप शादी-शुदा हैं?	(Kyaa aap shaa-dee shü-daa hain?)
सुमन	: हाँ, मैं शादी-शुदा हूँ।	(Haà, main shaa-dee shü-daa hoò.)
ललित	: आपके परिवार में कौन-कौन है?	(Aap-kay per-i-waar maỳ kawn-kawn hai?)
सुमन	: मेरे परिवार में मेरे पति और दो बच्चे हैं।	(May-ray per-i-waar maỳ may-ray puh-ti aur do b-uch-chay hain)
ललित	: आपके बच्चे कितने साल के हैं?	(Aap-kay b-uch-chay kit-nay saal kay hain?)
सुमन	: मेरा बेटा पाँच साल का है और बेटी दस साल की है।	(May-raa bay-Taa paà-ch saal kaa aur bay-Tee dus saal kee hai.)
ललित	: आप के पति क्या करते है?	(Aap kay puh-ti kyaa ker-tay hain?)
सुमन	: मेरे पति वकील है।	(May-ray puh-ti waqeel hain.)
ललित	: क्या आप भी काम करतीं हैं?	(Kyaa aap bhee kaam ker-tee hain?)
सुमन	: जी मैं एक चिकित्सक हूँ।	(Jee main ayk chi-kit-suk hoò.)
ललित	: आप से मिलकर ख़ुशी हुयी।	(Aap say mil-ker khu-shee huee.)
सुमन	: मुझे भी। फिर मिलेंगे।	(Mu-jhay bhee. Phir mil-aỳ-gay.)

Translation

Lalit	:	Hello, madam! What is your name?
Suman	:	Sir, my name is Suman.
Lalit	:	Ms. Suman, where are you from?
Suman	:	I am from India.
Lalit	:	From where in India?
Suman	:	I am from Kanpur.
Lalit	:	Are you married?
Suman	:	Yes, I am married.
Lalit	:	Who else are there in your family?
Suman	:	I have my husband and my two children in the family.
Lalit	:	How old are your children?
Suman	:	My son is five years old and my daughter is ten.
Lalit	:	What does your husband do?
Suman	:	My husband is a lawyer.
Lalit	:	Do you also work?
Suman	:	Yes, I am a doctor.
Lalit	:	It was a pleasure to meet you.
Suman	:	Me too. See you again.

Practice 2

Practice asking the following questions:

आपका नाम क्या है?	(Aap-kaa naam kyaa hai?)
आप कहाँ से हैं?	(Aap kuh-haȧ say haiṅ?)
_____ में कहाँ से है?	(_____ maẏ kuh-haȧ say?)
क्या आप शादीशुदा हैं?	(Kyaa aap shaa-dee-shudaa haiṅ?)
आपके परिवार में कौन-कौन है?	(Aap-kay peri-waar meiṅ kawn-kawn hai?)
आपके बच्चे कितने साल के हैं?	(Aap-kay b-uch-chay kit-nay saal kay haiṅ?)
आप के पति क्या करते हैं?	(Aap-kay puh-ti kyaa ker-tay haiṅ?) (*to a female about her husband*)
आपकी पत्नि क्या करतीं हैं ?	(Aap-kee p-ut-ni kyaa ker-teė haiṅ?) (*to a male about his wife*)
क्या आप भी काम करतीं हैं?	(Kyaa aap bhee kaam ker-teė haiṅ?) (*to a female*)
क्या आप भी काम करते हैं?	(Kyaa aap bhee kaam ker-tay haiṅ?) (*to a male*)

Practice 3

Translate the following questions and practice by asking these questions to a Hindi speaker.

1. What is your name?
2. Where are you from?
3. Where from in _____?
4. Who all are there in your family?
5. Are you married?

6. How old are your children?
7. What does your husband do?
8. What does your wife do?
9. Do you also work?

Practice 4
Learn how to answer to the questions by adding your information to the sentences written below.

मेरा नाम _____ है। (add your name)

1. मैं _____ से हूँ। (place)

2. _____ में, मैं _____ से हूँ। (country and city)

3. मेरे परिवार में _____ और _____ है। (people/relationship)

4. हाँ, मैं _____ हूँ। (married)

5. नहीं, मैं _____ नहीं हूँ। (unmarried)

6. मेरा बेटा _____ साल का है और बेटी _____ की है। (age)

7. मेरी पत्नि _____ है। (profession)

8. मेरे पति _____ हैं। (profession)

1.4 My Home मेरा घर

Objectives
By the end of this lesson you will be able to:
1. Describe your home in detail using simple and locative compound postpositions.
2. Understand and use gender-oriented nouns and pronouns, and their relationship with the postposition in a sentence.

📖 **Culture Note**

As mentioned earlier, Indians are naturally very inquisitive and ask many questions, which you may find awkward in answering. However, it is their attempt to learn as much about you so that they can feel comfortable and open. If you invite them to your house, they would want to see how beautifully you have set it up and decorated it. Don't hesitate showing them your house and they will appreciate it.

Nouns 🎧 01-07

कमरा	(kum-raa)	*masc.*	room
चारदीवारी	(chaar-dee-waa-ree)	*fem.*	boundary wall
बैठक	(bai-Thuk)	*fem.*	living room/drawing room
दरवाज़ा/किवाड़	(der-waa-zaa/ki-waarD)	*masc.*	door
रंग	(rung)	*masc.*	color
खिड़की	(khirD-kee)	*fem.*	window
रसोई	(rus-oee)	*fem.*	kitchen
फ़र्श	(fur-sh)	*masc.*	floor
सीढ़ी	(see-rDhee)	*fem. sing.*	stair/ladder
सीढ़ियाँ	(see-rDhi-yaȧ)	*fem. pl.*	stairs, staircase
रास्ता	(raas-taa)	*masc.*	path, road, way
सोने का कमरा	(so-nay kaa kum-raa)	*masc.*	bedroom
खाने का कमरा	(khaa-nay kaa kum-raa)	*masc.*	dining room
पढ़ने का कमरा	(perDh-nay kaa kum-raa)	*masc.*	study room
ग़ुसलखाना/बाथरूम	(gü-sul-khaa-naa)	*masc.*	bathroom
स्नानघर	(snaan-gher)	*masc.*	bathroom
काँच	(kaȧn-ch)	*masc.*	glass, mirror
केलू	(kay-loo)	*masc.*	clay shingle (for roof)
मंज़िल	(munzil)	*fem.*	story (of a building)
मकान	(muk-aan)	*masc.*	house
घर	(gher)	*masc.*	home
फाटक/गेट	(faa-Tuk)	*masc*	gate
आँगन	(aȧ-gun)	*masc.*	courtyard
छत	(Ch-ut)	*fem.*	roof/ceiling
बग़ीचा	(bug-ee-chaa)	*masc.*	garden
फूल	(phool)	*masc.*	flower

Adjectives

मंज़िला	(mun-zilaa)	*masc.*	storied
मंज़िली	(mun-zi-lee)	*fem.*	storied
हवादार	(huh-waa-daar)		ventilated
छोटी सी	(Cho-Tee see)	*fem. sing*	rather small
छोटा सा	(Cho-Taa saa)	*masc. sing.*	rather small
मुख्य	(mü-kh-yuh)		main

Simple Postpositions

में	(maẏ)		in
पर	(per)		on, at
से	(say)		from, by, with, for, since, than
ऊपर	(ooper)		above
नीचे	(nee-chay)		below
पास	(paas)		near

पीछे	(pee-Chay)		behind
का	(kaa)	*masc. sing.*	of (apostrophe s)
की	(kee)	*fem. sing.*	of (apostrophe s)
के	(kay)	*masc. pl.*	of (apostrophe s)

Compound Postpositions

X के ऊपर	(kay oo-per)	above X
X के नीचे	(kay nee-chay)	below X
X के सामने	(kay saam-nay)	front of X
X के आगे	(kay aa-gay)	in front of X, ahead of X
सामने, आगे	(saam-nay, aa-gay)	in the front, ahead
X के पीछे	(kay pee-chay)	behind of X
पीछे की तरफ़	(pee-chay kee ter-uf)	at the back side
साथ ही	(saa-th hee)	attached to
X के पास	(kay paas)	near X
आसपास	(aas-paas)	around, near by
की बगल में	(kee bug-ul maẏ)	next to X
चारों तरफ़	(chaa-ró ter-uf)	all around
दोनों तरफ़	(do-nó ter-uf)	both sides

Comparatives and Superlatives

से छोटा	(say Cho-Taa)		smaller than
से बड़ा	(say ber-Daa)		bigger than
सबसे	(sub-say)		of all
सबसे बड़ा	(sub-say ber-Daa)	*masc. sing.*	biggest of all
सबसे छोटी	(sub-say Cho-Tee)	*fem. sing./pl.*	smallest of all
सबसे पहले	(sub-say peh-lay)		first of all
सबसे ऊपर	(sub-say oo-per)		on the top
सबसे नीचे	(sub-say nee-chay)		at the bottom

Other

भी	(bhee)	also, as well
तो	(toe)	used to emphasize a person, pronouns, adjectives as "definitely" in positive sentences and "at all" in negative sentences.
चलो	(chuh-lo)	let's go

Grammar: Introduction to Nouns

Remember that Hindi has two main categories of nouns, marked and unmarked masculine and feminine, and these two have their subcategories: singular and plural.

1. A singular marked masculine noun ends in the dependent vowel ा, and its plural form ends in े.
2. A singular marked feminine noun ends in the dependent vowel ी or ई, and a marked feminine plural ends in ि याँ or इयाँ.
3. An unmarked masculine noun ends in a vowel other than the ा or in a consonant and remains the same in plural.
4. An unmarked feminine noun ends in a vowel other than ी or ई, or a consonant. To form the plural unmarked feminine, the vowel े with a dot over it or ें is added.

NOTE Male kinship terms such as uncle and grandfather never change to the plural form, but feminine kinship terms do change to the plural form.

Study the table below and get acquainted with the noun formations.

Marked *masc. sing.*	Marked *masc. pl.*	Marked *fem. sing.*	Marked *fem. pl.*
कमरा (kum-raa) room	कमरे (kum-ray) rooms	खिड़की (khi-rD-kee) window	खिड़कियाँ (khi-rD-ki-yaȧ) windows
दरवाज़ा (der-waa-zaa) door	दरवाज़े (der-waa-zay) doors	सीढ़ी (see-rDh-ee) stair	सीढ़ियाँ (see-rDhi-yaȧ) stairs
ग़ुसलख़ाना (ghü-sul-khaa-naa) bathroom	ग़ुसलख़ाने (ghü -sul-khaa-nay) bathrooms	लड़की (lerD-kee) girl	लड़कियाँ (lerD-ki-yaȧ) girls
बग़ीचा (bug-ee-chaa) garden	बग़ीचे (bug-ee-chay) gardens	रसोई (rus-oee) kitchen	रसोइयाँ (rus-oi-yaȧ) kitchens

Unmarked *masc. sing.*	Unmarked *masc. pl.*	Unmarked *fem. sing.*	Unmarked *fem. pl.*
घर (gher) house/home	घर (gher) houses/homes	छत (Ch-ut) roof/ceiling	छतें (Ch-ut-ain) roofs/ceilings
आँगन (aȧ-gun) courtyard	आँगन (aȧ-gun) courtyards	मेज़ (may-ze) table	मेज़ें (may-zaiṅ) tables

Unmarked *masc. sing.*	Unmarked *masc. pl.*	Unmarked *fem. sing.*	Unmarked *fem. pl.*
रोशनदान (ro-shun-daan) skylight (in a room)	रोशनदान (ro-shun-daan) skylight	मंज़िल (mun-zil) story (in a house)	मंज़िलें (mun-zil-ain) stories
आदमी (aad-mee) man	आदमी (aad-mee) men	झाड़ू (jhaa-rDoo) broom	झाड़ुएँ (jhaa-rdü-yė) brooms

Simple and Locative Compound Postpositions

Words which are known as prepositions in English are called postpositions in Hindi. The only difference between prepositions and postpositions is that a Hindi postposition is placed AFTER an object (the nouns) whereas a preposition comes BEFORE a noun. There are two types of postpositions in Hindi: simple and compound. Below are some examples:

Simple Postposition	Preposition*	Compound Postposition	Preposition*
में (maẏ)	in	X के अन्दर (kay under)	inside of X

* English equivalents

Preposition	Simple Postposition	Preposition	Compound Postposition
in	में (maẏ)		
inside	अन्दर (un-der)	inside of X	X के अन्दर (kay under)
outside	बाहर (baa-her)	outside of X	X के बाहर (kay baa-her)
on, at	पर (per)		X पर (per)
above	ऊपर (oo-per)	above X upon X	X के ऊपर (kay oo-per)
below, under	नीचे (nee-chay)	below X, under X	X के नीचे (kay nee-chay)
from, by, with, for, since, than	से (say)		
in the front, ahead	सामने, आगे (saam-nay, aa-gay)	in front of X, ahead of X	X के सामने, X के आगे (kay saam-nay, kay aa-gay)

Preposition	Simple Postposition	Preposition	Compound Postposition
behind	पीछे (pee-chay)	behind X	X के पीछे (kay pee-chay)
to the back side	पीछे की तरफ़ (pee-chay kee ter-uf)	to the back side of X	X के पीछे की तरफ़ (kay pee-Chay kee ter-uf)
near	पास (paas)	near X	X के पास (kay paas)
around	आसपास (aas-paas)	around X	X के आसपास (kay aas-paas)
far	दूर (doo-r)	far from X	X से दूर (say doo-r)
attached	साथ ही (saath-hee)	attached to X	X के साथ ही (kay saath hee)
adjacent	बगल में (bug-ul maẏ)	next to X	X की बगल में (kee bug-ul maẏ)

As mentioned earlier, a postposition changes the form of singular and plural marked masculine nouns. The changes that occur in the nouns due to the addition of a simple or a compound postposition make those changed nouns indirect. This change in linguistic terms is known as "oblique." Oblique literally means something that is not direct. There are two types of oblique in Hindi: singular and plural. See the table below to understand the concept of oblique in Hindi. It is the backbone of Hindi sentence structure.

Read the nouns and notice the changes to marked and unmarked nouns if a postposition is added.

Marked				Unmarked	
masc. sing.	*masc. sing. oblique*	*masc. pl.*	*masc. pl. oblique*	*masc. sing.*	*masc. pl. oblique.*
कमरा (kum-raa) room	कमरे में (kum-ray maẏ) in the room	कमरे (kum-ray) rooms	कमरों में (kum-rȯ maẏ) in the rooms	घर (gh-er) home	घरों के सामने (gher-oṅ kay saam-nay) in front of houses
दरवाज़ा (der-waa-zaa) door	दरवाज़े पर (der-waa-zay per) at the door	दरवाज़े (der-waa-zay) doors	दरवाज़ों पर (der-waa-zȯ per) at the doors	आँगन (aȧ-gun) courtyard	आँगनों के बीच में (aȧ-gun-ȯ kay beech maẏ) in the middle of the courtyards

Marked				Unmarked	
fem. sing.	*fem. sing. oblique*	*fem. pl.*	*fem. pl. oblique*	*fem. pl.*	*fem. pl. oblique*
खिड़की (khirD-kee) window	खिड़की से (khirD-kee say) from the window	खिड़कियाँ (khirD-kiyaā) windows	खिड़कियों का (khirD-kiyỏ kaa) windows'… (color)	छतें (Ch-ut-ain) roofs	छतों पर (Ch-ut-ỏ per) on the roofs
सीढ़ी (see-rDhee) stair	सीढ़ी पर (see-rDhee per) on the stair	सीढ़ियाँ (see-rDhi-yaā) stairs	सीढ़ियों पर (see-rDhi-yỏ per) on the stairs	बैठकें (baiTh-uk-ain) living rooms	बैठकों में (baiTh-uk-ỏ maẏ) in the living rooms

Read the words in Hindi on the left side and match them with their corresponding translation. You will notice that the Hindi locative postpositions are placed right after the location or a place.

Practice 1
The unmarked masculine noun घर does not change even if a postposition follows it:

1. घर में   (gher maẏ)   in front of the house
2. घर पर   (gher per)   near the house
3. घर के ऊपर   (gher kay oo-per)   above the house
4. घर के नीचे   (gher kay nee-chay)   behind the house
5. घर के सामने   (gher kay saam-nay)   around the house
6. घर के पीछे   (gher kay pee-chay)   below the house
7. घर के पास   (gher kay paas)   at home
8. घर के आसपास   (gher kay aas-paas)   in the house

Practice 2
The marked masculine noun कमरा becomes कमरे as soon as a postposition is added:

1. कमरे में   (kum-ray maẏ)   from the room
2. कमरे पर   (kum-ray per)   near the room
3. कमरे के ऊपर   (kum-ray kay oo-per)   in front of the room
4. कमरे के नीचे   (kum-ray kay nee-chay)   behind the room
5. कमरे के सामने   (kum-ray kay saam-nay)   above the room
6. कमरे के पीछे   (kum-ray kay pee-chay)   in the room
7. कमरे के पास   (kum-ray kay paas)   around the room
8. कमरे के आसपास   (kum-ray kaya aas-paas)   at the room
9. कमरे से   (kum-ray say)   below the room

NOTE Did you notice a change in the Hindi examples in the second set? The change that has occurred in the second set is to the form of the noun कमरा, a singular masculine marked noun, which changes as soon as a postposition is placed right after it, making it a plural masculine noun. This form, कमरे, is also known as "singular oblique" due to the inflection in a singular masculine noun. In the first set, the noun घर is an unmarked masculine noun and remains unchanged. When you use a postposition after a marked masculine noun, do not forget to change it to plural first.

Singular feminine nouns and unmarked masculine nouns do not change their form in the postpositional phrase; however, marked feminine plural, marked masculine plural, and unmarked masculine plural nouns altogether take a very different form in the postpositional phrase. This form is also known as the "plural oblique" due to the inflection in the plural masculine noun because of a postposition.

Practice 3
Now change all singular masculine marked nouns below into plural as shown in the examples above (on page 44).

1. बग़ीचा		4. कमरा	
2. दरवाज़ा		5. गुसलखाना	
3. रास्ता			

Practice 4.1
Label the pictures below using nouns from the column above and add a postposition as each picture indicates. Do not forget to change the form of your masculine nouns as you have done in the earlier exercise.

1. in the garden.

2. at the door

_____

_____

3. on the road   4. in the bedroom

_____   _____

Practice 4.2
Do you get the idea? Now describe each picture in a complete sentence.

1. _____

2. _____

3. _____

4. _____

Practice 5
Label each picture on next page with the correct postposition. Clues are given next to each blank. [Cat: बिल्ली]

	Clues
1. _____	at the stair
2. _____	on top of the toilet bowl
3. _____	on the bed
4. _____	above the computer
5. _____	between the chairs
6. _____	next to the plates

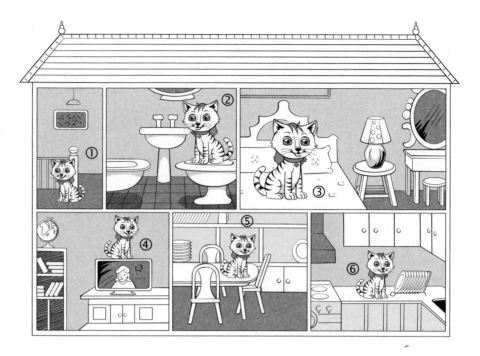

Practice 6 Pre-reading Exercise

Brainstorm about all the places or things in, around, at the back of, and in front of your house. Also think of the exact location of those places or objects. Make a list of those places and their location in Hindi. Then, draw a simple sketch to show the location of the places/things you have mentioned in your list.

(for your sketch and labelling)

Practice 7

Now read about the description of a house as it is seen from outside. Then circle all the postpositions, underline nouns, and highlight all the adjectives in the description.

यह मेरा घर है। मेरा घर बहुत बड़ा है। मेरा घर दो मंज़िला है। मेरे घर के आगे एक बहुत बड़ा बग़ीचा है। उस बग़ीचे में सुन्दर-सुन्दर फूल हैं और हरी-हरी घास भी है। बग़ीचे के पास एक छोटा सा रास्ता है। वहीं पर गाड़ी खड़ी करने की जगह भी है। उसके पास चार सीढ़ियाँ हैं। घर के चारों तरफ़, सफ़ेद रंग की चारदीवारी है। घर के पीछे, बहुत से पेड़ हैं। मेरे घर का रंग, बाहर से सफ़ेद और नीला है। उसकी छत का रंग, नीला है और वह छत केलू की है। घर का मुख्य दरवाज़ा भूरे रंग का है। मुख्य दरवाज़े की दोनों तरफ़, काँच की दो बड़ी-बड़ी खिड़कियाँ हैं। घर की दूसरी मंज़िल पर, सामने की तरफ़ एक बालकनी है। बालकनी के पीछे, एक दरवाज़ा और एक खिड़की है।

Yeh may-raa gher hai. May-raa gher ba-hut ber-Daa hai. May-raa gher do mun-zilaa hai. May-ray gher kay aa-gay ayk ba-hüt ber-Daa bug-ee-chaa hai. Üs bug-ee-chay maẏ sünder-sünder phool haiṅ aur her-ee her-ee ghaas bhee hai. Bug-ee-chay kay paas ayk Cho-Taa saa raas-taa hai. Vuh-heė per gaarDee kherDee ker-nay kee jug-uh bhee hai. Üskay paas chaar see-rDhi-yaȧ haiṅ.

Gher kay chaa-raẇ ter-uf, suf-aid r-ung kee chaar-dee-waa-ree hai. Gher kay pee-Chay, ba-hüt say pay-rD haiṅ. May-ray gher kaa r-ung, baa-her say suf-aid aur nee-laa hai. Üskee Ch-ut kaa r-ung, nee-laa hai. Veh Ch-ut kay-loo kee hai. Gher ka mü-kh-yuh der-waa-zaa bhoo-ray r-ung kaa hai. Mü-kh-yuh der-waa-zay kee do-nȯ ter-uf, kaȧ-ch kee doe ber-Dee ber-Dee khirD-ki-yaȧ haiṅ. Gher kee doos-ree mun-zil per, saam-nay kee ter-uf ayk baal-cony hai. Baal-cony kay pee-Chay, ayk der-waa-zaa aur ayk khirD-kee hai.

Translation

This is my house. My house is very big. It has two stories. In front is a huge garden. There are beautiful flowers growing in that garden, and there is green grass as well. Near the garden is a small pathway where there is a place to park a car. There are four steps near it. The boundary wall of the house is white in color. Behind the house are many trees. From the front, my house is white and blue in color. Its roof is blue and is made of *kèloo**. The main door is brown in color, and flanked by a big glass window on either side. The second story has a balcony at the front of the house, behind which is a door and a window.

---

* *Kèloo* is used as shingles to cover the rooftop of houses in places where it rains a lot. *Keloo*, made of black cotton soil and sand, is affordable and widely used on the slanting rooftops.

Practice 8 Post-Reading Activity

Now imagine your own house or apartment and write about it. Use the preceding text as an example. Use the list that you have made in the pre-reading activity.

Creative Writing

_____

_____

_____

_____

Practice 9 Asking Questions about a House

Based on what you have written, answer the following questions in Hindi. Remember that the answer to कैसा (kai-saa) and कैसी (kai-see) is always an adjective that describes the noun; it may be a shape, color, or size. For कितना (kit-naa), कितनी (kit-nee), and कितने (kit-nay) the answer is a number or amount; for कहाँ (kuh-haȧ), it is a location; for क्या (kyaa) it is a noun. Remember, when answering very simple questions, note how a question is asked and then replace only the question word with the answer.

Example:

Question: तुम्हारा घर कहाँ है?   (Tüm-haa-raa gher kuh-haȧ hai?)   Where is your home?

Answer: मेरा घर भारत में है।   (May-raa gher Bhaa-rut maẏ hai.)   My home is in India.

Answer the following questions.

1. तुम्हारा घर कैसा है?   (Tüm-haa-raa gher kai-saa hai?)   How is your house?

_____

2. तुम्हारा घर कितनी मंज़िला है?   (Tüm-haa-raa gher kit-nee mun-zilaa hai?)

   How many stories is your house? _____

Or तुम्हारे घर में कितनी मंज़िलें हैं?   (Tüm-haa-ray gher maẏ kit-nee mun-zil-ain haiṅ?)

   How many stories are there in your house? _____

3. बग़ीचा कहाँ है?   (Bug-ee-chaa kuh-haȧ hai?)   Where is the garden?

_____

4. बग़ीचे में क्या लगा है?   (Bug-ee-chay maẏ kyaa lug-aa hai?)

   What is planted in the garden? _____

5. बग़ीचे के पास क्या है?   (Bug-ee-chay kay paas kyaa hai?)   What is near the garden?

_____

6. क्या तुम्हारे घर के चारों तरफ़ चारदीवारी है?   (Kyaa tüm-haa-ray gher kay chaa-rȯ ter-uf chaar-dee-waa-ree hai?)   Do you have a boundary wall around your house?

_____

7. घर के पीछे क्या है? (Gher kay pee-Chay kyaa hai?) What is behind the house?

_____

8. तुम्हारे घर का रंग बाहर से कैसा है? (Tüm-haa-ray gher kaa ru-ung baa-her say kai-saa hai?)
   What color is your house on the outside?

_____

Practice 10
Write sentences to describe the house in the picture below.

Example: सीढ़ियाँ, दरवाज़े के सामने हैं। The stairs are in front of the door.
दरवाज़े के सामने सीढ़ियाँ हैं। In front of the door are stairs.

_____

_____

_____

Practice 11

Choose from the list of postpositions below and complete the sentences.

(की बग़ल में, के ऊपर, सबसे ऊपर, के सामने, से बड़ी, से छोटा, के साथ ही, पर)

1. मेज़, खिड़की _____ । The table is in front of the window.

2. खिड़की _____ एक मेज़ है। The window is in front of the table.

3. बैठक, रसोई और खाने के कमरे _____ । The living room is above the kitchen and the dining room.

4. रसोई और खाने के कमरे _____, बैठक है। Above the kitchen and the dining room is the living room.

5. गुसलखाना, सोने के कमरे _____ है। The bathroom is attached to the bedroom.

6. सोने के कमरे _____ गुसलखाना है। There is a bathroom attached to the bedroom.

7. पहली मंज़िल _____ रसोई और खाने का कमरा है। On the first floor is a kitchen and a dining room.

8. रसोई और खाने का कमरा पहली मंज़िल _____ है। The kitchen and the dining room are on the first floor.

9. सोने का कमरा _____ है। The bedroom is on the top floor.

10. _____ सोने का कमरा है। On the top floor is the bedroom.

11. बैठक, सोने के कमरे _____ है। The living room is bigger than the bedroom. (comparative)

12. सोने का कमरा बैठक _____ है। The bedroom is smaller than the living room. (comparative)

Comparatives and Superlatives

Unlike English, Hindi adjectives do not use a different form of the comparative and superlative forms. In order to change from the positive form of adjectives to the comparative, the postposition से is inserted before the adjective, regardless of whether it is masculine, feminine, or plural.

Example: से अच्छा, से बड़ा, से सुन्दर, से छोटा
से लम्बी, से छोटी, से बड़ी
से अच्छे, से बड़े

The sentence structure will be as follows:

Object of comparison/Subject + compared object + से + adjective + auxiliary verb

खिड़की,	दरवाज़े से	बड़ी	है।
(khirD-kee	der-waa-zay say	berDee	hai.)
The window	than the door	bigger	is

(The window is bigger than the door.)

यह कमरा	उस कमरे से	बड़ा	है।
(Yeh kum-raa	üs kum-ray say	berDaa	hai.)
This room	than that room	bigger	is

(This room is bigger than that room.)

NOTE One thing you would want to keep in mind is sometimes the word order of the subject and the object of comparison may change but the meaning does not change, because the noun/pronoun with which the subject is compared is always followed by the postposition से.

दरवाज़े से	खिड़की	बड़ी	है।
(der-waa-zay say)	khirD-kee	berDee	hai.)

(The window is bigger than the door.)

than/from

यह (*third person sing., close proximity to the speaker*)	+ से =	इस से is-say	than him/her/this (closer)
वह (*third person sing, distant proximity from the speaker*)	+ से =	उस से üs say	than him/her/that (distant)
ये (*honorific and plural, close proximity to the speaker*)	+ से =	इन से in-say	than him/her/them/these (honorific)
वे (*honorific and plural, shows distance from the speaker*)	+ से =	उन से ün say	than him/her/them/those (honorific)

Example:

यह खिड़की	उस खिड़की से	छोटी है ।	
(yeh khirD-kee	üs khirD-kee	say Cho-Tee hai.)	खिड़की
This window	than that window	is smaller	

(This window is smaller than that window.)

इस कमरे से	वह कमरा	बड़ा	है।
(is kum-ray say	veh kum-raa	berDaa	hai.)
Than this room	that room	bigger	is

(That room is bigger than this room.)

The verb in its original infinitive form (*m*) changes to the oblique case due to the postposition that follows it.

सोना + का + कमरा = सोने का कमरा (so-nay kaa kum-raa) room of/for sleeping, bedroom

पढ़ना + का + कमरा = पढ़ने का कमरा (perDh-nay kaa kum-raa) room of/for study, study room

Practice 1

Read the examples below to understand comparatives.

यह दरवाज़ा, उस दरवाज़े से छोटा है। This door is smaller than that door.
(Yeh der-waa-zaa, üs der-waa-zay say Cho-Taa hai.)

Or

उस दरवाज़े से यह दरवाज़ा छोटा है। Compared to that door, this door is smaller.
(üs der-waa-zay say, yeh der-waa-zaa Cho-Taa hai.)

Or

उस दरवाज़े से छोटा, यह दरवाज़ा है। Compared to that door, this door is smaller.
(üs der-waa-zay say Cho-Taa, yeh der-waa-zaa hai.)

वे खिड़कियाँ, इन खिड़कियों से बड़ी हैं। Those windows are bigger than these windows.
(Vay khirD-ki-yaȧ, in khirD-ki-yȯ say berDee hain̉)

Or

इन खिड़कियों से, वे खिड़कियाँ बड़ीं हैं। Compared to these windows, those windows are bigger.
(In khirD-ki-yȯ say, vay khirD-ki-yaȧ berDee hain̉.)

Or

इन खिड़कियों से बड़ी, वे खिड़कियाँ हैं।   Compared to these windows, those windows are bigger.
(In khirD-ki-yó say berDee, vay khirD-ki-yaá hain.)

मेरा घर, आपके घर से बड़ा है।   My house is bigger than your house.
(May-raa gher aap-kay gher say berDaa hai.)

Or

आपके घर से, मेरा घर बड़ा है।   Compared to your house, my house is bigger.
(Aap-kay gher say, may-raa gher berDaa hai.)

Or

आपके घर से बड़ा, मेरा घर है।   Compared to your house, my house is bigger.
(Aap-kay gher say berDaa, may-raa gher hai.)

Practice 2
Translate the following sentences into Hindi based on the examples given above.

1. His room is bigger than mine.

   _____

2. The study room is smaller than the bedroom.

   _____

3. The living room is more beautiful than the bedroom.

   _____

4. My father's bedroom is better than mine.

   _____

The superlative degree of adjectives has a fixed expression: सब से (*of all*) **+ adjective.**

Subject +	Object of Comparison +	सबसे	+	Adjective +	Auxiliary Verb
मेरे पिताजी	का घर	सबसे		बड़ा	है।
(May-ray pitaa-jee	kaa gher	sub-say		berDaa	hai.)

               (My father's house is the biggest.)

Practice 3

Complete the sentences based on the example given below. Choose the appropriate adjective from the options and add the superlative construction to complete each sentence.

Example:

This room is the biggest. यह कमरा <u>सबसे बड़ा</u> है।

(साफ़ लंबी हवादार सुंदर)

1.   इस कमरे की खिड़कियाँ _____ हैं। *(fem. pl.)*

2.   हमारे घर का बाग़ीचा _____ है। *(masc. sing.)*

3.   उसके घर का फ़र्श _____ है। *(masc. sing.)*

4.   इस घर की चारदीवारी _____ है। *(fem. sing.)*

Practice 4

The conversation below is about Roshan's new home. In this conversation you will learn how the locative postpositions such as "in front of," "behind," "above," and comparatives are used when describing a home.

Read along with the audio and circle all the simple postpositions, compound postpositions, and the comparative and superlative forms on the text below.

Part 1 [01-08]

राजन :   नमस्ते रौशन

रौशन :   नमस्ते राजन

राजन :   रौशन तुम कैसे हो?

रौशन :   मैं ठीक हूँ, तुम कैसे हो? अन्दर आओ।

राजन :   मैं भी ठीक हूँ। तुम्हारा घर तो बहुत सुंदर है। अपना घर दिखाओ।

रौशन :   ज़रूर, आओ देखो। हमारा घर दो मंज़िला है। चलो, पहले ऊपर चलें। ऊपर की मंज़िल पर चार कमरे हैं। सबसे पहले यह हमारा कमरा है। यह कमरा, दूसरे कमरों से बड़ा है। इसके साथ एक बड़ा सा गुसलखाना भी है। यह दूसरा कमरा है। यह हमारे कमरे से थोड़ा सा छोटा है। यह हमारे बच्चों का कमरा है। यह तीसरा कमरा बच्चों के पढ़ने का कमरा है। और यह है चौथा कमरा, यह हमारा फ़ैमिली रूम है।

राजन :   हर कमरे के साथ गुसलखाने भी हैं?

रौशन :   नहीं, एक हमारे कमरे के साथ है और दूसरा बच्चों के कमरे के साथ।

Romanization 1

Raaj-un   : Num-us-tay Raw-shun.

Raw-shun : Num-us-tay Raaj-un.

Raaj-un   : Raw-shun tüm kai-say ho?

Raw-shun : Maiṅ Theek hoȯ, tüm kai-say ho? Under aao.

Raa-jun   : Maiṅ bhee Theek hoȯ. Tüm-haa-raa gher toe bahüt sünder hai. Up-naa gher dhi-khaa-o.

Raw-shun : Zaroor, aao day-kho. Hum-aa-raa gher doe mun-zilaa hai, ch-ul-o peh-lay ooper ch-ul-aiṅ. Ooper kee mun-zil per ch-aar kum-ray haiṅ. Sub-say peh-lay yeh hum-aa-raa kum-raa hai. Yeh kum-raa, doos-ray kum-rȯ say berDaa hai. Is-kay saath ayk berDaa saa gü-sul-khaa-naa bhi hai. Yeh doos-raa kum-raa hai. Yeh hum-aa-ray kum-ray say thorDaa saa Cho-Taa hai. Yeh hum-aa-ray bu-uch-chȯ kaa kum-raa hai. Yeh tees-raa kum-raa buch-chȯ kay perDh-nay kaa kum-raa hai. Aur yeh hai chaw-thaa kum-raa, yeh hum-aa-raa family room hai.

Raaj-un   : Her kum-ray kay saath gü-sul-khaa-nay bhee haiṅ?

Raw-shun : Nuh-heeṅ ayk hum-aa-ray kum-ray kay saath hai aur doos-raa bu-uch-chȯ kay kum-ray kay saath.

Translation 1

Rajan   : Hello, Roshan.

Roshan   : Hello, Rajan.

Rajan   : How are you, Roshan?

Roshan   : I am fine. Tell me: how are you doing?

Rajan   : I am fine too. Your house is so beautiful, show me your house.

Roshan   : Why not? Definitely, come and see. Our home has two stories. Let's go upstairs first. On the upper floor are four rooms. First of all, this is our room. Attached to it is a bathroom. Here is the second room. It is a little smaller than our room. This is our children's room. And the third room is the children's study room. This is the fourth room: it is our family room.

Rajan   : Is a bathroom attached to every room?

Roshan   : No, one is attached to our room and the other one is attached to the children's room.

Part 2 🎧 01-09

Now listen to the second part of the conversation and answer the comprehension questions below.

राजन — वाह! तुम्हारे कमरे तो बहुत हवादार हैं, हर कमरे में बड़ी बड़ी खिड़कियाँ भी हैं। और सबसे ऊपर क्या है?

रोशन — सबसे ऊपर एक छत है। छत भी बहुत खुली और बड़ी है। चलो, अब नीचे चलते हैं।

राजन — ठीक है, चलो।

रोशन — यह हमारी बैठक है, इसकी बग़ल में यह हमारा रसोईघर है, और साथ ही खाने का कमरा है। यहाँ एक और गुसलखाना है। रसोईघर की बगल में, ऊपर जाने के लिए सीढ़ियाँ भी हैं। और पीछे की तरफ़ एक आँगन भी है।

राजन — वाह रोशन, तुम्हारा घर देखकर मज़ा आ गया।

Romanization 2

Raaj-un   : Vaah! tüm-haa-ray kum-ray toe bahut huw-aa-daar hain, her kum-ray maẏ-berDee khirD-ki-yaȧ bhee hain. Aur oo-per kyaa hai?

Raw-shun : Sub-say oo-per ayk Ch-ut hai. Ch-ut bhee bahut khu-lee aur berDee hai. Ch-ulo ub nee-chay chul-tay hain.

Raaj-un   : Theek hai, Ch-ul-o.

Raw-shun : Yeh hum-aa-ree baiTh-uk hai, iskee bug-ul maẏ yeh hum-aa-raa rus-oee gher hai, aur saath hee khaa-nay kaa kum-raa hai. Yuh-haȧ ayk güs-ul-khaa-naa hai. Rus-oee gher ki bug-ul maẏ ooper jaa-nay kay li-yay see-rDhi-yaȧ bhee hain. Aur pee-Chay ki ter-uf ayk aȧ-gun bhee hai.

Raaj-un   : Vaah Raw-shun, tüm-haa-raa gher day-kh-ker muz-aa aag-guh-yaa.

Practice 5 Comprehension Check

Now listen again and answer the following comprehension questions.

1. How many stories does Roshan's house have?
    रोशन का घर कितनी मंज़िला है/ रोशन के घर में कितनी मंज़िलें हैं?

    _____

2. What is on the top floor?
    सबसे ऊपर क्या है?

    _____

3. What is the third room for?
    तीसरा कमरा किसके लिए है?

    _____

4. How many bathrooms are there in the house?
    घर में कितने ग़ुसलख़ाने हैं?

    _____

5. What is behind the house?
    घर के पीछे क्या है?

    _____

6.	Where are the stairs in the house located?
	घर में सीढ़ियाँ कहाँ हैं?

_____

Translation 2

Rajan	:	Wonderful! Your rooms are so ventilated, and every room has big windows as well. And what is on the topmost floor?

Roshan	:	On the topmost floor is the terrace, which is also very open and big. Let's go downstairs now.

Rajan	:	OK, let's go.

Roshan	:	This is our living room, and next to it is our kitchen, and attached to it is the dining room. There is one more bathroom here. The stairs leading to the second level are next to the kitchen. And there is a courtyard at the back of the house.

Rajan	:	Wow! Roshan, I really like your house.

Practice 6

Create questions for the following answers.

1.	Answer: We have a two-story house.
	हमारा घर दो मंज़िला है? (Hum-aa-raa gher do mun-zilaa hai.)

	Question: _____

2.	Answer: This is our kitchen, and the dining room is attached to the kitchen.
	ये हमारा रसोईघर है, और साथ ही खाने का कमरा है।
	(Yeh hum-aa-raa rus-oee gher hai, aur saath hee khaa-nay kaa kum-raa hai.)

	Question: _____

3.	Answer: There is a courtyard behind the house.
	घर के पीछे की तरफ़ एक आँगन भी है।
	(Gher kay pee-Chay kee ter-uf ayk aà-gun bhee hai.)

	Question: _____

4.	Answer: That room is bigger than the other rooms.
	वह कमरा, दूसरे कमरों से बड़ा है।
	(Veh kum-raa, doos-ray kum-rò say berDaa hai.)

	Question: _____

5.   Answer: On the top floor is a terrace.
       सबसे ऊपर, एक खुली छत है I (Sub-say ooper, ayk khü-lee Ch-ut hai.)

Question: _____

1.5 My Daily Routine मेरी दिनचर्या

Objectives

By the end of this chapter, students will be able to:
1.   Describe their daily routine, including the time they take for each activity.
2.   Understand some cultural differences between the daily routines of their culture and
       the culture in India.
3.   Use the suitable words to describe their routine, e.g. *wake up, eat breakfast, wash
       face, get dressed, leave the house,* etc.

Vocabulary 01-10

Verbs -infinitive (to..) form

बताना	(but-aa-naa)	*v.t.*	to tell
उठना	(üTh-naa)	*v.i.*	to wake up
करना	(ker-naa)	*v.t.*	to do
बनाना	(bun-aa-naa)	*v.t.*	to make
पीना	(pee-naa)	*v.t.*	to drink
जाना	(jaa-naa)	*v.i.*	to go
घूमना	(ghoom-naa)	*v.i.*	to walk
नहाना	(nuh-aa-naa)	*v.i.*	to bathe
धोना	(dho-naa)	*v.t.*	to wash
खाना	(khaa-naa)	*v.t.*	to eat
देखना	(day-kh-naa)	*v.t.*	to watch, to see
सोना	(so-naa)	*v.i.*	to sleep
सो जाना	(so jaa-naa)	*comp. v.i.*	to go to sleep

Conjunct verbs (a noun + a verb)

मंजन करना	(mun-jun ker-naa)	*masc. v.t.*	to brush (teeth)
की मदद करना	(kee mud-ud ker-naa)	*fem. v.t.*	to help
व्यायाम/कसरत करना	(vyaa-yaam/kus-rut ker-naa)	*masc./fem. v.t.*	to exercise

Verbs with conjunctive participle कर

उठकर	(üTh-ker)	after getting up
पीकर	(pee-ker)	after drinking
करके	(ker-kay)	after doing

आकर	(aa-ker)		after coming back
नहाकर	(nuh-haa-ker)		after taking bath
पढ़कर	(perDh-ker)		after reading/studying
खाकर	(khaa-ker)		after eating
रुककर	(rük-ker)		after stopping
पहुँचकर	(puh-hüch ker)		after/upon arriving

Nouns

रसोई	(Rus-oo-ee)	*fem. sing.*	kitchen
शाम	(shaam)	*fem. sing.*	evening
रात	(raat)	*fem. sing.*	night
खाना	(khaa-naa)	*masc. sing.*	food
फल	(ph-ul)	*masc. sing.*	fruit
अख़बार	(ukh-baar)	*masc. sing.*	newspaper
बाग़	(baa-gh)	*masc. sing.*	garden
दफ़्तर	(duf-ter)	*masc. sing.*	office
पूजा	(poo-jaa)	*fem. sing.*	worship
सैर	(sair)	*fem. sing.*	brisk walk
हाथ	(haa-th)	*masc. sing.*	hand
मुँह	(müh)	*masc. sing.*	face
आराम	(aa-raam)	*masc. sing.*	rest
घंटा	(gh-un-Taa)	*masc. sing.*	hour

Adverbs

थोड़ी देर	(thorDee der)	for a while/for some time
फिर	(phir)	then
उसके बाद	(üs-kay baad)	after that
लगभग/क़रीब	(lug-bhug/ker-eeb)	approximately
तक	(tuk)	till

Adjectives

सात	(saat)	seven
आठ	(aaTh)	eight
दस	(dus)	ten
सवा	(suv-aa)	fifteen minutes after (time)
साढ़े	(saarDhe)	thirty minutes after (time)

Grammar: Habitual Present Tense and Conjunctive Participle ker कर

Habitual Present Tense: As the word suggests, this kind of grammatical structure indicates that an activity is done habitually or daily in the present time. The habitual form of the main verb is made up of the root of a verb and the suffix tá, tī, tè (ता, ती, ते) according to the gender and number of the subject; and the subject in such form is always in the direct case, as it is used in English, i.e., "I go to school every day."

Structure: Subject + Object (if any) + verb + Auxiliary Verb

मैं		खाना	खाता/ती	+ हूँ (with an object, food)
(Main	खा-naa		khaa-tee	hoṅ)
I	eat		food.	

वे		दफ़्तर	जाते +	हैं (no object)
(Vey	duf-ter		jaa-tey	hain.)
They go to the office.				

NOTE All transitive verbs in a sentence take an object, which gives an answer to the question word *What* (an inanimate object). An intransitive verb never have an object in a sentence.

i.e.:   What do you eat every day? }
        What do you make?   } Transitive verbs

        I get up at seven every day.   }
        She goes to school in the morning. } Intransitive verbs

Habitual Verb Conjugations with Pronouns

Pronoun	Verb	Auxiliary
मैं (main) I *(first person)*	जाता (jaa-taa) (to go) *masc. sing.* जाती (jaa-tee) *fem. sing.*	हूँ (hoṅ) हूँ
तुम (tüm) you *(second person familiar)*	खाते (khaa-taa) (to eat) *masc. sing.* खाती (khaa-tee) *fem. sing.*	हो (ho) हो
तुम लोग (tüm low-g) you people *(second person familiar)*	खाते (khaa-taa) (to eat) *masc. pl.* खाती (khaa-tee) *fem. pl.*	हो (ho) हो
आप (aap) you *(second person formal, pl./ honorific)*	पीते (pee-tay) (to drink) *m.pl./ honorific* पीतीं (pee-teṅ) *fem. pl./honorific*	हैं (hain) हैं

Pronoun	Verb	Auxiliary
यह/ वह (yeh/veh) he, she, this, that *(third person sing.)*	करता (ker-taa) (to do) *masc. sing.* करती (ker-tee) *fem. sing*	है (hai) है
तू (too) you *(second person sing. & intimate)*	देखता (deykh-taa) (to see) *masc. sing.* देखती (deykh-tee) *fem. sing.*	है (hai) है
ये/ वे (yay/vay) he, she, they, these, those *(third person pl. & honorific)*	बनाते (bun-aa-tay) (to make) *masc. pl./honorific* बनातीं (bun-aa-teė) *fem. pl./honorific*	हैं (hain) हैं

Practice 1

Learn to form verbs in the habitual tense. Add the suffix ता taa for masculine singular, ती tee for feminine singular, ते tay for masculine plural or honorific, and तीं teė for feminine plural or honorific. Refer the examples above and complete the table.

	Verb	*Masc. sing.*	*Masc. pl./ honorific*	*Fem. sing.*	*Fem. pl./ honorific*
	खाना (to eat)	खाता	खाते	खाती	खातीं
1.	पीना (to drink)				
2.	जाना (to go)				
3.	घूमना (to walk)				
4.	आना (to come)				
5.	करना (to do)				
6.	बनाना (to make)				

Practice 2

Choose the appropriate verb from the list given and conjugate them to complete the sentence. Take note of the subject and the auxiliary verb conjugation in bold.

(देखना पकाना जाना खाना करना)

1. क्या **तुम** रोज़ कसरत _____ **हो**? *(masc.pl.)*　　Do you exercise every day?

2. **राम** रोज़ _____ **है** । *(masc. sing)*　　Ram eats fruits every day.

3. **रेनू** स्कूल _____ **है** । *(fem. sing)*　　Renu goes to school.

4. **माँ** खाना _____ **हैं** । *(fem. honorific)* Mother makes food.

5. **मैं** रात को टी वी _____ **हूँ** । *(fem. sing)*　　I watch TV at night.

Practice 3

Translate the fallowing sentences into Hindi.

1. Ram goes to school at 7 in the morning.

    _____

2. Sheela prepares dinner at 8 in the evening.

    _____

3. She goes to library every day at 5.

    _____

4. He watches TV in the evening.

    _____

5. Ranu helps her mother in the kitchen.

    _____

Conjunctive Participle: Conjunctive participles कर ker or के kay in Hindi is used to join two verb phrases. कर ker can be translated as *after, after that, and then* or *upon* in English

Example:

After eating he goes for a walk.
खाना खाकर/खाके वह घूमता है ।
(Khaa-naa khaa-ker/khaa-kay veh ghoom-taa hai.)

or

He goes for a walk after eating./He eats, and then he goes for a walk.
वह खाना खाकर/खाके घूमता है ।
(Veh khaa-naa khaa-ker/khaa-kay ghoom-taa hai.)

Did you notice that the above sentence has two verbs in sequence खाकर and घूमता? In this type of verb form, the first verb root always carries the conjunctive participles कर ker, and the second verb in sequence is inflected based on the gender or the number of subject(s) and the tense in which the sentence is formed.

Practice 4

Let's practice forming verbs with the conjunctive participle कर. Refer the example above as a model, and fill in the table.

Verb	Verb root	Conjunctive participles कर/के	Complete form conjunctive participles कर /के
उठना (to wake up)	उठ	कर/के	उठकर/उठके
नहाना (to bathe)			
जाना (to go)			
खाना (to eat)			
सोना (to sleep)			
बनाना (to make)			

Let's practice joining two verb phrases using the conjunctive participle कर/के. Follow the example to complete the activity.

Example:

She studies; after that, she eats.

वह खाना खाती है और उसके बाद /फिर वह पढ़ती है ।

With conjunctive कर: वह खाना **खाकर** पढ़ती है ।

Practice 5

Rewrite the sentences in Hindi, using the example given above as a model.

1. The boy watches TV for a while after he reaches home.
    लड़का स्कूल से आता है फिर थोड़ी देर टी वी देखता है ।

    _____

2. Upon reaching home, Father reads the newspaper.
    पिताजी घर आते हैं और फिर अख़बार पढ़ते हैं ।

    _____

3. She helps her mother after she gets home.
    वह घर पहुँचती है उसके बाद अपनी माँ की मदद करती है ।

    _____

NOTE The verb करना takes the conjunction ke के, instead of ker कर, to avoid redundancy; however, the conjuction ke के can be used with all the other verb roots in colloquial speech.

Practice 6 🎧 01-11

Read along with the audio and underline the verbs in the habitual present tense form and the verbs with the conjunctive participle कर.

मैं रोज़ सुबह सात बजे उठती हूँ और उठकर मंजन करती हूँ । मंजन करने के बाद मैं चाय बनाती हूँ और एक कप चाय पीती हूँ । चाय पीकर थोड़ी देर घूमने के लिए बाग़ में जाती हूँ । वहाँ मैं कुछ व्यायाम करती हूँ । व्यायाम करके आठ बजे तक वापस घर आती हूँ । घर आकर नहाती हूँ । नहाकर मैं पूजा करती हूँ । पूजा करके नाशता बनाती हूँ । लगभग सवा आठ बजे मैं नाश्ता करती हूँ और अख़बार पढ़ती हूँ । अख़बार पढ़कर मैं दफ़्तर जाती हूँ । दफ़्तर में मैं लगभग आठ घंटे काम करती हूँ । शाम को करीब पाँच बजे मैं घर वापस आती हूँ । घर आकर मैं हाथ मुँह धोती हूँ, फिर चाय पीती हूँ, और थोड़ी देर आराम करती हूँ । थोड़ी देर आराम करके, शाम का खाना बनाती हूँ । क़रीब आठ बजे खाना खाती हूँ । खाना खाकर थोड़ी देर सैर के लिए जाती हूँ । सैर से आने के बाद, थोड़ी देर टी वी देखती हूँ और लगभग साढ़े दस बजे तक सो जाती हूँ ।

Romanization

Main rowz sub-uh saat buj-ay üTh-tee hoon aur üTh-ker mun-jun ker-tee hoon. Mun-jun ker-nay kay baad main chai bun-aa-tee hoon aur ayk cup chai pee-tee hoon. Chai pee-ker ThorDee der ghoom-nay kay li-yay baagh maẏ jaa-tee hoon. Vuh-haȧ kuCh vyaa-yaam ker-tee hoon. Vyaa-yaam ker-kay aaTh buj-ay tuk vaa-pus gher aa-tee hoon. Gher aa-ker nuh-haa tee hoon. Nuh-haa-ker/poo-jaa ker-tee hoon. Poo-jaa ker-kay naash-taa bun-aa-tee hoon. Lug-bhug suv-aa aaTh buj-ay main naash-taa ker-tee hoon aur ukh-baar perDh-tee hoon. Ukh-baar perDh-ker main duf-ter jaa-tee hoon. dufter maẏ main lug-bhug aaTh gh-un-Tay kaam ker-tee hoon. Shaam ko ker-eeb paȧch buj-ay main gher vaa-pus aa-tee hoon. Gher aa-ker main haath moohn dho-tee hoon, phir chai pee-tee hoon aur thorDi der aa-raam ker-tee hoon. thorDee der aa-raam ker-key sham kaa khaa-naa bun-aa-tee hoon. Ker-eeb aaTh buj-ay khaa-naa khaa-tee hoon. Khaa-naa khaa-ker thorDee der sair ke liye jaa-tee hoon. Sair se aa-nay kay baad thorDee der T.V dekh-tee hoon aur lug-bhug saarDhe dus buj-ay tuk so jaa-tee hoon.

Translation

I get up at 7 o'clock every day and then I brush my teeth. I then make tea and drink a cup of it. After my tea, I go to the garden for a walk. There I exercise a little bit. I return home approximately at 8 o'clock. I take a bath and pray. After I have finished praying, I prepare breakfast. Around 8.15, I have my breakfast and read the newspaper. Then I go to the office. In the office, I work for eight hours. I return home around 5 o'clock in the evening. Upon returning home, I freshen up and have a cup of tea. After which, I make dinner. I eat at round 8 o'clock. After my dinner, I go for a brisk walk. On reaching home, I watch television for a while. At about 10 o'clock, I go to sleep.

Practice 7

Based on the reading example, apply your own daily routine based on the schedule given. You can use following verbs to create your daily routine.

Helping words: उठना, नहाना, मंजन करना, घूमना, सैर करना, नाश्ता करना, चाय पीना, जाना, काम करना, पढ़ाई करना, मदद करना, व्यायाम करना, आराम करना, टी वी देखना, क़िताब पढ़ना, अख़बार पढ़ना, खेलना, खाना बनाना

My Monday Schedule

Time	Activities
7.00 to 8.00 am	Wake up, then brush teeth, take a shower. Then eat simple breakfast with family.
8.00 am	Leave home, take a bus to school.
8.55 am	Reach school.
9.00 am to 3.30 pm	In school. (Have lunch at 1 pm)
4.00 to 5.00 pm	Play basketball with friends, then go home.
5.00 to 7.00 pm	Study on my own. Finish up homework.
7.30 pm	Have dinner.
8.00 to 11.00 pm	Watch TV, listen to the radio or do reading.
11.00 pm	Go to bed

Creative Writing

_____

_____

_____

_____

_____

_____

_____

_____

Practice 8   🎧 01-12

Listening to the dialogue between two girls.

Script

सीमा	:	मीरा तुम स्कूल के बाद क्या करती हो?
मीरा	:	स्कूल के बाद, मैं पढ़ने के लिए लाइब्रेरी जाती हूँ ।
सीमा	:	लाइब्रेरी मे तुम कितनी देर रहती हो?
मीरा	:	लाइबेरा में, मैं एक घंटा रुककर पढ़ाई करती हूँ ।
सीमा	:	उस के बाद तुम क्या करती हो?
मीरा	:	एक घंटा पढ़ाई करके, मैं योगा करने जाती हूँ । वहाँ एक-डेढ़ घंटे योगा करती हूँ ।
सीमा	:	योगा करके सीधे घर जाती हो?
मीरा	:	हाँ, योगा करके, मैं सीधे घर जाती हूँ ।
सीमा	:	घर पहुँचकर क्या करती हो?
मीरा	:	घर पहुँचकर, नहाती-धोती हूँ, और थोड़ा आराम करती हूँ ।
सीमा	:	और उस के बाद?
मीरा	:	फिर मैं रसोई में माँ की मदद करती हूँ । लगभग आठ बजे हम खाना खाते हैं और थोड़ी देर टी वी देखकर मैं सो जाती हूँ ।

Listen to the dialogue again and now fill in the missing words.

सीमा : मीरा _____ स्कूल के बाद क्या _____

मीरा : स्कूल के बाद _____ पढ़ने के लिए लाइब्रेरी _____ ।

सीमा : लाइब्रेरी में _____ कितनी देर _____ _____

मीरा : लाइब्रेरी में, मैं एक घंटा _____ पढ़ाई करती हूँ ।

सीमा : तुम क्या करती हो?

मीरा : एक घंटा _____ _____ मैं योगा करने जाती हूँ । वहाँ एक-डेढ़ घंटे _____ करती हूँ ।

सीमा : योगा _____ _____ घर जाती हो?

मीरा : हाँ, योगा करके, मैं सीधे _____ _____ हूँ ।

सीमा : घर _____ _____ क्या करती हो?

मीरा : घर पहुँचकर, _____ _____ हूँ, और _____ _____ करती हूँ ।

सीमा : और उस के बाद?

मीरा : फिर मैं _____ _____ में माँ _____ _____ करती हूँ ।

_____ आठ बजे _____ खाना _____ _____ और थोड़ी देर टी वी

_____ मैं _____ _____ हूँ ।

Practice 9
Answer the questions on the dialogue in Hindi.

1. मीरा स्कूल के बाद कहाँ जाती है?
   Where does Meera go after school?

   _____

2. लाइब्रेरी में रुककर मीरा क्या करती है?
   What does Meera do in the library?

   _____

3. मीरा माँ की मदद कब करती है?
   When does Meera help her mother?

   _____

4. मीरा व्यायाम करके कहीं और भी जाती है?
   Does Meera go to some other places after her exercise?

   _____

5. घर पहुँचकर मीरा क्या-क्या करती है?
   What else does Meera do upon reaching home?

   _____

Romanization
Seema : Meera, tüm school kay baad kyaa ker-tee ho?
Meera : School kay baad main perDh-nay lay liye library jaa-tee hoȯ.
Seema : Library maẏ tüm kit-nee der reh-tee ho?
Meera : Library maẏ main ayk gh-un-Taa rük-ker perdh-aa-yee ker-tee hoȯ.
Seema : Üs-kay baad tüm kyaa ker-tee ho?
Meera : Ayk gh-un-Taa perDh-aa-yee ker-kay main yoga ker-nay jaa-tee joon. Vuh-haȧ
        ayk DerDh gh-un-Taa yoga ker-tee hoȯ.
Seema : Yoga ker-kay see-dhay gher jaa-tee ho?

Meera   :   Haȧ yoga ker-kay see-dhay gher jaa-tee hoȯ.

Seema   :   Gher puh-hünch-ker kyaa ker-tee ho?

Meera   :   Gher puh-hüch-ker nuh-haa-tee dho-tee hoon aur thorDaa aa-raam ker-tee hoȯ.

Seema   :   aur üs-kay baad?

Meera   :   phir main rus-o-yee mein maȧ kee mud-ud ker-tee hoon. Lug-bhug aaTh buj-ay hum khaa-naa khaa-tay hain aur ThorDee der T.V dekh-ker main so jaa-tee hoȯ.

Translation

Seema   :   Meera, what do you do after school?

Meera   :   After school, I go to the library to study.

Seema   :   How long do you stay in the library?

Meera   :   I stay there for an hour and study.

Seema   :   What do you do after that?

Meera   :   After studying for an hour, I go to do yoga. I do yoga for an hour.

Seema   :   Do you go directly home?

Meera   :   Yes, I go directly home after the exercise.

Seema   :   What do you do after reaching home?

Meera   :   Upon reaching home, I bathe, wash and rest for a while.

Seema   :   And after that?

Meera   :   Then I help my mom in the kitchen. At about 8 o' clock we eat, and after which, I watch TV for a while. I then go to sleep.

*Read the full dialogue on pages 79–80.

Traveling in India

2.1 At a Train Station in India भारत में रेल स्टेशन पर

Objectives

By the end of this lesson you will be able to converse with a person behind the ticket window and:

1. Buy a train ticket.
2. Ask for arrival and departure information using the verb लगना.
3. Cancel a train ticket.
4. Acquire and understand travel information.
5. Fill out a train reservation form using thematic vocabulary.

📖 **Culture Note**

Indian Railways, or भारतीय रेल, owned and operated by the Indian government, is one of the largest rail networks in the world. Indian Railways transports millions of people daily from one end of India to another. It is one of the safest modes of traveling in India where one can experience shades of Indian culture, landscapes, human behavior, and much more; the whole rail system covers approximately 65,000 km (40,000 mi) over 7,500 stations.

The 21st century has brought many technological advancements and India is also very much impacted by it. At present, many new and high-speed trains are running on tracks with all the amenities and comforts of travel. The train reservation system has also become computerized; however, human interaction cannot be ignored. Therefore in this lesson, we will show you how to survive using Hindi in India in such a scenario where technology has not yet fully arrived.

Vocabulary

Verbs

निकलना	(nik-ul-naa)	*v.i.*	to depart
चलना	(ch-ul-naa)	*v.i.*	to leave, to depart, to move
पहुँचना	(puh-hünch-naa)	*v.i.*	to arrive, to reach
भरना	(bh-er-naa)	*v.i.*	to fill in something or to fill up
जानना	(jaa-nuh-naa)	*v.i.*	to know
चाहना	(chaah-naa)	*v.i.*	to want
पैसे लगना	(pai-say lug-naa)	*v.i.*	to cost money
समय लगना	(sum-ay lug-naa)	*v.i.*	to take time
चाहिए	(chaa-hi-yay)	*aux. v.*	need

Adverbs

कब-कब	(cub-cub)	when, what times
सुबह	(süb-uh)	morning
बजे	(buj-ay)	o'clock
घंटे	(gh-un-Tay)	hours
तक	(tuk)	till, up till

Adjectives

सवा	(suv-aa)	fifteen [*time*] after
चार	(chaar)	four
पाँच	(paà-ch)	five
छह	(Ch-eh)	six
सौ	(saw)	hundred
साठ	(saa-Th)	sixty
निचली	(nich-lee)	lower
ऊपरी	(oop-er-ee)	upper
पहली	(peh-lee)	first
दूसरी	(doos-ree)	second
शाकाहारी	(shaa-kaa-haa-ree)	vegetarian
माँसाहारी	(maà-saa-haa-ree)	non-vegetarian

Nouns

यात्रा	(yaa-traa)	*fem.*	journey, travel
किराया	(kir-aa-yaa)	*masc.*	fare, rent
आरक्षण	(aa-ruk-shun)	*masc.*	reservation
गंतव्य	(gun-tuv-yuh)	*masc.*	destination
वापसी	(vaa-pus-ee)	*fem.*	return (from somewhere)
श्रेणी	(shray-rnee)	*fem.*	grade, class
विवरण	(viv-run)	*masc.*	detail
हस्ताक्षर	(hust-aak-sher)	*masc.*	signature

उम्र/आयु	(üm-ruh)	*fem.*	age
तारीख़	(Taa-ree-kh)	*fem.*	date
चयन	(ch-uh-y-uh-n-uh)	*masc.*	selection
स्त्री	(s-tree)	*fem.*	woman
पुरुष	(pü-rü-sh)	*masc.*	man
लिंग	(ling)	*masc.*	gender
स्थान	(sth-aan)	*masc*	place

Grammar

Lagna लगना is to express requirement (amount), cost, and time that something or someone takes.

Look at some of the examples that use लगना for cost, similar to the expressions "how much does it cost," "will it cost," "did it cost" and so forth. Sentence variations without using लगना will also be provided. Study the sentences below to understand the grammatical structure.

1. How much does a ticket from Delhi to Calcutta cost?
   दिल्ली से कलकत्ते का टिकट <u>कितने का लगता</u> है?
   (Dil-lee say c-ul-cutt-ay kaa Tik-ut kit-nay kaa lug-taa hai?)

2. How much will a ticket from Mumbai to Jaipur cost?
   मुम्बई से जयपुर का टिकट <u>कितने का लगेगा</u>?
   (Müm-bai say Jai-pür kaa Tik-ut kit-nay kaa lug-ay-gaa?)

3. How much did the ticket cost you?
   तुम्हें टिकट <u>कितने का लगा</u>?
   (Tüm-hay Tik-ut kit-nay kaa lug-aa?)

Answers for the above questions can be:

1. It costs 1,423 rupees from Delhi to Calcutta.
   दिल्ली से कलकत्ता के एक हज़ार चार सौ तेईस रुपये लगते हैं । (*habitual present*)
   (Dil-lee say Cul-cut-taa kay ayk huz-aar chaar saw tay-ees rü-puh-yay lug-tay hain.)

2. It will cost 1,300 rupees from Mumbai to Jaipur.
   मुम्बई से जयपुर के तेरह सौ रुपये लगेंगे । (*future*)
   (Müm-bai say Aag-raa kay tay-ruh saw rü-puh-yay lug-aẏ-gay.)

3. It cost me 800 rupees.
   मुझे टिकट आठ सौ रुपये का लगा । (*simple perfect*)
   (Müjhay Tick-uT aaTh sau rüp-uh-yay kaa lug-aa.)

In the above sentences, the intransitive verb लगना is changed based on the tense, i.e., habitual, future, or past. The intransitive verb लगना is also reflected in the gender of the noun "ticket," a masculine noun in Hindi.

Using the intransitive verb लगना with time:

1. How long does a train take to travel from Agra to Lucknow?
    ट्रेन को /गाड़ी को आगरा से लखनऊ पहुँचने में कितना समय लगता है? (habitual present)
    (Train ko/gaa-rDee ko Aag-raa say Luck-nuh-oo puh-hůṅch-nay maẏ kit-naa sum-ay lug-taa hai?)

2. How long will the train take to reach Ajmer?
    ट्रेन को /गाड़ी को अजमेर पहुँचने में कितना समय लगेगा? (future)
    (Train ko/gaa-rDee ko Uj-may-r puh-hůṅch-nay maẏ kit-naa sum-ay lug-ay-gaa?)

3. How long did the train take to get from Jaipur to Delhi?
    ट्रेन को /गाड़ी को जयपुर से दिल्ली पहुँचने में कितना समय लगा? (simple perfect)
    (Train ko/gaa-rDee ko Jai-pür say Dil-lee puh-hůṅch-nay maẏ kit-naa sum-ay lug-aa?)

4. Why is the train taking so long to arrive?
    ट्रेन को /गाड़ी को आने में इतना समय क्यों लग रहा है? (present progressive)
    (Train ko/gaa-rDee ko aa-nay maẏ it-naa sum-ay kẏo lug ruh-haa hai?)

Answers to the above questions can be:

1. It takes four hours for the train to travel from Agra to Lucknow.
    ट्रेन को /गाड़ी को आगरा से लखनऊ पहुँचने में चार घंटे लगते हैं ।
    (Train ko/gaa-rDee ko Aag-raa puh-hůṅch-nay maẏ chaar gh-un-Tay lug-tay haiṅ.)

2. It will take an hour for the train to reach Ajmer.
    ट्रेन को /गाड़ी को अजमेर पहुँचने में एक घंटा लगेगा ।
    (Train ko/gaa-rDee ko Uj-may-r puh-hůṅch-nay maẏ ayk gh-un-Taa lug-ay-gaa.)

3. It took five hours for the train to travel from Jaipur to Delhi.
    ट्रेन को /गाड़ी को जयपुर से दिल्ली पहुँचने में पाँच घंटे लगे ।
    (Train ko/gaa-rDee ko Jai-pür say Dil-lee puh-hůṅch-nay maẏ paaṅ-ch gh-un-Tay lug-ay.)

4. (Anything. For that, a reason is needed.)
    For example:

    There is a technical problem with the train engine.
    ट्रेन के इंजन में खराबी आ गयी है ।
    (Train kay in-jun maẏ koi kher-aa-bee aa gayee hai.)

Did you notice a change in the sentence structure? The main difference between the two structures using the same auxiliary verb लगना is the addition of a verb in the oblique form (indirect form: when a subject or object is blocked by a postposition) "आने में" and "पहुँचने में." Whenever you need to use a verb in such case, change the main verb into the oblique form like this:

Main verb	Oblique Form
आना (aa-naa)	आने में (aa-nay maẏ)
जाना (jaa-naa)	जाने में (jaa-nay maẏ)
निकलना (nik-ul-naa)	निकलने में (nikul-nay maẏ)

These days buying train tickets in India is computerized. You can go to the train station and book your ticket; you may also do it from the comfort of your home, or you can use a travel agent. The purpose here is to use the language with locals because it is possible that some of the stations are not yet fully equipped with the computerized reservation system.

Read the vocabulary for inquiring about the cost of a ticket and the train schedule.

Practice 1 Vocabulary-Building Exercise
Match each word on the left column with the correct definition on the right column.

1. यात्रा   the price of transportation
2. किराया   a place where a person ends his/her journey
3. आरक्षण   to come back from somewhere
4. गंतव्य   to go from one place to another
5. ऊपरी   a pre-arrangement to secure space
6. वापसी   at an upper level
7. श्रेणी   the act of inscribing your name
8. निकलना   to depart
9. विवरण   to move
10. भरना   age
11. हस्ताक्षर   a grade of seating arrangement in a plane or a train
12. चाहना   the date of the month
13. चाहिए   to fill out
14. चलना   a detailed description
15. उम्र   to desire
16. तारीख़   indicates need

Practice 2 Pre-Listening Exercise

Fill in the blanks with the appropriate Hindi word.

मुझे दिल्ली से आगरा के दो टिकट _____ ।

1. (need)

पहले आपको यह फ़ॉर्म _____ होगा ।

2. (to fill out)

पहले मैं यह _____ चाहता हूँ कि, दिल्ली से आगरा के लिए ट्रेन _____ हैं?

3. (to know)   4. (what times)

देखिए, दिल्ली से आगरा के लिए _____ दो गाड़ियाँ हैं ।

5. (morning)

_____ है नई दिल्ली-भोपाल शताब्दी ऐक्सप्रैस, यह दिल्ली से सुबह छह बजे _____ है

6. (first)   7. (departs)

_____ है दिल्ली-लखनऊ स्वर्ण शताब्दी ऐक्सप्रैस, यह सुबह _____ छह बजे

8. (second)   9. (fifteen after)

निकलती है ।

दोनों गाड़ियाँ _____ से स्टेशन से चलतीं हैं?

10. (which)

ये दोनों _____ नई दिल्ली स्टेशन से ही _____ हैं ।

11. (trains)   12. (departs)

अच्छा, और इनको आगरा पहुँचने में _____ है?

13. (How much time does it take?)

दिल्ली- भोपाल-शताब्दी को _____ और छह मिनट लगते हैं ।

14. (two hours)

यह नई दिल्ली _____ आगरा कैन्ट _____ जाती है और दूसरी गाड़ी को दो

15. (from)   16. (to)

घंटे और छत्तीस मिनट । यह टूंडला तक _____ है ।

17. (goes)

अच्छा, और इनका _____ कितना _____ है?

18. (fare)   19. (costs)

सुबह _____ गाड़ी के चार सौ पाँच रुपये लगते हैं और सवा छह बजे वाली

  20. (the one at six o'clock)

गाड़ी का किराया _____ रुपये है।

  21. (four hundred sixty)

एक फ़ॉर्म _____ ।

  22. (please give me)

यह _____ ।

  23. (please take)

Practice 3 🎧 02-02

Now listen to the conversation and read along with it. Then complete the activities that follow.

यात्री	: मुझे दिल्ली से आगरा के दो टिकट चाहिएँ।
क्लर्क	: पहले आपको यह फ़ॉर्म भरना होगा। यह लीजिए, यह फ़ॉर्म भर दीजिए।
यात्री	: लेकिन पहले मैं यह जानना चाहता हूँ कि, दिल्ली से आगरा के लिए ट्रेन कब-कब हैं?
क्लर्क	: देखिए, दिल्ली से आगरा के लिए सुबह दो गाड़ियाँ हैं। पहली है नई दिल्ली-भोपाल शताब्दी ऐक्सप्रैस, यह दिल्ली से सुबह छह बजे निकलती है और दूसरी है दिल्ली-लखनऊ स्वर्ण शताब्दी ऐक्सप्रैस, यह सुबह सवा छह बजे निकलती है।
यात्री	: दोनों गाड़ियाँ कौन से स्टेशन से चलती हैं?
क्लर्क	: ये दोनों गाड़ियाँ नई दिल्ली स्टेशन से ही चलती हैं।
यात्री	: अच्छा, और इनको आगरा पहुँचने में कितना समय लगता है?
क्लर्क	: दिल्ली-भोपाल शताब्दी को दो घंटे और छह मिनट लगते हैं, यह नई दिल्ली से आगरा कैन्ट तक जाती है और दूसरी गाड़ी को दो घंटे और छत्तीस मिनट लगते हैं और यह टूंडला तक जाती है।
यात्री	: अच्छा, और इनका किराया कितना लगता है?
क्लर्क	: सुबह छह बजे वाली गाड़ी के चार सौ पाँच रुपये लगते हैं और सवा छह बजे वाली गाड़ी का किराया चार सौ साठ रुपये है।
यात्री	: अच्छा, एक फ़ॉर्म दे दीजिए।
क्लर्क	: यह लीजिए।

Romanization

Yaat-ree : Mü-jh-ay Dill-lee say Aag-raa kay doe Tick-uT chaa-hi-yay.

Clerk : Peh-lay aap-ko yeh form bher-naa ho-gaa. Yeh lee-ji-yay, yeh form bher dee-ji-yay.

Yaat-ree : Lay-kin peh-lay maiṅ yeh jaan-naa chaa-h-taa hoṅ ki Dill-lee say Aag-raa kay li-yay Train cub-cub haiṅ?

| Clerk | : | Day-khi-yay, Dill-lee say Aag-raa kay li-yay süb-uh doe gaarD-iyaà hain. Peh-lee hai Nuh-yee Dill-lee-Bho-paal Shut-aab-dee Express, yeh Dill-lee say süb-uh Cheh buj-ay nik-ul-tee hai aur doos-ree hai Dill-lee-Luckh-nuh-oo Sw-urn Shut-aab-dee Express, yeh süb-uh suh-vaa Cheh buj-ay nik-ul-tee hai. |

Yaat-ree : Doe-nò gaarD-iyaan kawn say station say ch-ul-tee hain.

Clerk : Yay doe-nò gaarD-iyaà Nuh-ee Dill-lee station say hee ch-ul-teen hain.

Yaat-ree : Uch-Chaa, aur in-ko Aag-raa puh-hünch-nay maỳ kit-naa sum-ay lug-taa hai?

Clerk : Dill-lee-Bho-paal Shut-aab-dee ko doe gh-un-Tay aur Cheh min-uT lug-tay hain. Yeh Nuh-ee Dill-lee say Aag-raa Cant tuk jaa-tee hai aur doos-ree gaa-rDee ko doe gh-un-Tay aur Chh-ut-tees min-uT lug-tay hain aur yeh ToonD-laa tuk jaa-tee hai.

Yaat-ree : Uch-Chaa, aur in-kaa kir-aa-yaa kit-naa lug-taa hai?

Clerk : Süb-uh Cheh buj-ay waa-lee gaarD-ee kay chaar saw paàch rüp-puh-yay lug-tay hain aur suh-vaa Cheh buj-ay waa-lee gaarD-ee kaa kir-aa-yaa chaar saw saaTh rüp-puh-yay hain.

Yaat-ree : Uch-Chaa, ayk form day dee-ji-yay.

Clerk : Yeh lee-ji-yay.

Translation

Traveler : I need two tickets from Delhi to Agra.

Clerk : First of all, you have to fill out this form. Here, take this form and fill it out.

Traveler : But first, I want to know the schedule of trains from Delhi to Agra?

Clerk : Look, there are two trains in the morning from Delhi to Agra. The first is the New Delhi-Bhopal Shatabdi Express. It departs at 6 in the morning, and the second one is the Delhi-Lucknow Swarna Shatabdi Express. It departs at 6:15 in the morning.

Traveler : What station do they depart from?

Clerk : Both of them depart from the New Delhi Station.

Traveler : And how much time do they take to reach Agra.

Clerk : The Delhi-Bhopal Shatabdi Express takes two hours and six minutes, and it goes up to Agra Cant; the second one takes two hours and 36 minutes and goes up to Tundla.

Traveler : And how much are the fares?

Clerk : The train that goes at 6 a.m. costs 405 rupees, and the fare for the train at 6:15 is 460.

Traveler : OK. Then please give me one form.

Clerk : Here.

Practice 4 Pre-Reading Exercise
Read and categorize the words in the appropriate columns.

(निचली, स्त्री, भरना, गंतव्य, पता, यात्री, सही, हस्ताक्षर, वापसी, चलना, चाहिए, विवरण, ऊपरी, पहली, निकलना)

Nouns	Adjectives	Verbs
स्थान		

Practice 5 Production
Now fill out a mock train reservation form and provide your details as required.

यात्रा का विवरण/जानकारी

यात्री का पूरा नाम _____

घर का पूरा पता _____

_____

ट्रेन पर चढ़ने का स्थान _____ गंतव्य स्थान _____

ट्रेन संख्या और नाम _____ यात्रा की तारीख़ _____

श्रेणी _____

क्रम संख्या	नाम	लिंग (स्त्री/पुरुष)	आयु/उम्र	सीट का चयन
1.				निचली बर्थ/ ऊपरी बर्थ
2.				
3.				शाकाहारी/ माँसाहारी खाना

यात्री के हस्ताक्षर

2.2 Travel Arrangements यात्रा प्रबंध

Objectives

By the end of this lesson, you will be able to:

1. Make travel arrangements in India, book a flight, and indicate your preferences regarding time, food, and seats.
2. Express your needs regarding travel dates and the urgency of your need, using internal compulsion, conjunct verb and causatives.
3. Understand travel related advisories, suggestions, instructions and do's and don'ts, using the subjunctive forms.

Vocabulary

Nouns

सेवा	(say-waa)	*fem.*	service
तारीख़	(taa-ree-kh)	*fem.*	date
जगह	(jug-uh)	*fem.*	place, space
वापसी	(vaap-us-see)	*fem.*	return
महीना	(muh-hee-naa)	*masc.*	month
किराया	(kiraa-yaa)	*masc.*	fare, rent
समय	(sum-ay)	*masc.*	time
आगमन	(aag-mun)	*masc.*	arrival
प्रस्थान	(prus-thaan)	*masc.*	departure
गंतव्य	(gun-tuv-yuh)	*masc.*	destination

Adjectives

खाली	(khaa-lee)	*masc.*	empty
सस्ता	(sus-taa)	*masc.*	cheap
दुगुना	(dü-gü-naa)	*masc.*	double
माँसाहारी	(maà-saa-haa-ree)		non-vegetarian
आने-जाने का	(aa-nay-jaa-nay kaa)	*masc.*	round trip (fare)

Verbs

ढूँढ़ना	(Dhoò-Dh-naa)	*v.t.*	to look for
बताना	(but-aa-naa)	*v.t.*	to tell
मंगाना	(m-ung-aa-naa)	*v.t.*	to order
निकलना	(nik-ul-naa)	*v.t.*	to depart
पहुँचना	(puh-hünch-naa)	*v.t.*	to arrive
कर देना	(ker-day-naa)	*comp. v.t.*	to do
वापस आना	(vaa-pus aa-naa)	*conj. v.i.*	to return (from somewhere)
पता करना	(p-ut-aa ker-naa)	*conj. v.i.*	to find out

NOTE Conjunct verbs are the combination of a noun and a verb, or an adjective and a verb.

Examples of Conjunct Verbs
वापस (noun-return) + आना (to come) = to return/to come back from somewhere.
1. I will come back tomorrow.
    मैं कल वापस आऊँगा।
    (main k-ul vaa-pus aa-oon-gaa.)

पता (noun-address) + करना (to do) = to find out
2. I need to find out about this train.
    मुझे इस ट्रेन के बारे में पता करना है।
    (müJh-ay is train kay baa-re main puh-taa ker-naa hai.)

Grammar

Internal compulsion in Hindi is used when the subject of a sentence feels an internal obligation toward oneself. Generally, it is used to express sentences such as "I have to go," "she/he has to wash her/his clothes," and "they have to meet." In this type of construction, the subject is always indirect and is blocked by the postposition को, and the verb is conjugated according to the gender and the number of the object (noun) closest to the verb. If there is no object (noun) present in the sentence or is not needed, the verb will appear in its original masculine form (infinitive form: *jaa-naa* "to go," and *so-naa* "to sleep"). These verbs are mainly intransitive verbs such as "to go," "to sleep," "to bathe," "to come," and "to wake up." For intransitive verbs, one cannot find an answer to the question "what" (a noun/object). Transitive verbs on the other hand do carry an object in a sentence and one can always find an answer to the question "What?"

Structure 1
A sentence without any inanimate object
Subject + को + object (a noun) + auxiliary verb है, हैं, था, थी, थे

I have to go to London.
मुझको लंदन जाना है
(Mü-Jh-ko Lon-don jaa-naa hai.)

She has to sleep.
उसको सोना है।
(Üs-ko so-naa hai.)

Structure 2
A sentence with an inanimate object or a material thing (noun)

I have to eat ice cream.
(मुझे आइसक्रीम खानी है।) *(fem. sing.)*
(Mü-Jh-ay ice-ceam khaa-nee hai.)

The girl has to sing a song.
(लड़की को गाना गाना है।) *(masc. sing.)*
(LerD-kee ko gaa-naa gaa-naa hai.)

The woman has to buy saris.
(औरत को साड़ियाँ खरीदनीं हैं।) *(fem. pl.)*
(Awe-rut ko saa-rD-iyaaṅ kher-eed-nee haiṅ.)

The man has to buy fruits.
(आदमी को फल खरीदने हैं।) *(masc. pl.)*
(Aad-mee ko ph-ul kher-eed-nay hain.)

Pronouns with को

NOTE The postposition को always follows a person, an animal, or any living thing.

मुझको/मुझे	(mü-jh-ko/ mü-jh-ay)	*first person*	to me
तुमको/तुम्हें	(tüm-ko/tüm-haẏ)	*second person, informal*	to you
आपको	(aap-ko)	*second person, formal*	to you
हमको/हमें	(hum-ko/hum-aẏ)	*first person, pl.*	to us
इसको/इसे	(is-ko/is-ay)	*third person, sing.*	to him/to her
उसको/उसे	(üs-ko/üs-ay)	*third person, sing.*	to him/to her
इनको/इन्हें	(in-ko/in-haẏ)	*third person, sing., honorific/pl.*	to him/to her
उनको/उन्हें	(ün-ko/ün haẏ)	*third person, sing., honorific/pl.*	to him/to her/ to them

Noun with को

लड़के को	(lerD-kay ko)	*marked masc. sing.*	to the boy
लड़कों को	(lerD-kaẇ ko)	*marked masc. pl.*	to the boys
लड़की को	(lerD-kee ko)	*marked fem. sing.*	to the girl
लड़कियों को	(lerD-ki-yȯ ko)	*marked fem. pl.*	to the girls

Proper Nouns with को

पॉल को	(Paul ko)	to Paul
कैथी को	(Kai-thee ko)	to Kathy

Sample sentences

1. तुमको/तुम्हें क्या मंगाना है? (tüm-ko kyaa m-ung-aa-naa hai?)	What do you have to/like to order?
2. आपको कहाँ जाना है? (Aap-ko kuh-haȧ jaa-naa hai?)	Where do you have to go?
3. इसको/उसको हवाईअड्डे पहुँचना है। (Is-ko h-uw-aa-ee uD-day puh-hünch-naa hai.)	He/she has to reach the airport.
4. पॉल को खाना खाना है। (Paul ko khaa-naa khaa-naa hai.)	Paul has to have (wants to eat) food.
5. कैथी को चाय पीनी है‌। (Kathy ko chaay pee-nee hai.)	Kathy has to (wants to) drink tea.

Practice 1

To practice the Hindi internal compulsion, label these pictures with a sentence in which you will identify what the subject has to do (chores or something he/she has to do or wants to do for him/herself).

1. I have to travel/go.
जाना

4. We have to reach there soon.
पहुँचना

7. He has to phone his mother.
फोन *(m)* करना

_____ _____ _____

2. I want to buy tickets.
खरीदना

5. They have to depart.
निकलना

8. I need to find out the fare.
किराया *(m)* पता करना

_____ _____ _____

3. I have to order
vegetarian food.
खाना *(m)* मंगाना

6. She needs to sleep
on the plane.
सोना

9. I have to come back on 9th.
वापस आना

_____ _____ _____

Causative verbs: "to have done"

As the word "causative" suggests, a person causes an action to be done by another individual. The Hindi language uses two types of causatives: first and second.

The first causative is used when a person himself/herself directly does an action that benefits an individual or a living thing, or causes someone else to do the action for him/her; the intermediary agent is not present in the first causative. In the second causative, a person causes an intermediary agent to do the work for him/her, which is followed by the postposition से.

You must remember that:

1. All causative verbs are transitive verbs.
2. Not all transitive verbs can be changed into their causative form.
3. Causative verbs are formed by adding वा to an intransitive verb stem.
4. When any external or intermediary agent is mentioned, it is always followed by the postposition से.
5. In the second causative, a subject never carries out the action by him/herself. He/she causes a second party to perform the task.
6. The main verb in this type of sentence structure can be conjugated in various tenses.
7. Causatives in Hindi take shape through the morphological method.
    a. "**Aa आ**" or "**la ला**" is placed between a verb root and the infinitive suffix ना to form a first causative verb.
    b. Then "**aa आ**" or "**vaa वा**" is placed between the verb root and infinitive suffix ना to form a second causative verb.
8.

Verb infinitive	Verb root	First Causative	Second Causative
करना	कर	करा	करवा
(ker-naa)	(ker)	(ker-aa)	(ker-waa)

Look at these two types of causatives in a sentence:

Structure: First Causative (without an intermediary agent)

Subject + Object + Causative Verb + Auxiliary Verb

मैं   काम   कराता   हूँ।   I have the work done.

(main kaam karaa-taa hoṅ.)

Structure: Second Causative (with an intermediary agent)

Subject + Intermediary Agent + से + Object + Causative Verb + Auxiliary Verb

मैं   उससे   काम   कराता/ करवाता   हूँ।

(main üs-say kaam karaa-taa hoṅ.)

I   have him   do the work.

मैं उससे काम करवाता हूँ   I have him do the work.
मैं उससे काम कराता हूँ

The following are the forms of pronouns when followed by the postposition से:

By you	तुम से, आपसे	(tüm-say aap say)
By him/her	इस से, उस से	(is-say üs-say)
By them	इन से, उन से	(in-say ün-say)

Verbs conjugated in the causative

Verbs	First Causative	Second Causative
करना to do	कराना to have done (self)	से करवाना to have done (by someone else)
मंगाना to order	मंगाना to order (self)	से मंगवाना to cause to deliver
पहुँचना to arrive	पहुँचाना to deliver (self)	से पहुंचवाना to have delivered (something by someone)

Practice 2
Read the sentences below for the practice.

Without an Intermediary Agent	*With an Intermediary Agent*
मैं रिज़र्वेशन करवाता/कराता हूँ।	मैं उससे रिज़र्वेशन करवाता हूँ।
(main ri-zer-vay-shun ker-waa-taa/ ker-aa-taa hoȯ.)	(main üs-say ri-zer-vay-shun ker-waa-taa hoȯ.)
I have the reservation done.	I have him/her make the reservation.
I buy the tickets.	I buy the tickets from him/her.
मैं रिज़र्वेशन कराऊँगा/ करवाऊँगा।	मैं उससे रिज़र्वेशन करवाऊँगा।
(main ri-zer-vay-shun ker-aa-oon-gaa/ ker-waa-oȯ-gaa.)	(main üs-say ri-zer-vay-shun ker-waa-oȯ-gaa.)
I will have the reservation done.	I will have him/her make the reservation.
I will buy the tickets.	I will buy the tickets from him/her.
मैं रिज़र्वेशन करा/करवा रहा हूँ।	मैं उससे रिज़र्वेशन करवा रहा हूँ।
(main ri-zer-vay-shun ker-aa/ker-waa ruh-haa hoȯ.)	(main üs-say ri-zer-vay-shun ker-waa ruh-haa hoȯ.)
I am having the reservation done.	I am having him/her make the reservation.
I am buying the tickets.	I am buying the tickets from him/her.
मैंने रिज़र्वेशन कराया/करवाया।	मैंने उससे रिज़र्वेशन करवाया।
(mai-nay ri-zer-vay-shun ker-aa-yaa/ ker-waa-yaa.)	(mai-nay üs-say ri-zer-vay-shun ker-waa-yaa.)
I made the reservation.	I had him/her make the reservation.
I bought the tickets.	I bought the tickets from him/her.

मुझे रिज़र्वेशन कराना/करवाना है।
(müJh-ay ri-zer-vay-shun ker-aa-naa/
ker-waa-naa hai.)
I have to have the reservation done.
I have to buy the tickets.

मुझे उससे रिज़र्वेशन करवाना है।
(müJh-ay üs-say ri-zer-vay-shun ker-waa-naa
hai.)
I have to have him/her make the reservation.
I have to buy the tickets from him/her.

मुझे रिज़र्वेशन कराना/करवाना चाहिए।
(müJh-ay ri-zer-vay-shun ker-aa-naa/
ker-waa-naa chaah-iyay.)
I should have the reservation done.
I should buy the tickets.

मुझे उससे रिज़र्वेशन करवाना चाहिए।
(müJh-ay üs-say ri-zer-vay-shun ker-waa-
naa chaah-iyay.)
I should have him/her make the reservation.
I should buy the tickets from him/her.

मुझे रिज़र्वेशन कराना/करवाना पड़ेगा।
(müJh-ay ri-zer-vay-shun ker-aa-naa/
ker-waa-naa perD-ay-gaa.)
I must have the reservation done.
I will have to make the reservation.

मुझे उससे रिज़र्वेशन करवाना पड़ेगा।
(müJh-ay üs-say ri-zer-vay-shun ker-waa-
naa perD-ay-gaa.)
I must have him/her make the reservation.
I will have to buy the tickets from him/her.

In order to practice causative verbs in Hindi, use verbs other than the verbs on your vocabulary list.

Practice 3

Observe the changes that occur when a verb is changed into the first and second causative forms, and then practice the same with other verbs in the columns.

Verbs	First causative (action to be done by the doer himself/herself)	Second causative (action caused to be done by an intermediary agent)
सोना (ओ) (so-naa) to sleep	सुलाना उ (sü-laa-naa)	से सुलवाना उ (sül-waa-naa)
1. बोलना (bowl-naa) to speak		
2. खोलना (kho-l-naa) to open		
घूमना (ऊ) (ghoom-naa) to take a walk	घुमाना उ (ghü-maa-naa)	से घुमवाना (say ghüm-waa-naa)
3. छूटना (Choo-T-naa) to depart/leave		
जुड़ना (उ) (jürD-naa) to connect	जुड़ाना उ (jürDaa-naa)	से जुड़वाना (say jürD-waa-naa)
4. खुलना (khü-l-naa) to open		
5. रुकना (rük-naa) to stop		

Verbs	First causative (action to be done by the doer himself/herself)	Second causative (action caused to be done by an intermediary agent)
निकलना (इ) (nik-ul-naa) to leave	निकालना इ (nik-aa-l-naa)	से निकलवाना (nik-ul-waa-naa)
6. मिलना (mil-naa) to meet		
7. बिकना (bik-naa) to be sold		
जीतना (ई) (jeet-naa) to win	जिताना इ (jit-aa-naa)	से जितवाना (say jit-waa-naa)
8. सीखना (see-kh-naa) to learn		
9. खींचना (kheen-ch-naa) to pull		
जगना (अ) (jug-naa) to wake up	जगाना आ (jug-aa-naa)	से जगवाना (say jug-waa-naa)
10. जलना (juh-ul-waa-naa) to burn		
11. चलना (chuh-ul-naa) to walk		

Practice 4 Pre-Listening Exercise

Many of you must have traveled by plane before, and had the experience of booking your tickets. Do you remember what you asked the travel agent? Try to recall all that you asked and make a list of these. What vocabulary did you use to communicate with the travel agent regarding your travel

Questions

1. _____

2. _____

3. _____

4. _____

5. _____

Vocabulary

1. _____   4. _____   7. _____   10. _____

2. _____   5. _____   8. _____   11. _____

3. _____   6. _____   9. _____   12. _____

Practice 5

Now practice your vocabulary by labeling these pictures and then listen to the conversation.

1. Booking a ticket

4. Dates

7. Empty Seats

_____

_____

_____

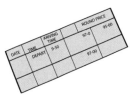

2. Airfare

5. Ticket

8. Round trip

_____

_____

_____

3. Arrival and Departure

6. Non-vegetrian

9. Cheap

_____

_____

_____

10. Expensive   11. Destination

_____   _____

Practice 6 Vocabulary-Building Exercise
Choose the best synonym for the underlined word from the three choices given.

1. गाड़ी के <u>प्रस्थान</u> का समय सात बजे है।
    a. आगमन   b. जाना   c. आना

2. न्यूयॉर्क जाने वाला <u>विमान</u> गेट नम्बर दस से जाएगा।
    a. बस   b. हवाई जहाज़   c. गाड़ी

3. विदेश जाने का हवाई जहाज़ का टिकट <u>सस्ता</u> नहीं होता।
    a. महंगा   b. महंगा नहीं   c. बहुत महंगा

4. हमारा विमान <u>गंतव्य</u> पर पहुँच गया है।
    a. पहुँचने वाली जगह   b. रुकने वाली जगह   c. चलने वाली जगह

Practice 7 Part 1 🎧 02-04
Listen to the conversation and then complete the activities that follow.

ट्रैवल एजेंट : एशिया ट्रैवल, हाँ जी बोलिए, मैं आपकी क्या सेवा कर सकता हूँ?
कॉलर   : जी मुझे इस महीने की अट्ठारह तारीख़ के लिए एक रिज़र्वेशन करवाना है।
ट्रैवल एजेंट : जी कहाँ का रिज़र्वेशन करवाना है?
कॉलर   : जी, मुझे लंदन जाना है।
ट्रैवल एजेंट : कौनसी उड़ान से जाना चाहेंगे?
कॉलर   : कोशिश कीजिए जैट एयरवेज़ से।
ट्रैवल एजेंट : ठीक है, मैं अभी पता करके बताता हूँ कि फ़्लाइट में जगह खाली या नहीं। अच्छा, आपको वापस
             कब आना है?
कॉलर   : अ ssss वापस, दो हफ़्ते बाद यानि अगले महीने की तीन तारीख़ को।
ट्रैवल एजेंट : आपको कौनसी क्लास का टिकट चाहिए?
कॉलर   : इकोनोमी का। सबसे सस्ता वाला ढूँढ़िएगा।
ट्रैवल एजेंट : ठीक है, थोड़ी देर रुकिए, मैं अभी बताता हूँ।
कॉलर   : ठीक है।

Romanization Part 1

Travel Agent : Asia Travels, haan jee bo-li-yay, main aap-kee kyaa say-waa ker suk-taa hoȯ.

Caller : Jee mü-jh-ay is muh-hee-nay kee uTThaa-ruh taa-re-kh kay li-yay ayk reservation ker-waa-naa hai.

Travel Agent : jee, kuh-haṅ kaa reservation ker-waa-naa-hai?

Caller: jee, mü-jh-ay London jaa-naa hai.

Travel Agent : kawn-see ürD-aan say jaa-naa chaa-ay-ng-ay?

Caller : ko-shi-sh kee-ji-yay Jet Airways say.

Travel Agent : Theek-hai, main ub-hee p-ut-aa ker-kay b-ut-a-taa hoȯ ki flight maẏ jug-uh khaa-lee hai yaa nuh-heė. Uch-Chaa, aap-ko vaa-p-us cub aa-naa hai?

Caller : uhhh. ...vaa-p-us, doe huf-tay baad, yaa-ni ug-lay muh-hee-nay kee teen taa-ree-kh ko.

Travel Agent : aap-ko kawn see class kaa Tik-uT chaa-hi-yay?

Caller : economy kaa. Sub-say sus-taa waa-laa Dhoȯ-Dhi-yay-gaa.

Travel Agent : Theek hai, tho-rDee day-r ruk-i-yay, main ub-hee b-ut-aa-taa hoȯ.

Caller : Theek hai.

Part 2 🎧 02-05

ट्रेवल एजेंट : हं ssss, अट्ठारह की फ़्लाइट का किराया दुगुना है। क्या आप बाद की फ़्लाइट लेना चाहेंगे? ... गुरुवार इक्कीस तारीख़ और वापसी पाँच को, ठीक है?

कॉलर : वैसे टिकट कितने का है?

ट्रेवल एजेंट : आने-जाने के सिर्फ़ चालीस हज़ार रुपये, जैट एयरवेज़ से।

कॉलर : यही सबसे सस्ता है?

ट्रेवल एजेंट : जी हाँ,....... यह सीट बुक कर दूँ?

कॉलर : हाँ कर दीजिए

ट्रेवल एजेंट : ठीक है तो ..... आपकी फ़्लाइट होगी 3957। नई दिल्ली से लंदन, हीथ्रो हवाइअड्डे तक।

कॉलर : और...... फ़्लाइट निकलने और पहुँचने का क्या समय है?

ट्रेवल एजेंट : वह नई दिल्ली से रात को दस बजे निकलती है और लंदन सुबह पौने सात बजे पहुँचती है।

कॉलर : ठीक है, और हाँ मैं माँसाहारी खाना मँगाना चाहूँगा।

ट्रेवल एजेंट : ज़रूर, नो प्रॉब्लम, जी आपका नाम?

Travel Agent : hmmm uT-Thaa-r-uh kee flight kaa ki-raa-yaa dü-gü-naa hai. Kyaa aap baad kee flight lay-naa chaah-aẏ-gay? Gü-rü-waar ik-kees taa-ree-kh aur vaa-p-us-ee paȧ-ch ko, Theek hai?

Caller : vai-say Tik-uT kit-nay kaa hai?

Travel Agent : aa-nay jaa-nay kay sirf chaa-lees h-uz-aar rü-puh-yay, Jet Airways say.

Caller : yuh-uh-hee sub-say s-us-taa hai?

Travel Agent : jee haaṅ ... yeh seat book ker doȯ?

Caller : haȧ ker dee-ji-yay.

Travel Agent : Theek hai, tow. ... Aap-kee flight ho-gee 3957. Nuh-ee Dill-lee say London Hethrow h-uw-aa-ee uD-Day t-uk.

Caller : aur ... Flight nik-ul-nay aur p-hünch-nay kaa kyaa sum-ay hai?

Travel Agent	:	veh nuh-ee Dill-lee say raat ko d-us b-uj-ay nik-ul-tee hai aur London süb-uh pawn-ay saat b-uj-ay p-hünch-tee hai.
Caller	:	Theek hai, aur haȧ, maiṅ maȧ-saa-haa-ree khaa-naa m-ung-aa-naa chaa-hoȯ-gaa.
Travel Agent	:	zer-oor, no problem, jee aap-kaa naam?

Practice 8 Listening Exercise

Listen to the conversation in two parts between a customer and a travel agent, and circle the verbs that you hear in the audio. Translate them as you listen, writing down on the blanks provided.

1. बोलना _____   9. मंगाना _____

2. करना _____   10. निकालना _____

3. बताना _____   11. माँगना _____

4. करवाना _____   12. जाना _____

5. पहुंचना _____   13. देना _____

6. सोना _____   14. लेना _____

7. खाना _____   15. कर देना _____

8. आना _____

Practice 9 Post-Listening Exercise
Listen once again and answer the questions.

1. कॉलर को कब का रिज़र्वेशन करवाना है?
   For what day does the caller need the reservation?

   _____

2. कॉलर को कहाँ जाना है?
   Where does the caller need to travel?

   _____

3. कॉलर को वापस कब आना है?
    When does the caller have to return?

4. कॉलर को कौनसी क्लास का टिकट चाहिए?
    What class ticket does the caller need?

5. जैट एयरवेज़ का भारत से लंदन आने-जाने का किराया कितना है?
    What is the round trip airfare from India to London by Jet Airways?

6. उड़ान के दिल्ली से निकलने और लंदन पहुँचने का समय क्या है?
    What is the flight departure time from Delhi and the arrival time in London?

7. यात्री यात्रा के दौरान कैसा खाना खाना चाहता है?
    What does the traveler want to eat during the flight?

Translation
Part 1

Travel Agent : Asia Travel. Yes, how may I help you?
Caller   : Yes, I'd like to make a flight reservation for the 18th of this month.
Travel Agent : OK. Where do you want to go?
Caller   : Well, I have to go to London
Travel Agent : What airline would you prefer?
Caller   : Try Jet Airlines.
Travel Agent : OK. Let me check if there are seats available or not. OK and when do
                     you want to return?
Caller   : Uh, return, in two weeks, and that is on the third of next month.
Travel Agent : What class ticket do you want?
Caller   : Economy class. Find the cheapest one.
Travel Agent : OK. Wait for a while, I'll tell you right away.
Caller   : OK.

Part 2

Travel Agent : Well, the price for the flight on 18th is double. Would you like a later flight, say on Thursday the 21st and then return on 5th, is that OK?

Caller : By the way, how much is the fare?

Travel Agent : It's only 40,000 rupees round-trip with Jet Airways.

Caller : Is this the cheapest one?

Travel Agent : Yes. Should I book this ticket?

Caller : OK then, book it.

Travel Agent : OK, then [pause] your flight will be flight 3957 from New Delhi to London, Heathrow Airport.

Caller : OK, go ahead please. What are the departure and arrival times for the flight?

Travel Agent : It leaves New Delhi at 10:00 p.m. and arrives in London at 6:45 a.m.

Caller : Alright. And oh, I'd like to request a non-vegetarian meal.

Travel Agent : Sure, no problem. And could I have your name please?

Travel-related Advice and Suggestions

Before reading the travel-related suggestions and advice below, think about what information you would need to gather in order to book an airline ticket. Write down all that information. Do you talk to a travel agent or do you buy tickets online?

Besides reinforcing the grammar and vocabulary that you have learned above in the conversation, you will be introduced to the subjunctive form of verb in Hindi, which is used to give suggestions, advice, and instructions. In this way, you will be able to understand travel advice, advisories, and dos and don'ts.

Remember: When general information is relayed to the public, then the polite pronoun आप āp is generally used for the purpose of subject-verb agreement; however, it is often implied when it is written on information boards or notice boards.

This reading will focus only on the polite form of subjunctives in Hindi.

Examples:

Verb (infinitive)	Subjunctive form with आप	Translation
ध्यान रखना (dhyaan ruh-kh-naa)	ध्यान रखें (dhyaa-n rukh-aẏ)	please remember
कोशिश करना (ko-shish ker-naa)	कोशिश करें (ko-shish ker-aẏ)	please try to
बुक करवाना (book ker-waa-naa)	बुक करवायें (book ker-waa-aẏ)	please have tickets booked

Verb (infinitive)	Subjunctive form with आप	Translation
जल्द से जल्द लेना (juld say juld lay-naa)	जल्द से जल्द लें (juld say juld aẏ)	please buy as soon as possible
बात करना (say baat ker-naa)	से बात करें (say baat ker-kar-aẏ)	please talk to
लिखना (li-kh-naa)	लिखें (likh-aẏ)	please write down

Practice 1

Read the instructions and advice below. Underline the verbs in the subjunctive form and in the internal compulsion. Translate them into English.

आपको विदेश जाना है या देश में ही हवाई यात्रा करनी है? आपको एक अच्छी एयरलाइन्स से टिकट बुक कराना है? तो उसके लिए नीचे लिखी बातों का ध्यान रखें... .

1. तय करें ...
   a. यात्रा की तारीख़ ।
   b. गंतव्य स्थान ।
   c. आपको एक तरफ़ा टिकट खरीदना है या दो तरफ़ा ।

_____

2. सूची बनायें और लिखें कि...
   a. आपके साथ कितने बच्चे हैं, कितने वयस्क हैं, और कितने बुज़ुर्ग हैं ।
   b. उनके नाम और उम्र क्या-क्या है ।

_____

3. ट्रैवल एजेंट को बतायें कि...
   a. टिकट के साथ आपको और क्या-क्या बुक करवाना है ।
   b. आपको फ़र्स्ट क्लास में टिकट बुक करवाना है या इकॉनॉमी में ।
   c. विमान में आपको सीट कहाँ चाहिए? खिड़की के पास, बीच में या गलियारे की कोने वाली सीट ।

_____

4. ट्रैवल एजेंट से पूछें कि...
   a. यात्रा में कैसा खाना मिलता है ।
   b. आप कितना सामान ले जा सकते हैं ।
   c. सामान का भार कितना हो ।
   d. विमान के आगमन, प्रस्थान और गंतव्य पर पहुँचने का समय क्या है ।

_____

Practice 2 Post-Reading Exercise
Answer the following questions in Hindi:

1. हवाई यात्रा से पहले किसकी सूची बनानी चाहिए? सूची लिखें।
   What kind of list should be made before the air travel? List them.

   1. _____

   2. _____

   3. _____

2. हवाई यात्रा से पहले ट्रैवल एजेंट से क्या-क्या पूछना चाहिए? दो बातें बताइये।
   What should one ask a travel agent in terms of air travel? State two things.

   1. _____

   2. _____

NOTE Internal compulsion also suggests "a desire" colloquially in Hindi, which in English is expressed through "want, like to, need to" and "would like to" constructions.

2.3 Hiring an Auto Rickshaw ऑटो रिक्शा करना

Objectives
By the end of this lesson, you will be able to communicate with an auto rickshaw driver and:
1. Set a price for hiring an auto rickshaw while bargaining with the driver.
2. State your destination using internal compulsion.
3. Ask for the availability of the transportation using the future tense.
4. Stop an auto on the way using the neutral imperative and give an order using the familiar imperative.

> 📖 **Culture Note**
> An auto rickshaw is an indispensable form of urban transportation in India. It is a motorized version of a hand-pulled or cycle rickshaw. It is also known as a three-wheeler and is cheaper than hiring a private taxi to travel shorter distances. Those who visit India are much fascinated by the auto rickshaw and prefer an auto rickshaw over a taxi.

Vocabulary

Verbs

आना	(aa-naa)	*v.i.*	to come
बैठना	(bai-Th-naa)	*v.i.*	to sit
रुकना	(rük-naa)	*v.i.*	to stop, to stay, to halt
जाना	(jaa-naa)	*v.i.*	to go
चलना	(ch-ul-naa)	*v.i.*	to go, to walk, to move
लेना	(lay-naa)	*v.i.*	to take, to charge (money)
उतरना	(üter-naa)	*v.i.*	to get off
लगना	(lug-naa)	*v.i.*	to cost
देना	(day-naa)	*v.i.*	to give
दे देना	(day-day-naa)	*comp. v.t.*	to give away, to hand over

Miscellaneous

कितना	(kit-naa)	question word *(masc. sing.)*	how much, how many
कहाँ पर	(kuh-haả per)	question word	at what place, where
यहाँ से	(yuh-haả say)		from here
कौन सी	(kawn-see)	question word *(fem.)*	which one
तक	(tuk)	*postposition*	till
तो	(toe)	*emphatic particle*	then, so, indeed, just
बहुत	(buh-hüt)	*adj.*	a lot, many
ज़्यादा	(zyaa-daa)	*adj.*	a lot, more, very many
चलना है तो	(ch-ul-naa hai toe)	*conditional sentence*	if (you) want to go
सवारी	(s-uv-aa-ree)	*fem.*	passenger, ride
अरे !	(err-ay)	an interjection, to call someone	hey!
वाला	(waa-laa)	*suffix masc. sing.,* generally used with professions such as a tea vendor, fruit vendor etc.	the one who...
ऑटो वाले!	(auto waa-lay)	an interjection, to call someone	auto rickshaw driver
हमेशा	(hum-ay-shaa)	*adv.*	always
अगर	(ug-er)	*conditional*	if

Grammar

Reviewing Internal Compulsion

The previous section "Travel Arrangements" provided you the grammar explanation and some practice of this structure. The same concept is reinforced here.

Read a few sentence that use the Internal Compulsion.

1. आपको कहाँ जाना है? (Aap-ko kuh-haả jaa-naa hai?) Where would you like to go?
आपको कहाँ उतरना है? (Aap-ko kuh-haả üter-naa hai?) What is your destination?/ Where do you need to get off?

2. आपको कितना रुकना है? (Aap-ko kit-naa rük-naa hai?)   How long is your stay?/How much/long do you have to stay?

3. क्या आपको वापस भी जाना है? (Kyaa aap-ko vaap-us bhee jaa-naa hai?)   Would you also be going back?/Do you also need to go back?

Future Tense

The future tense in Hindi is made up of a verb root and the suffix ऊँगा oȯ-gaa, ऊँगी oȯ-gee, ओगे o-gay, ओगी o-gee, एगा ay-gaa, एगी aẏ-gee, ऐंगे aẏ-gay and ऐंगीं aẏ-gee. Like English, the future tense in Hindi also uses the pronouns "I," "you," "we," and "they" as the subject of a sentence, and the verb conjugates in gender and number with the subject directly.

Sentence structure

Subject + object + verb root + ऊँगा, ऊँगी, ओगे, ओगी, एगा, एगी, ऐंगे and ऐंगीं
(direct)   (future suffix-gender/number)

Example:

Subject	Verb root	Future suffix	Full form	In a sentence
मैं (maiṅ) I	जा (jaa) go	ऊँगा (masc. sing.) (oȯg-aa) will	जाऊँगा (first person sing.) (jaa-oȯ-gaa) will go	मैं जाऊँगा। (maiṅ jaa-oȯ-gaa) I will go.
मैं (maiṅ) I	जा (jaa) go	ऊँगी (fem.sg.) (oȯ-gee) will	जाऊँगी (first p. sg.) (jaa-oȯ-gee) will go	मैं जाऊँगी। (maiṅ jaa-oȯ-gee) I will go.
यह/वह (yeh/veh) he, she, it	उतर (üter) get off	एगा (masc. sing.) (ay-gaa) will	उतरेगा (üt-ray-gaa) will get off	यह/वह उतरेगा (yeh/veh üt-ray-gaa) He will get off.
यह/वह (yeh/veh) he, she, it	चल (ch-ul) leave/depart	एगी (fem.sg.) (ay-gee) will	चलेगी (ch-ul-ay-gee) will leave/depart	यह/वह चलेगी (yeh/veh ch-ul-ay-gee) It will depart/leave.
तू (too) you	ले (lay) take	एगी (fem. sing.) (gy-gee) will	लेगी (lay-gee) will take	तू लेगी (too lay-gee) You will take.
तुम (tüm) you	आ (aa) come	ओगे (masc. sing.) (o-gay) will	आओगे (informal, sing) (aao-gay) will come	तुम आओगे। (tüm aao-gay) You will come.

Subject	Verb root	Future suffix	Full form	In a sentence
तुम (tüm) you	आ (aa) come	ओगी *(fem. sing.)* (o-gee) will	आओगी *(informal, sing.)* (aao-gee) will come	तुम आओगी । (tüm aao-ge) You will come.
आप/हम/ये/वे (aap/hum/ yay/vay) you	बैठ (baiTh) sit	एंगे *(masc. pl. honorific)* (aẏ-gay) will	बैठेंगे *(formal, pl.)* (baiTh-aẏ-gay) will sit down	आप/ हम/ये/वे बैठेंगे । (aap baiTh-aẏ-gay) You will sit down.
आप/हम/ये/वे (aap/hum/ yay/vay) you/we/he/ she/they	बैठ (baiTh) sit	एंगी *(fem. pl. honorific)* (aẏ-gee) will	बैठेंगी *(formal, pl.)* (baiTh-aẏ-gay) will sit down	आप/हम/ये/वे बैठेंगी । (aap baiTh-aẏ-gee) We will sit down.
आप/हम/ये/वे (yay/vay) you/we/he/ she/they	रुक (rük) stop/stay	एंगी *(fem. pl. honorific)* (aẏ-gee) will	रुकेंगी *(formal, pl.)* (rük-aẏ-gay) will stop/stay	आप/हम/ये/वे रुकेंगी । (aap-aẏ-gee) You will stop/stay.

Examples:

आप कहाँ जायेंगे? (Aap kuh-haȧ jaa-aẏ-gay?) Where would you like to go?

तुम वहाँ चलोगे? (Tüm vuh-haȧ ch-ul-ogay?) Will you take us/go there?

तुम कितना लोगे? (Tüm kit-naa lo-gay?) How much will you charge?

पैसे कितने लगेंगे? (Pai-say kit-nay lug-aẏ-gay?) How much money will it cost?

मैं तो पचास रुपये दूँगा/ दूँगी/देंगे । (Main to puch-aas rüpuh-yay doȯ-gaa, doȯ-gee, daẏ-gay.)
I will give you only 50 rupees.

Practice 1

Fill in the table with the appropriate conjugation of the future tense of the verbs.
Follow the example given on the first row.

Verb	मैं *(masc./ fem.)*	तुम *(masc./ fem.)*	तू *(masc./ fem.)*	आप/हम *(masc. pl./ fem. pl.)*	यह/वह *(masc. sing./ fem. sing.)*	ये/वे *(masc. pl./ fem. pl.)*
चलना (ch-ul-naa) to move	चलूँगा/ चलूँगी	चलोगे/ चलोगी	चलेगा/ चलेगी	चलेंगे/ चलेंगी	चलेगा/ चलेगी	चलेंगे/ चलेंगी
रुकना (rük-naa) to stop						
बैठना (Bai-Th-naa) to sit						
उतरना (Üter-naa) to get off						

📖 **Culture Note: The Neutral and the Familiar Imperative**

The neutral imperative form can be used with तुम, आप, and तू, and it is especially used in the market when one is buying things such as fruits and vegetables from the vendors, or receiving services from vendors —such as rickshaw drivers, auto rickshaw drivers, and all vendors who do manual labor in Indian society. This does not mean that you are in any way degrading them; this imperative is more of a suggestion and a request instead of a command or an order. Neutral imperatives are verbs in their infinitive form. On the other hand people use polite imperatives when dealing with shop owners who have relatively bigger businesses such as bookstores, clothing stores, sweets stores, jewelry stores, and shoe stores.

In the familiar imperative, the verb conjugates with the second person familiar pronoun such as तुम आओ, तुम बैठो, तुम बोलो, तुम चलो, तुम देखो, and तुम रुको. The familiar imperative is used mainly to give orders and commands to a person who is familiar to you: your friend or a person younger than you. Colloquially, it is also used in the day-to-day language by rickshaw drivers, auto rickshaw drivers, vegetable vendors, shop owners, especially in the Delhi, Rajasthan, Haryana, and Punjab regions, and to a great extent by educated people as well. In Utter Pradesh, the polite imperative is widely used.

Practice 2 Pre-Listening Exercise
Match the vocabulary with their Hindi meaning.

1. from here   चलना
2. to give (compound verb)   बैठना
3. passenger   पैसे लगना
4. hey!   दे देना
5. if you want to go   अरे
6. to sit   यहाँ से
7. to go   अगर तुम जाना चाहते हो तो
8. to cost   सवारी

Practice 3

Listen to the conversation between an auto rickshaw driver and a passenger. Then underline all the verbs that you hear. Next, answer the questions that follow.

सवारी   : अरे ऑटो वाले!!! रुकना।
ऑटो चालक : आओ बहन जी बैठो। कहाँ पर जाना है?
सवारी   : कनाट प्लेस जाना है, चलोगे?
ऑटो चालक : कितनी सवारियाँ हैं?
सवारी   : तीन। कितना लोगे?
ऑटो चालक : कनाट प्लेस पर कहाँ जाना है?
सवारी   : हनुमान मंदिर पर उतरना है।
ऑटो चालक : यहाँ से हनुमान मंदिर तक के एक सौ पच्चीस लगेंगे।
सवारी   : एक सौ पच्चीस रुपए तो बहुत ज़्यादा हैं, ठीक बोलो भई।
ऑटो चालक : ज़्यादा नहीं हैं बहन जी, आपसे ज़्यादा नहीं लूँगा।
सवारी   : हम हमेशा अस्सी में जाते हैं। अस्सी रुपये देंगे,चलना है तो चलो।
ऑटो चालक : अस्सी तो बहुत कम हैं बहन जी। आप पिचानवे दे देना।
सवारी   : अच्छा चलो ठीक है।
ऑटो चालक : बैठो

Romanization
S-uv-aa-ree   : Err-ay!!! auto waa-lay rük-naa.
Auto chaa-luk : Aao beh-hen jee bai-Tho. Kuh-haȧ per jaa-naa hai?
S-uv-aa-ree   : Connaught place jaa-naa hai, ch-ul-o-gay?
Auto chaa-luk : Kit-nee s-uv-aa-ri-yaȧ hain?
S-uv-aa-ree   : teen. Kit-naa low-gay?
Auto chaa-luk : Connaught place per kuh-haȧ jaa-naa hai?
S-uv-aa-ree   : Huh-nü-maan mun-dir per üter-naa hai?
Auto chaa-luk : Yuh-haȧ say Huh-nü-maan mun-dir tuk kay ayk saw p-uch-ees lug-aẏ-gay.
S-uv-aa-ree   : Ayk saw p-uch-ees rü-p-yay toe b-hüt zyaa-daa hain, Theek bo-lo bhaa-ee.

Auto chaa-luk	:	Zyaa-daa nuh-heė haiṅ beh-hen jee, aap-say zyaa-daa pai-say nuh-heeṅ loȯ-gaa.
S-uv-aa-ree	:	Hum hum-ay-shaa üs-see maẏ jaa-tay haiṅ. Us-see rü-p-yay daẏ-gay, ch-ul-naa hai toe ch-ul-o.
Auto chaa-luk	:	Us-see toe buh-hüt cum haiṅ beh-hen jee. Aap pich-aan-way day day-naa.
S-uv-aa-ree	:	Uch-Chaa ch-ul-o Theek hai.
Auto chaa-luk	:	Bai-Tho.

Practice 4

1. Write the Hindi sentences that used the expression to ask for the fare.

_____

2. Write down the Hindi phrase that used an interjection.

_____

Practice 5

Provide the Hindi sentences that translate to the following.

1. We always pay eighty rupees.

_____

2. We will give only eighty rupees.

_____

3. If you want to go, then let's go.

_____

Translation

Passenger	:	Hey auto rickshaw driver!!! Stop for me.
Auto Rickshaw Driver	:	Come sister, have a seat. Where do you need to go?
Passenger	:	Will you take us to Connaught Place?
Auto Rickshaw Driver	:	How many passengers are there?
Passenger	:	Three. How much will you charge?
Auto Rickshaw Driver	:	Where do you have to get off at Connaught Place?
Passenger	:	We have to get off at Hanuman Temple.
Auto Rickshaw Driver	:	It will cost 125 rupees from here to Hanuman Temple.
Passenger	:	125 rupees!! This is too much, say the right price.
Auto Rickshaw Driver	:	It is not too much; I will not charge you higher.

Passenger	:	We always go with 80 rupees. We will pay only 80; if that suits you, then let's go.
Auto Rickshaw Driver	:	80 is too low. OK, you can give me 95.
Passenger	:	OK then let's go.
Auto Rickshaw Driver	:	Come, have a seat.

Practice 6 🎧 02-09

Listen again and fill in the blank spaces with the word that you hear.

Choose the words from the list in parenthesis.
(चलो ठीक है, बैठो, रुकना, उतरना, सवारियाँ, चलो, कितना, कहाँ, जाना, लगेंगे,चलोगे, ज़्यादा नहीं है, ठीक बोलो भई, लूँगा, देंगे, दे देना, चलो)

सवारी: अरे ऑटो वाले!!! _____ ।
                              (1)

ऑटो चालक: आओ बहन जी _____ । कहाँ पर _____ है?
                                   (2)

सवारी: कनाट प्लेस जाना है, _____ ।
                                  (3)

ऑटो चालक: कितनी _____ हैं?
                           (4)

सवारी: तीन । _____ लोगे?
                      (5)

ऑटो चालक-कनाट प्लेस पर _____ जाना है?
                           (6)

सवारी: हनुमान मंदिर पर _____ है ।
                      (7)

ऑटो चालक: यहाँ से हनुमान मंदिर तक के एक सौ पच्चीस _____ ।
                                       (8)

सवारी: एक सौ पच्चीस रुपए तो बहुत ज़्यादा हैं, _____ _____
                                                   (9)

_____ ।

ऑटो चालक: _____ _____ _____ । बहन जी,
                       (10)

आपसे ज़्यादा नहीं _____ ।
                           (11)

सवारी: हम हमेशा अस्सी रुपये में _____ हैं,चलना है तो _____ ।
                                    (12)

ऑटो चालक: अस्सी तो बहुत _____ हैं, चलो आप पिचानवे _____ ।
                           (13)

सवारी: अच्छा _____ _____ _____ ।
$\quad\quad\quad\quad\quad$ (14)

ऑटो चालक: _____ ।
$\quad\quad\quad\quad\quad$ (15)

2.4 Hiring a Cycle Rickshaw साइकिल रिक्शा करना

Objective

By the end of this lesson, you will know how to hire a cycle rickshaw in India, bargain with the rickshaw driver, and set the price.

> 📖 **Culture Note**
>
> The cycle-rickshaw *Wala* is the job title of people who provide the three-wheeled cycle-carriage transportation in India. The cycle-carriage is the traditional mode of transportation. In India, it is a very common sight to see people being pulled by a cycle rickshaw even to this day, and you can ride the rickshaw for short distance travel for a very reasonable price (prices vary according to the rickshaw driver and the distance). These rickshaw *walas* are very hardworking people, just like any person of the working class in India. Therefore, when it is the time to set the price for your short distance travel, you can negotiate the price, but be fair.

Vocabulary

Nouns

भैया/भाई	(bh-iyaa/bhaa-ee)	*masc.*	brother
रिक्शे वाला	(rick-shay waa-laa)	*masc.*	rickshaw driver
बाबू जी	(baa-boo jee)	*masc.*	sir
चौक	(chawk)	*masc.*	square (in a city)
रुपया	(rüp-uh-yaa)	*masc.*	rupee
चढ़ाई	(ch-urDh-aa-ee)	*fem.*	climb/hike/incline

Adverbs

दूर	(doo-r)		far
तुरंत	(tü-runt)		immediately

Adjectives

कितना	(kit-naa)	*masc.*	how much
बहुत	(buh-hüt)		a lot, too much
कुछ	(kü-Ch)		few, a little
कम	(k-um)		less

तीस	(tees)		thirty
पचपन	(p-uch-pun)		fifty five

Verbs

जाना	(jaa-naa)	*v.i.*	to go
आना	(aa-naa)	*v.i.*	to come
लेना	(lay-naa)	*v.t.*	to take/to charge
लौटना	(law-Taa-naa)	*v.t.*	to return (from somewhere)
वापस आना	(vaa-pus aa-naa)	*v.i.*	to return (from somewhere)
सुनना	(sün-naa)	*v.t.*	to listen
बैठना	(bai-Th-naa)	*v.i.*	to sit
समझना	(sum-ujh-naa)	*v.t.*	to understand
ले आना	(lay-aa-naa)	*v.i.*	to bring
लाकर छोड़ना	(laa-ker Cho-rD-naa)	*v.t.*	to bring and drop
कम करना	(k-um ker-naa)	*v.t.*	to reduce
दे देना	(day day-naa)	*comp. v.t.*	to give away
बता देना	(but-aa-day-naa)	*comp. v.t.*	to tell

Grammar

In this section we will introduce the emphatic particles भी and तो, the suffix वाला, and imperatives with simple and compound verbs, and the future tense in simple and compound verbs.

Grammar Practice

The emphatic particle भी bhee: Just as English uses "too," "also," and "as well as" to emphasize a noun, pronoun, adjective, adverb or verb, Hindi also uses the emphatic particle भी bhee to emphasize a particular part of speech or a phrase. In Hindi, भी always follows immediately after a word or a phrase. In a negative sentence, the negation नहीं follows the emphatic particle भी. Sometimes while translating भी from Hindi to English, other techniques such as intonation pattern, tone, and pitch convey the meaning.

Read the examples below:
I will also go there.
मैं भी वहाँ जाऊँगा। (main bhee vuh-haȧ jaa-oȯ-gaa.) (follows the pronoun)

There, I will take an auto as well as a cycle rickshaw.
मैं वहाँ ऑटो लूँगा और **साइकिल रिक्शा भी** लूँगा। (main vuh-haȧ auto loon-gaa aur cycle rick-shaa bhee loȯ-gaa.) (follows the noun)

That place is far from here as well.
वह जगह यहाँ से **दूर भी** तो है। (veh jug-uh yuh-haȧ say door bhee to hai.) (follows the adverb)

I need to go there and return (as well).

मुझे वहाँ जाकर **आना भी** है। (müJh-ay vuh-haä jaa-ker aa-naa bhee hai.) (follows the verb)

Practice 1

Translate and revise the following sentences to practice using the emphatic particle भी. Use the example below as a model:

I will go by bus today.   Will you also be going by bus?

मैं आज बस से जाऊँगा।   क्या तुम भी आज बस से जाओगे?

1. I need to return today.   Do you also have to return today?

_____

2. I want to ride a cycle rickshaw.   Would you also ride the cycle rickshaw?

_____

The emphatic particle तो literally does not mean anything, but its meaning is conveyed mainly through intonation, tone, and stress. Just like the emphatic particle भी, the emphatic particle तो also follows a pronoun, noun, adverb, adjective, or verb. The negation in a negative sentence always follows the emphatic particle तो.

Read the examples below and understand the pattern.

You are not going there but **I will** go.
तुम वहाँ नहीं जा रहे हो, लेकिन **मैं तो** जाऊँगा।
(tüm vuh-haä nuh-heé jaa ruh-hay ho, laykin main toe jaa-oö-gaa.)

You go there; **I will not** go.
तुम जाओ, **मैं तो नहीं** जाऊँगा।
(tüm jaa-o, main toe nuh-heé jaa-oö-gaa.)

Note that the stress in both the English sentences is on the pronoun "I" conveying "definitely" in the positive sentence and "at all" in the negative sentence. However sometimes it is hard to find the words in English that express तो: the inflection of the voice conveys the stress/meaning in such a case.

मुझे तो बस में बैठना बिल्कुल पसंद नहीं है।   **I don't like** to sit in the bus at all.
(müjh-ay toe bus main baiTh-naa bil-kül puh-us-und nuh-heé.)

मैं रिक्शे पर बैठना तो चाहता हूँ लेकिन...।   **I do want to ride** the rickshaw; however.....
(main rick-shay per baiTh-naa toe chaah-taa hoö lay-kin.)

वह जगह **दूर तो** है, लेकिन मुझे वहाँ जाना है।
(veh jug-uh doo-r toe hai, lay-kin müjh-ay vuh-haȧ jaa-naa hai.)

Although that place **is far away**, I need to go there.

उसकी गाड़ी **छोटी तो** है, लेकिन अच्छी है।
(üs-kee gaarD-ee Cho-Tee toe hai lay-kin uch-Chee hai.)

Though his car **is small**, it is good.

The suffix वाला "wālā"

The suffix वाला which literally means "the one who," "the one that is," "which is," is a widely used suffix in Hindi. It can be used with possessive pronouns, with demonstrative pronouns, with professions, with adjectives, with adverbs, and with nouns. It is mainly used in the service industry such as the "tea vendor," "milkman," "vegetable vendor," and "the one who drives a bus." When it is joined with possessive pronouns, demonstrative pronouns, adjectives, and adverbs, वाला waa-laa works as an adjective and inflects based on the gender of the noun: in feminine form, it becomes वाली waa-lee and for plural, it becomes वाले waa-lay.

Examples:

With possessives (as an adjective)	With demonstrative pronouns	With adjectives	With adverbs	With nouns (indicates ownership)	With the professions
मेरा वाला (may-raa waa-laa) मेरी वाली (may-ree waa-lee) मेरे वाले (may-ray waa-lay) the one that is mine	यह वाला (yeh waa-laa) यह वाली (yeh waa-lee) this one	काला वाला (kaa-laa waa-laa) काली वाली (kaa-lee waa-lee) काले वाले (kaa-lay waa-lay) black one/ black ones	ऊपर वाला (oo-per waa-laa) ऊपर वाली (oo-per waa-lee) ऊपर वाले (oo-per waa-lay) the one above	पैसे वाला (pai-say waa-laa) पैसे वाली (pai-say waa-lee) पैसे वाले (pai-say waa-lay) the one with money	चाय वाला (chai waa-laa) चाय वाली (chai waa-lee) चाय वाले (chai waa-lay) the one who sells tea
तुम्हारा वाला (Tüm-haa-raa waa-laa) तुम्हारी वाली (Tüm-haa-ree waa-lee) तुम्हारे वाले (Tüm-haa-ray waa-lay) the one that is yours	ये वाले (yay waa-lay) ये वाली (yay waa-lee) these ones/ those ones	नया वाला (nuh-yaa waa-laa) नयी वाली (nuh-yee waa-lee) नये वाले (nuh-yay waa-lay) new one/ new ones	नीचे वाला (nee-chay waa-laa) नीचे वाली (nee-chay-waa-lee) नीचे वाले (nee-chay waa-lay) the one below	दुकान वाला (dü-kaan waa-laa) दुकान वाली (dü-kaan waa-lee) दुकान वाले (dü-kaan waa-lay) shop owner	रिक्शे वाला (rick-shay waa-laa) रिक्शे वाला (rick-shay waa-lee) रिक्शे वाले (rick-shay waa-lay) rickshaw driver

With possessives (as an adjective)	With demonstrative pronouns	With adjectives	With adverbs	With nouns (indicates ownership)	With the professions
आपका वाला (aap-kaa waa-laa) आपकी वाली (aap-kaa waa-lee) आपके वाले (aap-kay waa-lay) the one that is yours	वह वाला (veh waa-laa) वह वाली (veh waa-lee) that one	बड़ा वाला (berDaa waa-laa) बड़ी वाली (berDee waa-lee) बड़े वाले (berDay waa-lay) big one/ big ones	इधर वाला (idh-er waa-laa) इधर वाली (idh-er waa-lee) इधर वाले (idh-er waa-lay) of this side	मकान वाला (muck-aan waa-laa) मकान वाली (muck-aan waa-lee) मकान वाले (muck-aan waa-lay) home-owner	दूध वाला (doo-dh waa-laa) दूध वाली (doo-dh waa-lee) दूध वाले (doo-dh waa-lay) milkman
तेरा वाला (tay-raa waa-laa) तेरी वाली (tay-ree waa-lee) तेरे वाले (tay-ray waa-lay) the one that is yours	वे वाले (vay waa-lay) वे वाली (yay-waa-lee) those ones		उधर वाला (üdh-er waa-laa) उधर वाली (üdh-er waa-lee) उधर वाले (üdh-er waa-lay) of that side	कपड़े वाला (cup-rDay waa-laa) कपड़े वाली (cup-rDay waa-lee) कपड़े वाले (cup-rDay waa-lay) cloth-shop owner	सब्ज़ी वाला (sub-zee waa-laa) सब्ज़ी वाली (sub-zee waa-lee) सब्ज़ी वाले (sub-zee waa-lay) vegetable vendor
इसका वाला (is-kaa waa-laa) इसकी वाली (is-kee waa-lee) इसके वाले (is-kay waa-lay) his/her			यहाँ वाला (yuh-haȧ waa-laa) यहाँ वाली (yuh-haȧ waa-lee) यहाँ वाले (yuh-haȧ waa-lay) the one here	बरतन वाला (ber-tun waa-laa) बरतन वाले (ber-tun waa-lee) बरतन वाले (ber-tun waa-lay) utensil store owner	बस वाला (b-us waa-laa) बस वाले (b-us waa-lee) बस वाले (b-us waa-lay) bus driver

With possessives (as an adjective)	With demonstrative pronouns	With adjectives	With adverbs	With nouns (indicates ownership)	With the professions
उसका वाला (üs-kaa waa-laa) उसकी वाली (üs-kee waa-lee) उसके वाले (üs-kay waa-lay) the one that is his/her			सुबह वाला (süb-uh waa-laa) सुबह वाली (süb-uh waa-lee) सुबह वाले (süb-uh waa-lay) the one from/of morning		किताब वाला (kit-aab waa-laa) किताब वाली (kit-aab waa-lee) किताब वाले (kit-aab waa-lay) bookseller
इनका वाला (in-kaa waa-laa) इनकी वाली (in-kee waa-lee) इनके वाले (in-kay waa-lay) the one that is his/her/their			दूर वाला (doo-r waa-laa) दूर वाली (doo-r waa-lee) दूर वाले (doo-r waa-lay) the distant one		

Imperatives

Imperatives in the Hindi language are used in commands, requests, and instructions. They do not change regardless of the gender or the number of the subject; rather, they conjugate based on the first, second, or third person pronouns. There are altogether six types of imperatives commonly used in Hindi in regular conversation:

1. The Familiar/Informal
2. The Formal/Polite
3. The Formal/Polite (subjunctive)
4. The Intimate
5. The Neutral
6. The Extra-Polite Future Imperative

The familiar or informal imperative is formed by adding the suffix ओ o to the roots ending in the long ā आ vowel or in the dependent form ो o to the root of a verb not ending in any vowel. The suffix यो is added to the verb stem that ends in the long I ी ee vowel in Hindi. It is generally used to give commands and orders. The pronoun तुम tüm is used as a subject of the familiar imperative sentence.

Infinitive	Verb root + suffix ओ, यो, ो	Familiar imperative with तुम (you)
जाना to go	जा + ओ	जाओ (tüm) go
सुनना to listen, hear	सुन + ओ	सुनो (sü-no) listen
पीना to drink	पि + यो	पियो (pi-yo) drink

The formal or polite imperative is formed by adding the suffix इये to the regular verb stem, and the suffix जिये is used with five irregular verb roots: करना, लेना, देना, पीना, and सीना. As the word "polite" suggests, it is used to make a request of a person who is not an acquaintance, who is higher in position or more senior in age, and a teacher; it is also used to give instructions and directions. It is always used with the pronoun आप.

Infinitive (irregular verbs)	Root + suffix	Formal imperative with आप (you)
जाना to go	जा + इये	जाइये (jaa-yay) please go
सुनना to listen, hear	सुन + इये	सुनिये (sün-i-yay) please listen
करना to do	की + जिये	कीजिये (kee-ji-yay) please do

The formal subjunctive imperative is formed by adding ँ yain to the verb root ending in the long vowel ā आ and the dependent ो vowel with the nasal marker. It is always used with the pronoun आप and never used with तुम and तू. The subjunctive imperatives are used to provide instructions in advertisements and in giving directions.

Infinitive	Root + suffix	Subjunctive imperative with आप (you)
जाना to go	जा + एँ	जायें/जाएँ (jaa-yain) please go
सुनना to listen, hear	सुन + एँ	सुनें (sün-ain) please listen
करना to do	कर + एँ	करें (ker-ain) please do

The intimate imperative uses only the verb stem as its form and is generally used to issue commands and orders. The pronoun तू is used as the subject of an intimate imperative sentence. It is used with younger siblings, children, servants, mother, and God. It shows the relationship as either very intimate, as with one's mother and God, or between a master and a servant.

Infinitive	Verb root	Intimate imperative with तू (you)
जाना to go	जा	जा (jaa) go
सुनना to listen, hear	सुन	सुन (sün) listen
करना to do	कर	कर (ker) do

The neutral imperative uses the infinitive form of a verb, and it can be used with तुम tüm, तू too, or आप aap.

This form of imperative is widely used in the marketplace with hawkers: while buying from vegetable vendors, fruit vendors, roadside vendors, and the like. It is also used in very informal settings, where a person can use it with any pronoun as mentioned above. The neutral imperative generally indicates that the request being made may or may not be fulfilled. It is suggestive in nature.

Infinitive	Verb root + ना suffix	Neutral imperative with तू , तुम, आप (you)
जाना to go	जा + ना	जाना (jaa-naa) go
सुनना to listen, hear	सुन + ना	सुनना (sün-naa) listen
करना to do	कर + ना	करना (ker-naa) do

The extra-polite future imperative is formed by adding इयेगा iyay-gaa, or इएगा i-ayga to regular verbs, and the suffix जियेगा ji-yay-gaa is used with five irregular verb roots: करना ker-naa, लेना lay-naa, देना day-naa, पीना pee-naa, and सीना see-naa. The future suffix गा conveys that the polite request will or may be completed in future. It is generally used to show high esteem toward the individual addressed. This form is always used with the pronoun आप.

Infinitive	Verb root + suffix इयेगा or जियेगा	Formal imperative with आप (you)
जाना to go	जा + इयेगा	जाइयेगा (jaa-i-yay-gaa) please go
सुनना to listen, hear	सुन + इयेगा	सुनियेगा (süni-yay-gaa) please listen
करना to do (irregular verb)	की + जियेगा	कीजियेगा (kee-ji-yay-gaa) please do

By now, you must have a relatively good understanding of how Hindi imperatives are formed. Let's see the extra-polite imperative, the suffix वाला waa-laa, and the emphatic particles भी bhee and तो toe used in conversation.

Using compound verbs and their underlying meaning

The compound verb in Hindi is a unique grammatical feature not found in the English language. Therefore it is difficult for a second language learner to use it in general conversation.

The compound verb is made up of two verbs: the main verb is followed by another verb. There are a few particular sets of compound verbs in Hindi, which provide shades of meaning. They slightly differ in meaning and tone from regular verbs. In this book, we will briefly touch on only one form of the Hindi compound verb: the compound with देना. This is the one that is widely used in conversations.

Main verb + देना + auxiliary verb

These are a few combinations: दे देना, कर देना, ला देना, रख देना, बता देना, सुना देना, and उतार देना. In these combinations, the compound verb देना implies that the action benefits someone else, not the doer of the action. देना is a transitive verb and is always used with another transitive verb. The compound verb is never used in the progressive tense and in negative sentences.

Below are examples comparing the meaning of a simple verb with that of a compound verb. The simple verb conjugation suggests the certainty of an action, while the compound verb conjugation shows uncertainty as one of the shades of meaning.

देना		दे देना	
मुझे पैसे दो	order	मुझे पैसे दे दो	pleading
मुझे पैसे दीजिए	command	मुझे पैसे दे दीजिए	requesting
मुझे कल पैसे दीजिएगा	polite command	मुझे कल पैसे दे दीजिएगा	providing leeway

Practice 2

Change the sentences below from their regular imperative forms to the compound form as shown in the example above.

1. मेरा काम करो!   (कर देना – informal)

_____

2. यह बैग वहाँ रखिए।   (रख देना – polite)

_____

3. तुम मेरे दोस्त को <u>बताना</u> कि मैं कल आऊँगा।   (बता देना – neutral)

_____

4. तुम मुझे बाज़ार में <u>उतारना</u>।   (उतार देना – neutral)

_____

Practice 3 Vocabulary-Building Exercise
Match the words on the left column with their corresponding sentences on the right column.

भैया   1. मेरा घर बहुत.......... है। (far)

दूर   2. तुम्हारे पास कितने.............हैं? (Rupees)

कम   3. रिक्शे वाले ...., रुकना। (brother)

रुपये   4. मुझे.............तक जाना है। (square)

चढ़ाई   5. पैसे थोड़ा..............करो। (reduce)

तुरंत   6. उस रास्ते पर बहुत..............है। (climb)

चौक   7. वह .... वहाँ पहुँच गया। (immediately)

Practice 4 Pre-Listening and Vocabulary-Building Exercise
Read the dialogue and fill in the blanks by translating the English words into Hindi.

रमेश – _____ भैया! ओ रिक्शे वाले _____!
         1. (hey, listen)   2. (brother)

रिक्शे वाला – हां _____,कहाँ जाना है आपको।
                  3. (sir)

रमेश – मुझे _____ तक जाना है। कितना पैसा _____?
            4. (square)   5. (will take)

रिक्शे वाला – बाबू _____ रूपया।
                  6. (thirty)

रमेश – तीस रुपये? तीस रूपये तो _____ हैं भाई।
                        7. (a lot)

रिक्शे वाला – बाबू चौक _____ भी तो है। और रास्ते में _____ है।
   8. (far)   9. (uphill grade also)

रमेश – _____ नहीं करोगे?
   10. (a little less)

रिक्शे वाला – बाबू दो रुपया कम _____ ।
   11. (give, compound form)

रमेश – अच्छा क्या तुम मुझे वहाँ से वापस यहाँ _____ भी सकते हो?
   12. (bring and drop)

रिक्शे वाला – क्या आप _____ ही वापस लौटेंगे।आपको वहाँ _____ देर लगेगी?
   13. (immediately)   14. (how much)

रमेश – हाँ, वहाँ एक _____ पर कुछ दस पन्द्रह _____ है, फिर वापस आना है।
   15. (shop)   16. (a minute's work)

रिक्शे वाला – ठीक है, मैं आपको _____ भी _____ ।
   17. (return/back)   18. (to bring)

रमेश – वहाँ _____ - _____ का क्या लोगे?
   19. (going and coming)

रिक्शे वाला – बाबू अब हमने एक तरफ़ का _____, जो समझियेगा _____ ।
   20. (have told you)   21. (give, polite compound form)

रमेश – मैं तुम्हें चौक तक जाने और वापस _____ का पचपन रूपये _____ ।
   22. (return)   23. (will give)

रिक्शे वाला – ठीक है बाबू, _____ रमेश – चलो।
   24. (please come and sit)

Practice 5 🎧 02-11

Listen to the conversation and underline the unknown or forgotten words.

रमेश   : सुनो भैया! ओ रिक्शे वाले भैया!
रिक्शे वाला : हाँ बाबू जी,कहाँ जाना है आपको।
रमेश   : मुझे चौक तक जाना है। कितना पैसा लोगे?
रिक्शे वाला : बाबू तीस रूपया।
रमेश   : तीस रुपये ? तीस रूपये तो बहुत हैं भाई।
रिक्शे वाला : बाबू चौक दूर भी तो है। और रास्ते में चढ़ाई भी है।

रमेश	:	कुछ कम नहीं करोगे?
रिक्शे वाला	:	बाबू दो रुपया कम दे दीजियेगा।
रमेश	:	अच्छा क्या तुम मुझे वहाँ से वापस यहाँ लाकर छोड़ भी सकते हो?
रिक्शे वाला	:	क्या आप तुरंत ही वापस लौटेंगे? आपको वहाँ कितनी देर लगेगी?
रमेश	:	हाँ, वहाँ एक दुकान पर कुछ दस पन्द्रह मिनट का काम है,फिर वापस आना है।
रिक्शे वाला	:	ठीक है, मैं आपको वापस भी ले आऊँगा।
रमेश	:	वहाँ आने और जाने का क्या लोगे?
रिक्शे वाला	:	बाबू अब हमने एक तरफ़ का बता दिया, जो समझियेगा दे दीजियेगा।
रमेश	:	मैं तुम्हें चौक तक जाने और वापस लौटने का पचपन रूपये दूँगा।
रिक्शे वाला	:	ठीक है बाबू, आइये बैठिये।
रमेश	:	चलो।

Romanization

Rum-ay-sh	:	Sü-no bh-i-yaa! O rick-shay waa-lay bh-i-yaa!
Rick-shay waa-laa	:	Haà baa-boo jee, kuh-haaṅ jaa-naa hai aap-ko?
Rum-ay-sh	:	Mü-jh-ay chawk t-uk jaa-naa hai. Kit-naa paisa lo-gay?
Rick-shay waa-laa	:	Baa-boo tees rü-puh-yaa.
Rum-ay-sh	:	Tees rü-puh-yay toe b-hüt haiṅ bha-ee.
Rick-shay waa-laa	:	Baa-boo chawk doo-r bhee toe hai. Aur raas-tay maẏ ch-urDh-aa-ee bhee hai.
Rum-ay-sh	:	Kü-Ch k-um nuh-heeṅ ker-o-gay?
Rick-shay waa-laa	:	Baa-boo dow rüp-uh-yaa k-um day dee-ji-yay-gaa.
Rum-ay-sh	:	Uch-Chaa kyaa tüm mü-Jh-ay vuh-haà say vaa-pus yuh-haà laa-ker Cho-rD bhee suk-tay ho?
Rick-shay waa-laa	:	Kyaa aap tü-runt hee vaa-p-us law-Tayn-gay? Aap-ko vuh-haà kit-nee day-r lug-ay-gee?
Rum-ay-sh	:	Haà, vuh-haà ayk dü-kaan per kü-Ch dus pun-druh min-uT kaa kaam hai, phir vaa-pus aa-naa hai.
Rick-shay waa-laa	:	Theek hai, maiṅ aap-ko vaa-pus bhee lay aa-oò-gaa.
Rum-ay-sh	:	Yuh-haà aa-nay aur jaa-nay kaa kyaa lo-gay?
Rick-shay waa-laa	:	Baa-boo ub hum-nay ayk ter-uf kaa but-aa di-yaa, jo sum-ujh-i-yay-gaa day dee-ji-yay-gaa.
Rum-ay-sh	:	Main tüm-haẏ chawk tuk jaa-nay aur vaa-pus lawT-nay kaa p-uch-pun rüp-uh-yay doò-gaa.
Rick-shay-waa-laa	:	Theek hai baa-boo, aa-i-yay baiTh-i-yay.
Rum-ay-sh	:	Ch-ul-o.

Practice 5.1
Write down the sentences from the conversation that express "to cost money," "to charge," and "to take time."

Hindi Sentences

1. _____

2. _____

3. _____

Practice 5.2
Write down the sentences that best match the translation for "I have some work there and then I have to come back" and "How much will you charge for both ways?"

1. _____

2. _____

Practice 5.3
Write down the sentences containing the compound verbs and translate them into English.

Hindi Sentences   English Translation

1. _____   _____

2. _____   _____

3. _____   _____

4. _____   _____

Practice 6 Post-Listening Activity
Translate the following sentences into Hindi.

1. I have to go to the nearby market.

_____

2. What will you charge me for that?

   _____

3. Will you also be coming back?

   _____

4. Sir, it is very far away.

   _____

5. How long will you take over there?

   _____

6. Thirty rupees is too much.

   _____

7. Can you wait there for 10 to 15 minutes?

   _____

8. You can give me whatever you think is OK. (Use the compound verb दे देना in translation.)

   _____

9. Please come and sit down.

   _____

Translation

Ramesh	:	Hey brother, hey rickshaw wala!
Rickshaw wala	:	Yes sir.
Ramesh	:	I have to go to the plaza/square. How much will you charge?
Rickshaw wala	:	Sir, 30 rupees.
Ramesh	:	Thirty bucks? It's a lot brother. 30 rupees?
Rickshaw wala	:	Sir, the square is too far. And you know there is an uphill grade on the way.
Ramesh	:	Will you not reduce a bit?
Rickshaw wala	:	OK you can give 2 rupees less.

Ramesh	:	Well, can you bring me back from there and drop me off here?
Rickshaw wala	:	Will you come back immediately after? How much time will you take there?
Ramesh	:	I have just 10–15 minutes' work at a shop, and then I have to come back.
Rickshaw wala	:	Well, then I will bring you back too.
Ramesh	:	What will you charge for a round trip?
Rickshaw wala	:	Sir, I have told you the price for one side, now whatever you think is OK, just give it to me.
Ramesh	:	I will give you 55 rupees to go to the square and come back.
Rickshaw wala	:	OK sir, please come and sit down.
Ramesh	:	Let's go.

Practice 7 Comprehension Check
Answer the following questions in Hindi.

1. रमेश को कहाँ जाना है?
    Where does Ramesh have to go?

    _____

2. रिक्शेवाला ज़्यादा पैसे क्यों माँग रहा है?
    Why is the rickshaw driver asking for a higher price?

    _____

3. रिक्शेवाला रमेश को कितने रुपये में ले जाने को तैयार हुआ?
    What rate was agreed upon by the rickshaw driver and Ramesh?

    _____

4. रमेश को चौक क्यों जाना है?
    What is Ramesh's purpose in going to the square?

    _____

5. रमेश को बाज़ार में कितनी देर तक रुकना है?
    How long will Ramesh stay in the square?

    _____

*Read the full dialogue on pages 131–132.

CHAPTER

At the Bank

3.1 Inquiring about Opening a Bank Account बैंक में खाता खोलने की जानकारी लेना।

Objectives

By the end of this lesson, you will be able to:

1. Converse with a bank manager on how to open a bank account.
2. Inquire about documents needed for opening a bank account and the bank's opening hours.
3. Understand the causative verbs to have the needed work done and external compulsion, when you are forced to act upon something unexpected.
4. Use the vocabulary for banking terms in India

📖 **Culture Note**

One of the biggest steps taken to advance India is bank privatization. For Europeans and Americans this is nothing new, but for India, privatized banks have been around only since the beginning of this century, yet they have already caught up with the status of large first-world banks. The new banking system has given people the opportunity to access their bank account from wherever they may be, from the vast numbers of ATM machines to online banking. Inside the banks, you will find your experience pleasant, whether you are a traveler or a local; the banks are known for their care and customer service, helping with all of your needs.

Vocabulary

Nouns

खाता	(khaa-taa)	*masc.*	account
दूतावास	(doo-taa-vaas)	*masc.*	embassy
जानकारी	(jaan-kaa-ree)	*fem.*	information
सप्ताह	(suh-up-taah)	*masc.*	week

निवास	(ni-waas)	*masc.*	residence
परिचय	(per-ich-ay)	*masc.*	introduction
तस्वीर	(tuh-us-veer)	*fem.*	picture
प्रमाण पत्र	(pruh-um-aan puh-utrh)	*masc.*	letter of proof/certificate
पहचान पत्र	(peh-chaan puh-utrh)	*masc.*	identification card
क़ाग़ज़ात	(kaag-zaat)	*masc.*	documents
बचत	(buh-uch-ut)	*fem.*	savings
नौकरी	(naw-ker-ee)	*fem.*	job
इंतज़ार	(int-zaar)	*masc.*	wait
भुगतान	(bhüg-taan)	*masc.*	payment
बकाया	(buck-aa-yaa)	*masc./adj.*	remainder/remaining
राशि	(raa-shi)	*fem.*	amount
मुद्रा	(müd-raa)	*fem.*	currency
दस्तख़त/हस्ताक्षर	(dust-kh-ut/h-us-taak-sh-er)	*masc.*	signature
रुपया	(rü-puh-yaa)	*masc.*	rupee/money
पैसा	(pai-saa)	*masc.*	coin/money
सिक्का	(sik-kaa)	*masc.*	coin

Adjectives and Adverbs

अपना	(up-naa)	*reflexive pron., masc.*	your, my, his, her Ex. He has to do <u>his work</u>. उसको <u>अपना काम</u> करना है। (üs-ko up-naa kaam ker-naa hai.)
अपनी	(up-nee)	*reflexive pron., fem.*	your, my, his, her Ex. She has to read <u>her book</u>. उसको <u>अपनी क़िताब</u> पढ़नी है। (üs-ko up-nee ki-taab perDh-nee hai.)
अपने	(up-nay)	*reflexive pron. masc. pl./ oblique*	your, my, his, her Ex. I have to go to <u>my bank</u>.) मुझे <u>अपने बैंक</u> (को) जाना है। (*oblique*) (müJh-ay up-nay bank jaa-naa hai.)
पूरा	(poo-raa)	*adj.*	complete
चालू	(chaa-loo)	*adj.*	checking/running
बचत	(buh-uch-ut)	*adj.*	savings (account)
कम से कम	(k-um-say k-um)	*adv.*	at least

Verbs

खोलना	(khol-naa)	*v.t.*	to open
खुलवाना	(khül-waa-naa)	*caus. v.t.*	to have opened
करना	(ker-naa)	*v.t.*	to do
जमा कराना	(jum-aa ker-aa-naa)	*v.t.*	to deposit
करवाना	(ker-waa-naa)	*caus. v.t.*	to have done

भरना	(bher-naa)	*v.t.*	to fill out
देखना	(day-kh-naa)	*v.t.*	to see
दिखाना	(di-khaa-naa)	*v.t.*	to show
चैक भुनवाना	(check bhün-waa-naa)	*caus. v.t.*	to have cashed the check
बदलना	(bud-ul-naa)	*v.t.*	to exchange
बदलवाना	(bud-ul-waa-naa)	*caus. v.t.*	to have exchanged
निकलवाना	(nik-ul-waa-naa)	*caus. v.t.*	to have withdrawn
गिनना	(gin-naa)	*v.t.*	to count

Grammar

The External Compulsion and Causative Verbs

Hindi has three types of compulsion, of which you have already learned two: the internal compulsion, and the moral compulsion. The third type is the external compulsion, which suggests that some kind of external force is compelling a person to act. A few examples of the external compulsion in English are:

1. Even though I was very tired, *I had to cook* for my guests, who came unannounced.
2. Because I am going to live there for a few years, *I will have to open* a bank account there.
3. Everyone *has to be at work* at 7:45 sharp. Our supervisor is very strict.

In all the examples above, the person or the people are compelled to act due to some kind of external force (whether he/she likes it or not).

Structure of the External Compulsion

Subject with को + object (*masc./fem., pl.*) + verb (infinitive) + पड़ना/होना (compulsion auxiliary in any tense)

मुझे/मुझको	बैंक	जाना	पड़ता है/ होता है (*habitual*)
(müJh-ko	bank	jaa-naa	perD-taa hai/ho-taa hai.)
I have to go to the bank. (everyday)			

मुझे/मुझको	बैंक	जाना	पड़ेगा/ होगा (*future*)
(müJh-ko	bank	jaa-naa	perD-ay-gaa/ho-gaa.)
I will have to go to the bank.			

NOTE The auxiliary होना in place of पड़ना can be used only with the habitual and future tenses in compulsion.

मुझे /मुझको	बैंक	जाना	पड़ा (*simple perfect*)
(müJh-ay/müJh-ko	bank	jaa-naa	perD-aa.)

I had to go to the bank.

मुझे /मुझको	बैंक	जाना	पड़ रहा है (*present progressive*)
(müJh-ko	bank	jaa-naa	perD-ruh-haa hai.)

I am having to go to the bank. (I am being forced to go the bank.)

Practice 1 [03-02]

Listen to the sentences below, transcribe them, and then translate them into English.

	Transcription	**Translation**
1.	_____	_____
2.	_____	_____
3.	_____	_____
4.	_____	_____
5.	_____	_____
6.	_____	_____
7.	_____	_____
8.	_____	_____
9.	_____	_____
10.	_____	_____

Causative verbs have been covered in Chapter 2 "Traveling in India." Here we will review some of them and practice them in a different context. Remember, the function of a causative verb is that either the subject himself or herself causes work to be done or he/she has someone else do it.

Practice 2

Read aloud the sentences below and practice the causative verb form used in banking. This will help you in communicating your banking needs.

मुझे खाता खुलवाना है।	I have to have an account open.
मुझे चालू खाता खुलवाना है।	I have to have a checking account open.
मुझे बचत खाता खुलवाना है।	I have to have a savings account open.
मुझे चैक भुनवाना है।	I have to have the check cashed.
मुझे पैसे निकलवाने हैं।	I have to withdraw the money.
मुझे करेंसी/मुद्रा बदलवानी है।	I have to have the currency exchanged.
मुझे पैसे जमा करवाने/कराने हैं।	I have to deposit the money.
मुझे अपना चालू खाता बंद करवाना/कराना है।	I have to close my checking account.

Practice 3 Vocabulary-Building

Match the English words on the left to the corresponding Hindi words on the right.

1.	work	कोई
2.	when	सकना
3.	week	काग़ज़ात
4.	to stay	बात करना
5.	account	भरना
6.	to have opened	काम
7.	documents	कब
8.	any	सप्ताह
9.	to talk to	करना पड़ेगा
10.	to tell	जानकारी
11.	will have to do	देना
12.	can	दिखाना
13.	to fill out	खाता
14.	to give	खुलवाना
15.	information	जमा कराना
16.	to show	बताना
17.	to deposit	फिर
18.	to close	आऊँगा/ आऊँगी
19.	then	बंद होना
20.	I will come	ठहरना

Practice 4 🎧 03-03

Listen to a dialogue between two acquaintances and read along with it.

Script

डेविड : सुनील जी नमस्ते आप कैसे हैं?

सुनील : नमस्ते डेविड, मैं ठीक हूँ तुम कैसे हो? भारत कब आये?

डेविड : मैं ठीक हूँ और भारत एक सप्ताह पहले ही आया हूँ।

सुनील : तुम अभी कहाँ ठहरे हो? और यहाँ कैसे आये? बैंक में कोई काम है?

डेविड : हाँ सुनील, बैंक में मुझे खाता खुलवाना है। क्या तुम मुझे बता सकते हो कि इस के लिये मुझे क्या करना होगा?

सुनील : हाँ हाँ क्यो नहीं, सबसे पहले तुम्हें बैंक मैनेज़र से बात करनी पड़ेगी, उसके बाद एक फ़ार्म भरना होगा जिसमें तुम को अपने बारे में पूरी जानकारी देनी होगी, कुछ काग़ज़ात दिखाने पड़ेंगे, खाते में कुछ रुपये जमा कराने पड़ेंगे और तुम्हारा खाता खुल जायेगा।

डेविड : क्या अभी बैंक बंद हो गया है?

सुनील : हाँ, अभी तो बैंक बंद हो गया है। तुम्हें कल आना पड़ेगा।

डेविड : बैंक कितने बजे खुलता है और कितने बजे बंद होता है?

सुनील : बैंक तो सुबह दस बजे खुलता है और शाम को पाँच बजे बंद होता है।

डेविड : ठीक है सुनील जी बहुत बहुत धन्यवाद मैं फिर कल सुबह दस बजे आऊँगा। नमस्ते।

Romanization

Day-vid : Sü-neel jee num-us-tay, aap kai-say haiṅ?

Sü-neel : Num-us-tay Day-vid, maiṅ Theek hoṅ, tüm kai-say ho? Bhaa-rut cub aa-yay?

Day-vid : Maiṅ Theek hoṅ aur ayk sup-taah peh-lay hee aa-yaa hoṅ.

Sü-neel : tüm ub-hee kuh-haà Theh-ray ho? Aur yuh-haaṅ kai-say aa-yay? Bank maẏ ko-ee kaam hai?

Day-vid : Haà Sü-neel, Bank maẏ mü-jhay khaa-taa khül-waa-naa hai. Kyaa tüm mü-Jhay but-aa suk-tay ho ki is-kay li-yay mü-Jhay kyaa ker-naa ho-gaa?

Sü-neel : Haà haaṅ kyó nuh-heé, sub-say peh-lay tüm-haẏ Bank Manager say baat ker-nee perD-ay gee, üs-kay baad ayk form bh-er-naa perD-ay-gaa jis-maẏ tüm-ko up-nay baa-ray maẏ poo-ree jaan-kaa-ree day-nee ho-gee, küCh kaag-zaat dikh-aa-nay perD-aẏ-gay, khaa-tay maẏ küCh rüp-ay-yay jum-aa ker-aa-nay perD-ay-gay aur tüm-haa-raa khaa-taa khül jaa-yay-gaa.

Day-vid : Kyaa ub-hee bank b-und ho g-yaa hai?

Sü-neel : Haà, ub-hee toe bank b-und ho guh-yaa hai. tüm-haiṅ k-ul aa-naa perD-ay-gaa.

Day-vid : Bank kit-nay buj-ay khül-taa hai aur kit-nay buj-ay b-und ho-taa hai?

Sü-neel : Bank toe sü-buh dus buj-ay khül-taa hai aur sham ko paà-ch buj-ay bund ho-taa hai.

Day-vid : Theek hai Sü-neel jee buh-hüt buh-hüt dhuh-unya-vaad, maiṅ ph-ir k-ul sü-buh aa-oṅ-gaa. num-us-tay.

Translation

David : Hello Sunil ji, how are you?

Sunil : Hello David. I am fine. How are you? When did you come to India?

David : I am fine. I just arrived here a week ago.

Sunil : Where are you staying? What brings you here? Do you have some work in the bank?

David : Yes, Sunil, I have to open a bank account. Can you tell me what I have to do for that?

Sunil : Yes, yes, why not. First of all, you will have to talk to the bank manager, then you will have to fill out a form in which you will have to provide personal information, you will have to show some documents, you will have to deposit some money and that's all—your bank account will be opened.

David : Has the bank closed already?

Sunil : Yes, currently the bank is closed. You will have to come back tomorrow.

David : What time does it open and what time does it close?

Sunil : It opens at ten in the morning and closes at five in the evening.

David : OK Sunil, thank you so much. I will come tomorrow at ten in the morning then. Goodbye.

Practice 5

Listen again and answer the following questions in Hindi.

1. डेविड भारत कब आया?
   When did David come to India?

   _____

2. डेविड को बैंक में क्या काम है?
   What work does David have at the bank?

   _____

3. सुनील के अनुसार, बैंक में डेविड को सबसे पहले क्या करना पड़ेगा?
   According to Sunil, what does David have to do first of all at the bank?

   _____

4. बैंक कितने बजे खुलता है और कितने बजे बंद होता है?
   What time does the bank open and close?

   _____

Practice 6

Translate the following sentences into Hindi.

1. You will have to deposit 5,000 rupees in the checking account.

   _____

2. What do I have to do to open a checking account?

   _____

3.   Do you have any information about the bank?

_____

4.   I have to open a savings account.

_____

3.2 Opening a Bank Account बैंक में खाता खोलना

Objectives
By the end of this lesson, you will be able to:
1.   Converse with a bank employee.
2.   Provide your personal information to the bank employee.
3.   Pronounce, read and listen to the Hindi words for important documents needed to open a bank account.

Grammar: Review

The External Compulsion and Causative Verbs

Pre-Listening Exercise
1.   *Brainstorm for a few minutes and think what documents your bank requires from you in order to open a checking or savings account. Write down your answers on a piece of paper.*

2.   *What phrases would you use in order to communicate with a bank employee when you need to open a bank account? Write them down below.*

_____

_____

Practice 1
Label the pictures in Hindi with the appropriate phrase, noun, or verb from the selection below.

1. Depositing   3. To cash   5. To fill (a form)   7. To exchange 9. Amount   11. Wait
2. Withdrawing 4. To show   6. Currency   8. Proof   10. Signature

1.

2.

3.

4.

5.

6.

7.

8.

9.

10.

11.

Practice 2

Choose the correct word to fit the sentence.

1. मुझे _____ खुलवाना है। (account)

   a. बचत   b. खाता   c. परिचय

2. बैंक में आपको अपना _____ पत्र दिखाना पड़ेगा। (identification)

   a. कागज़ात   b. परिचय   c. निवास

3. बैंक में मुझे बहुत देर तक _____ करना पड़ा। (wait)

   a. चैक   b. बक़ाया   c. इंतज़ार

4. मुझे बैंक में चैक _____ है। (to cash)

   a. खुलवाना   b. निकलवाना   c. भुनवाना

5. मैंने पिछले साल बैंक में दस हज़ार रुपयों की _____ की। (savings)

   a. बचत   b. नौकरी   c. राशि

6. खाता खोलने के लिए आपको पाँच हज़ार रुपये की _____ जमा करवानी पड़ेगी। (amount)

   a. पैसे   b. राशि   c. मुद्रा

Practice 3

Read along as you listen to the dialogue below that is between a customer and a bank manager. Then fill in the Hindi word for the English counterpart, given in parenthesis below each blank.

मैनेज़र- नमस्ते जी, आइये बैठिये _____ मैं आपकी क्या _____ कर सकता हूँ?
                                     1. (please tell)   2. (service)

निकोल : मैं आपके बैंक में _____ खोलना चाहती हूँ।
                                   3. (account)

मैनेज़र : आप कैसा खाता _____ चाहती हैं?
                                   4. (to have opened)

निकोल : जी मैं आपके बैंक में _____ खाता खुलवाना चाहती हूँ। इसके लिए मुझे क्या करना होगा?

5. (savings)

मैनेजर : आपका नाम?

निकोल : मेरा नाम निकोल है।

मैनेजर : आप कहाँ काम करतीं हैं?

निकोल : मैं अमरीकी _____ में काम करती हूँ।

6. (embassy)

जी मैं चाणक्यपुरी में गुप्ता _____ में रहती हूँ।

7. (residence)

मैनेजर : आप भारत में _____ _____ रहेंगी?

8. (how many years)

निकोल : जी चार साल

Script 1 🎧 03-04

मैनेज़र : नमस्ते जी, आइये बैठिये, बताइये मैं आपकी क्या सेवा कर सकता हूँ?

निकोल : मैं आपके बैंक में ख़ाता खोलना चाहती हूँ।

मैनेज़र : आप कैसा खाता खुलवाना चाहती हैं?

निकोल : जी मैं बचत खाता खुलवाना चाहती हूँ। उसके लिए मुझे क्या करना होगा?

मैनेजर : आपका नाम?

निकोल : मेरा नाम निकोल है।

मैनेजर : आप कहाँ काम करतीं हैं?

निकोल : मैं अमरीकी दूतावास में काम करती हूँ।

मैनेज़र : आप कहाँ रहती हैं?

निकोल : जी मैं चाणक्यपुरी में गुप्ता निवास में रहती हूँ।

मैनेज़र : आप भारत में कितने साल रहेंगी?

निकोल : जी चार साल।

Romanization 1

Manager	:	Num-us-tay jee, aa-i-yay bai-Th-i-yay, but-aa-i-yay aap-kee kyaa say-waa ker suk-taa hoȯ?
Nicole	:	Main aap-kay bank maẏ khaa-taa khol-naa chaah-tee hoȯ.
Manager	:	Aap kai-saa khaa-taa khül-waa-naa chaah-teė hain?
Nicole	:	Jee, main buh-uch-ut khaa-taa khül-waa-naa chaah-tee hoȯ. Üs-kay li-yay mü-jhay kyaa ker-naa ho-gaa?
Manager	:	Aap-kaa naam?
Nicole	:	May-raa naam Nicole hai.
Manager	:	Aap kuh-haȧ kaam ker-tee hain?
Nicole	:	Main Um-ree-kee doo-taa-vaas maẏ kaam ker-tee hoȯ.

Manager : Aap kuh-haȧ reh-teė hain?
Nicole : Main chaa-nukyuh-püree maẏ Güp-taa Niwaas maẏ reh-tee hoȯ.
Manager : Aap bhaa-rut maẏ kit-nay saal ruh-haẏ-gee?
Nicole : Jee chaar saal.

Translation 1

Manager : Greetings, please have a seat. How may I help you today?
Nicole : I would like to open an account in your bank.
Manager : What type of account would you like to open?
Nicole : I want to open a savings account; what do I have to do?
Manager : What is your name?
Nicole : My name is Nicole.
Manager : Where do you work?
Nicole : I work at the US Embassy.
Manager : Where do you live?
Nicole : I live in Chanakyapuri, in the Gupta residence.
Manager : How many years will you be staying in India?
Nicole : Four years.

Script 2  03-05

मैनेज़र : अच्छा तो आप को सब से पहले एक फ़ार्म भरना होगा। उस में आपको अपनी पूरी जानकारी देनी होगी।
निकोल : फ़ॉर्म के साथ और क्या-क्या काग़ज़ात चाहिए?
मैनेज़र : एक तस्वीर उसके साथ ही दो पहचान पत्र, निवास स्थान का प्रमाण पत्र, और अपने दफ़्तर से नौकरी का प्रमाण पत्र फ़ार्म के साथ जमा कराना होगा।
निकोल : सभी काग़ज़ातों के साथ मुझे कितने रूपये जमा कराने पड़ेंगे?
मैनेज़र : आप को कम से कम एक हज़ार रूपये जमा कराने पड़ेंगे?
निकोल : जी बहुत-बहुत धन्यवाद, तो फिर मैं फ़ार्म भर कर सभी काग़ज़ातों के साथ कल सुबह आती हूँ।
मैनेज़र : ठीक है, फिर आपसे कल मुलाक़ात होगी।

Romanization 2

Manager : Uch-Chaa toe aap-ko sub-say peh-lay yeh form bher dee-ji-yay. Is-may aap-ko up-nee poo-ree jaan-kaa-ree day-nee ho-gee.
Nicole : Form kay saa-th aur kyaa-kyaa kaag-zaat chaa-hi-yaẏ?
Manager : Ayk tus-veer laa-nee ho-gee, üs-kay saa-th hi doe peh-chaan p-ut-ruh, ni-waas sth-aan kaa prum-aan p-ut-ruh aur up-nay duf-ter say nau-ker-ee kaa prum-aan p-ut-ruh form kay saath jum-aa ker-aa-nay hȯ-gay.
Nicole : Sub-hee kaag-zaatȯ kay saath mü-jhay kit-nay rüp-uh-yay juh-um-aa ker-aa-nay perD-aẏ-gay?
Manager : Aap ko kum say kum ayk huz-aar rüp-uh-yay juh-um-aa ker-aa-nay perD-aẏ-gay.
Nicole : Jee buh-hüt buh-hüt dh-unyuh-vaad, toe phir main form bher-kay sub-hee kaag-zaa-tȯ kay saath k-ul süb-uh aa-tee hoȯ.
Manager : Theek hai phir aap-say k-ul mül-aa-quaat ho-gee.

Practice 4

Now, read along as you listen to the second part of the dialogue. Then fill in the Hindi word for the English counterpart, given in parenthesis below the blanks.

मैनेज़र : _____ आप को सब से पहले एक _____ _____ । उस में
        1. (OK then)   2. (will have to fill out a form)

आपको अपनी _____ _____ देनी होगी ।
             3. (complete information)

निकोल : फ़ॉर्म के साथ और क्या-क्या _____ चाहिए?
                       4. (documents)

मैनेज़र : एक _____ उसके साथ ही दो _____, _____ का प्रमाण पत्र,
           5. (photo)   6. (identification card) (residence)

और अपने दफ़्तर से नौकरी का _____ _____, फ़ॉर्म के साथ _____ होंगे ।
                    7. (certificate of proof)   8. (to deposit)

मैनेज़र : आप को _____ एक हज़ार रूपये जमा कराने पड़ेंगे?
              9. (at least)

निकोल : जी बहुत-बहुत धन्यवाद, तो कल मैं फ़ॉर्म भर कर सभी _____ के साथ सुबह 10 बजे
     आऊँगी ।   10. (documents)

मैनेज़र : ठीक है, फिर आपसे कल _____ होगी ।
                    11. (meeting)

Translation 2

Manager : Well, first of all you need to fill out a form in which you will have to give your complete information.

Nicole : What documents are needed along with the form?

Manager : You will have to bring your photograph along with two photo IDs, proof of residence and proof of your employment, all of which you will have to submit with the form.

Nicole : How much money will I have to deposit?

Manager : You will have to deposit at least 1,000 rupees.

Nicole : OK thanks. I will come back tomorrow with the completed form and all the documents.

Manager : OK then, I will see you tomorrow.

Practice 5 Post-Listening Exercise
Listen to the recording again.

1. Write down the type of documents needed to open a bank account in India.

    _____

2. How much money is needed to open an account?

    _____

3. Why does Nicole have to come again the next day?

    _____

3.3 Cashing a Check चैक भुनवाना

Objectives
By the end of this lesson you will be able to:
1. Deposit into and withdraw money from your bank account in India.
2. Answer the bank teller's questions regarding the deposit and withdrawal of money.

Grammar: Review Causative Verbs

Remember that the causative verb in Hindi expresses an action that a subject causes to happen. There are two types of causative verbs: First Causative and Second Causative Verbs.

In a First Causative sentence, the subject directly causes the action to happen.

Subject + Indirect object + को + Direct Object (if any) + Verb Transitive + auxiliary
माँ   बच्चे   को   सुला   रही   है।
(maà buh-uch-chay ko sü-laa ruh-hee hai.)
Mother is putting the child to sleep.

माँ   अपने बच्चे   को खाना   खिला   रही   है।
(maà up-nay buh-uch-chay ko khaa-naa khi-laa ruh-hee hai.)
A mother is feeding food to her child.

A Second Causative Verb always needs an intermediary agent to make things happen for the subject. In this case the intermediary agent is always followed by the postposition से *(by)*. Sometimes use of the intermediary agent is not required.

Subject + intermediary agent + से + Object + verb root with suffix वा + auxiliary (if any)

मैं रोज़   अपने बेटे से   खाना   बनवाती   हूँ।

(main row-z up-nay bay-Tay say khaa-naa bun-waa-tee hoon.)

I have my son make the food every day.

मैं रोज़   खाना   बनवाती   हूँ।

(main row-z khaa-naa bun-waa-tee hoon.)

I have the food cooked every day.

Practice 1 Pre-Listening Exercise
Match the vocabulary on the left with its English meanings.

1.	दस्तख़त	should I do
2.	सेवा	two thousand five hundred
3.	निकलवाना	signature
4.	कर देना	service
5.	करूँ	behind
6.	के पीछे	to do
7.	ढाई हज़ार	to withdraw

Practice 2
You are at a bank in India to deposit a check. Do your part as a customer by completing the dialogue, either answering or asking a question.

बैंक कर्मचारी: जी कहिए, आपकी क्या सेवा कर सकते हैं?

आदमी   : _____

बैंक कर्मचारी : नकद जमा करवाएँगे है या चैक?

आदमी   : _____

बैंक कर्मचारी : ज़रा चैक पर दस्तख़त भी कर दीजिए।

आदमी   : _____

बैंक कर्मचारी : चैक के पीछे।

आदमी   : _____

बैंक कर्मचारी : आपको इस चैक में से पैसे निकलवाने भी हैं?

आदमी   : _____

बैंक कर्मचारी : कितने निकलवाने हैं?

आदमी   : _____

बैंक कर्मचारी : यह लीजिए आपके ढाई हज़ार रुपये।

आदमी   : _____

Check your answers against the dialogue below.

Script 🎧 [03-06]

बैंक कर्मचारी :	जी कहिए, आपकी क्या सेवा कर सकते हैं?
आदमी :	मुझे पैसे जमा करवाने हैं।
बैंक कर्मचारी :	नक़द जमा करवाएँगे है या चैक?
आदमी :	चैक जमा करवाना है।
बैंक कर्मचारी :	ज़रा चैक पर दस्तख़त भी कर दीजिए।
आदमी :	कहाँ करूँ?
बैंक कर्मचारी :	चैक के पीछे।
आदमी :	यह लीजिए दस्तख़त कर दिए।
बैंक कर्मचारी :	आपको इस चैक में से पैसे भी निकलवाने हैं?
आदमी :	हाँ, पैसे भी निकलवाने हैं।
बैंक कर्मचारी :	कितने निकलवाने हैं?
आदमी :	ढाई हज़ार निकाल दीजिए।
बैंक कर्मचारी :	यह लीजिए आपके ढाई हज़ार रुपये।
आदमी :	बहुत-बहुत धन्यवाद।

Romanization

Bank kerm-chaa-re	: Jee kuh-hi-yay, aap-kee kyaa say-waa ker suk-tay hain?
Aad-me	: Mü-jhay pai-say j-um-aa ker-waa-nay hain.
Bank kerm-chaa-re	: Nuq-ud j-um-aa ker-waa-aaẏ-gay yaa check?
Aad-me	: Check j-um-aa ker-waa-naa hai.
Bank Kerm-chaa-re	: Zer-aa check per dust-kh-ut bhee ker dee-ji-yay.
Aad-me	: Kuh-haȧ ker-oȯ?
Bank Kerm-chaa-re	: Check kay pee-chay.
Aad-me	: Yeh lee-ji-yay dust-kh-ut ker di-yay.
Bank Kerm-chaa-re	: Aap-ko is check maẏ say pai-say bhee nik-ul-waa-nay hain?
Aad-me	: Haȧ pai-say phee nik-ul-waa-nay hain.
Bank Kerm-chaa-re	: Kit-nay nik-ul-waa-nay hain?

Aad-me	:	Dhaa-ee huz-aar nik-aal dee-ji-yay.
Bank Kerm-chaa-re	:	Yeh lee-ji-yay aap-kay Dhaa-ee huz-aar rüp-uh-yay.
Aad-me	:	Buh-hüt buh-hüt dh-unyuh-vaad.

Translation

Bank Teller	:	How can I help you today?
Man	:	I would like to make a deposit.
Bank Teller	:	Will that be cash or check?
Man	:	I'm depositing a check.
Bank Teller	:	Here, can you please sign the check?
Man	:	Where should I sign?
Bank Teller	:	On the back of the check.
Man	:	All right. Here you go.
Bank Teller	:	Would you like to withdraw any cash?
Man	:	That would be great.
Bank Teller	:	How much would you like to withdraw?
Man	:	I would like to withdraw twenty-five hundred rupees.
Bank Teller	:	Here is your twenty-five hundred rupees.
Man	:	Thanks for everything.

*Read the full dialogue on page 146.

CHAPTER

4

Shopping in India

4.1 In the Marketplace बाज़ार में

Objectives

By the end of this lesson you will be able to:

1. State the names of some common fruits, vegetables, and herbs.
2. Buy produce, using the common phrases provided in the lesson.
3. Bargain with produce vendors using the familiar and neutral imperatives.
4. Understand and use the measurement/weighing system in India.
5. Show your agreement or disagreement on a price stated by the vendor.

> 📖 **Culture Note**
>
> If you are going to live in India for a period of time, you will definitely need a house, and in order to run your kitchen, you will need to buy food from the market, especially vegetables and fruits. It is important to know that India's climate is tropical, and fruits and vegetables are not available year-round. Although the open market policy has opened up the world market and cold storages have enhanced the availability of off-season produce mostly in metropolitan and big cities, off-season produce is not easily available elsewhere.

Vocabulary

सब्ज़ी	(sub-zee)	*fem.*	vegetable
फूल गोभी	(phool go-bhee)	*fem.*	cauliflower
पत्ता गोभी	(putt-aa go-bhee)	*fem.*	cabbage
मटर	(mut-er)	*fem.*	pea
शिमला मिर्च	(shim-laa mir-ch)	*fem.*	capsicum/bell pepper
गाजर	(gaa-jer)	*fem.*	carrot
मूली	(moo-lee)	*fem.*	radish
हरी मिर्च	(her-ee mir-ch)	*fem.*	green chili
आलू	(aa-loo)	*masc.*	potato
प्याज़	(pyaaz)	*masc.*	onion

अदरक	(ud-ruck)	*fem.*	ginger
धनिया	(dh-un-iyaa)	*masc.*	cilantro
टमाटर	(Tum-aa-Ter)	*masc.*	tomato
पालक	(paa-luck)	*masc.*	spinach

Qualitative Adjectives

ताज़ा/ ताज़ी/ ताज़े	(taa-zaa/taa-zee/ taa-zay)	*masc. sing./ fem./masc. pl.*	fresh
बासी	(baa-see)		old, stale
महंगा/ महंगी/ महंगे	(mehṅ-gaa/mehṅ-gee/ mehṅ-gay)	*masc. sing./ fem./masc. pl.*	expensive
सस्ता/ सस्ती/ सस्ते	(sus-taa/sus-tee/ sus-tay)	*masc. sing./ fem./masc. pl.*	cheap
गला हुआ/ गली हुयी/ गले हुए	(g-ul-aa hüa/g-ul-ee hü-ee/g-ul-ay hü-ay)	*masc. sing./ fem./masc. pl.*	softened, tender
सड़ा हुआ/ सड़ी हुयी/ सड़े हुए	(serD-aa hüaa/ serD-ee hü-ee/ serD-ay hü-ay)	*masc. sing./ fem./masc. pl.*	rotten

Quantitative Adjectives

इतना	(it-naa)	*masc. sing.*	this much
इतना सा/सी/ से!	(it-naa-saa/see/say)	*masc. sing./ fem./masc. pl.*	so little
थोड़ा	(tho-rDaa)	*masc. sing.*	little
थोड़ा सा/ सी/ से	(tho-rDaa saa/ see/say)	*masc. sing./ fem./masc. pl.*	very little, a little bit
ज़रा	(zer-aa)		little
ज़रा सा/सी/ से	(zer-aa saa/see/say)	*masc. sing./ fem./masc. pl.*	very little, a little bit
बहुत सारा/सारी/सारे	(buh-hüt saa-raa/ saa-re/saa-ray)	*masc. sing./ fem./masc. pl.*	lots of
थोड़ा कम	(tho-rDaa kum)		a little less
बहुत ज़्यादा	(buh-hüt zyaa-daa)		a lot

Units of Measure

ग्राम	(graa-m)		gram
पाव भर	(paav bher)		quarter kilo
किलो	(kilo)		kilo
आधा किलो	(aa-dhaa kilo)		half kilo
सवा किलो	(s-uv-aa kilo)		one and one quarter kilo
दर्जन	(der-zen)		dozen
गुच्छा	(guch-Chaa)	*masc. sing.*	bunch
टुकड़ा	(Tük-rDaa)	*masc. sing.*	piece

Currency

पैसे	(pai-say)	*masc. pl.*	money, coin money
रुपया	(rü-puh-yaa)	*masc. sing.*	rupee
रुपये	(rü-puh-yay)	*masc. pl.*	rupees
छुट्टे/खुल्ले	(ChüT-Tay/khül-lay)	*masc. pl.*	change (coins)
रेज़गारी	(rayz-gaa-re)	*fem. sing.*	change (coins)
पिचहत्तर पैसे	(pich-hutter pai-say)	*masc. pl.*	quarter of a rupee/75 paise
पचास पैसे	(p-uch-aas pai-say)	*masc. pl.*	half rupee/50 paise
डेढ़ रुपये	(DerDh rü-puh-yay)	*masc. pl.*	a rupee and a half
ढाई रुपये	(Dhaa-ee rü-puh-yay)	*masc. pl.*	two rupees and a half
सौ रुपये	(saw rü-puh-yay)	*masc. pl.*	hundred rupees

Verbs

देना	(day-naa)	*v.t.*	to give
लेना	(lay-naa)	*v.t*	to take, to charge
तोलना	(tol-naa)	*v.t.*	to weigh
डालना	(Daal-naa)	*v.t.*	to put
दाम लगाना	(daam lug-aa-naa)	*v.t.*	to price
भाव लगाना	(bhaav lug-aa-naa)	*v.t.*	to price
बोलना	(bowl-naa)	*v.t.*	to say, to tell, to speak

Useful Phrases When Buying Fruits and Vegetables

1.	कैसे दिये?	(kai-say di-yay)	*masc. pl.*	What is the price?
2.	कैसी दी?	(kai-see dee)	*fem. sing.* [single item]	What is the price?
3.	कैसी दीं?	(kai-see deè)	*fem. pl.*	What is the price?
4.	क्या भाव दिया?	(kyaa bhaav di-yaa)	*masc.sing.* [single item]	How much is it for?
5.	क्या भाव दी?	(kyaa bhaav dee)	*fem. sing.*	How much is it for?
6.	क्या भाव दिये?	(kyaa bhaav di-yay)	*masc. pl.*	How much is it for?
7.	कितने का दिया?	(kit-nay kaa di-yaa)	*masc. sing.*	How much is it for?
8.	ठीक दाम लगाओ।	(Theek daam lug-aa-o)		Say the right price.
9.	ठीक बोलो।	(Theek bo-lo)		Give me your best price.
10.	थोड़ा कम करो।	(tho-rDa kum ker-o)		Reduce a little bit (price)
11.	ठीक से तोलो।	(Theek say tol-o)		Weigh properly/correctly
12.	और डालो।	(awr Daa-lo)		Put more, add more
13.	कुल कितने पैसे हुए?	(kül kit-nay pai-say hü-yay)		How much is the total?

NOTE These phrases are used mainly in buying produce and food items, not for books, clothing, furniture, shoes, or tickets.

Grammar

Reviewing the Familiar Imperative and the Neutral Imperative

The familiar imperative is used with people you are familiar with: younger siblings, friends, and market vendors selling produce, and other people who do business on a very small scale. It is used mainly to give orders and commands using the second person pronoun तुम. It uses the verb root + the dependent or independent ओ vowel. However, when the familiar imperative is used with a compound verb, the intensity of a command or an order is lessened. On the other hand, the neutral imperative can be used with anyone and with any form of pronouns, such as आप, तुम, तू, and तुम. The neutral imperative is not used to give orders; rather, it is suggestive and implies a request. But when the neutral imperative is used in a strong negative sentence using मत m-ut ("don't"), it leans towards a command.

Sample Sentences

Practice 1

Read the sentences below along with the audio and pay attention to the inflection or the tone:

1.	सब्ज़ी वाले !!! रुको।	*familiar*	(sub-zee vaa-lay!!! rü-ko.)
2.	सब्ज़ीवाले !!! रुकना।	*neutral*	(sub-zee vaa-lay!!! rük-naa.)
3.	दो किलो मटर दे दो।	*familiar*	(doe kilo mut-ter day doe.)
4.	दो किलो मटर देना।	*neutral*	(doe kilo mut-ter day-naa.)
5.	पाव भर हरी मिर्च दे दो।	*familiar*	(paav ber her-ee mir-ch day doe.)
6.	पाव भर हरी मिर्च देना।	*neutral*	(paav ber her-ee mir-ch day-naa.)
7.	थोड़ी सी अदरक भी डाल दो।	*familiar*	(thorD-ee see ud-ruk bhee Daal doe.)
8.	थोड़ी सी अदरक भी डाल देना।	*neutral*	(thorD-ee see ud-ruk bhee Daal day-naa.)
9.	एक गुच्छा धनिया भी डाल देना।	*neutral*	(ayk güch-Chaa dh-un-iyaa bhee daal-day-naa.)
10.	सौ के खुल्ले दे दो।	*familiar*	(saw kay khül-lay day doe.)
11.	सौ के खुल्ले देना।	*neutral*	(saw kay khül-lay day-naa.)
12.	ठीक दाम लगाओ।	*familiar*	(Theek daam l-ug-aao.)
13.	ठीक दाम लगाना।	*neutral*	(Theek daam l-ug-aa-naa.)
14.	ताज़े टमाटर दो, सड़े हुए मत दो।	*familiar*	(taa-zay Tum-aa-Ter doe, serD-ay hü-ay mut doe.)
15.	ताज़े टमाटर देना, सड़े हुए मत देना।	*neutral*	(taa-zay Tum-aa-Ter doe, serD-ay hü-ay mut day-naa.)
16.	गली हुई सब्ज़ियाँ मत डालो।	*familiar*	(g-ul-ee hü-ee sub-zi-yaà mut Daa-lo.)
17.	गली हुई सब्ज़ियाँ मत डालना।	*neutral*	(g-ul-ee hü-ee sub-zi-yaà mut Daal-naa.)
18.	बासी गोभी मत डालो, अच्छी गोभी दो।	*familiar*	(baa-see go-bhee mut Daa-lo uch-Chee go-bhee doe.)

19. बासी गोभी मत डालना,   *neutral*   (baa-see go-bhee mut Daa-lo uch-Chee
    अच्छी गोभी देना।   go-bhee day-naa.)

Practice 2 Pre-Listening Exercise

Match the Hindi words with their English meaning.

1.	गोभी	fresh
2.	गाजर	wholesale market
3.	मूली	to say
4.	बैंगन	to put
5.	ताज़ी	cost
6.	धनिया	How much is it?
7.	भाव	pricey
8.	महंगी	carrot
9.	मंडी	change (money)
10.	दाम लगाना	cilantro
11.	बोलना	eggplant
12.	डाल देना	radish
13.	खुल्ले	cauliflower
14.	कितने हुए?	to price

Practice 3 🎧 04-03

Listen to the conversation between a female customer and a vegetable vendor on a street in India, and complete the activities that follow.

सब्ज़ी वाला : गोभी लो, पालक लो, गाजर लो, मटर लो, बैंगन लो, मूली लो।

ग्राहक : अरे सब्ज़ी वाले ज़रा रुकना!

सब्ज़ी वाला : आया बहनजी। बोलो आपको क्या दूँ?

ग्राहक : तुम्हारे पास आज क्या-क्या है?

सब्ज़ी वाला : मेरे पास ताज़ी पत्ता गोभी है, फूल गोभी है, गाजर है, टमाटर है, धनिया है, शिमला मिर्च है। आपको क्या चाहिए?

ग्राहक : ये फूल गोभी क्या भाव दी?

सब्ज़ी वाला : फूल गोभी बहनजी पच्चीस रुपये किलो है।

ग्राहक : इतनी महंगी!! ठीक दाम बोलो। सब्ज़ी मंडी में तो ये बीस रुपये किलो है।

सब्ज़ी वाला : बीस रुपये किलो तो पाँच दिन पहले का भाव है बहनजी। आज बाज़ार में सब्ज़ियाँ बहुत महंगी हो गयी हैं। बोलो कितनी दूँ?

ग्राहक : बीस में दोगे तो लूँगी।

सब्ज़ी वाला : चलो आपको बाइस रुपये किलो दे दूँगा। ये लो।

ग्राहक : और टमाटर कैसे दिए? एक किलो टमाटर भी देना और ठीक दाम लगाना। साथ में हरे धनिये का गुच्छा, दो चार हरी मिर्च और एक अदरक का टुकड़ा भी डाल देना।

सब्ज़ी वाला : ये लो बहन जी, एक किलो टमाटर पच्चीस रुपये के, ये धनिये का गुच्छा, ये हरी मिर्च और अदरक।

ग्राहक : कुल कितने हुए?

सब्ज़ी वाला   : इन सबके मिला के पचास रुपये दे दो।
ग्राहक   : सौ के खुल्ले है?
सब्ज़ी वाला   : हाँ बहन जी, ये लो आपके बाक़ी के पचास रुपये।

Practice 4 Post-Listening Exercise

1. Write the words that have been used in the conversation to address someone and translate them.

    a. _____

    b. _____

2. Give the names of the vegetables that the vendor has.

    a. _____   c. _____   e. _____

    b. _____   d. _____   f. _____

3. Write down the sentence where the customer expressed surprise, and then translate it into English.

    _____

    _____

4. Give the verbs that were used in the familiar imperative and neutral imperative forms.

    Familiar
    a. _____   b. _____   c. _____   d. _____

    Neutral
    a. _____   b. _____   c. _____   d. _____

5. What sentence provides the closest translation to "How much is the total?" Give the sentence in Hindi.

    _____

6. In how many ways did the customer ask for the price? Write them down.

    _____

Practice 5
Listen again and choose the correct word for each blank space.

1. अरे सब्ज़ी वाले ज़रा रुकना _____.   रूकना   रुकना (to stop)

2. _____ बहनजी। बोलो आपको क्या दूँ?   गया   आया (to come)

3. तुम्हारे _____ आज क्या-क्या है?   पासा   पास (to have)

4. आपको क्या _____?   चाहना   चाहिए (to need)

5. फूल गोभी क्या _____?   भाव दी   भाव दिये (what is the price–*fem.*)

6. इतनी _____ !! ठीक दाम बोलो।   सस्ती   महंगी (costly)

7. बीस में _____ तो लूँगी।   लोगे   दोगे (will give)

Practice 6
How would you say the following sentences in Hindi?

1. I need a quarter kilo of carrots. _____

2. How much are the tomatoes? _____

3. What is the total (price) for all of these? _____

4. You are asking for too much. _____

5. So expensive! Say the right price. _____

6. Give me a bunch of cilantro. _____

7. Also add a few green chilies and a piece of ginger. _____

8. Do you have change for five hundred rupees? _____

Romanization

Sub-ze Waa-laa : Go-bhee lo, paa-luck lo, gaa-jer lo, mut-ter lo, bang-un lo, moo-lee lo.

Graa-huk : Err-ay sub-zee Waa-lay zer-aa rük-naa.

Sub-ze Waa-laa : Aa-yaa beh-hen-jee. Bo-lo aap-ko kyaa doȯ?

Graa-huk : tüm-haa-ray paas aaj kyaa-kyaa hai?

Sub-ze Waa-laa : May-ray paas taa-zee putt-taa go-bhee hai, gaa-jer hai, Tum-aa-Ter hai, dh-un-iyaa hai, shim-laa mirch hai. Aap ko kyaa chaa-hi-yay?

Graa-huk : Yeh phool go-bhee kyaa bhaav dee?

Sub-zee Waa-laa : Phool go-bhee beh-hen jee p-uch-chees rüp-uh-yay ki-lo hai.

Graa-huk : It-nee meh-ang-ee!! Theek daam bo-lo. Sub-zee mun-Dee maẏ toe yeh bees rüp-uh-yay kilo hai.

Sub-zee Waa-laa : Bees rüp-uh-yay kilo toe beh-hen jee paȧch din peh-lay kaa bhaav hai. Aaj bazar mein sub-zi-yaȧ buh-hüt meh-an-gee ho guh-yee hain. Bow-low kit-nee doȯ?

Graa-huk : Bees maẏ doe-gay toe loȯ-gee.

Sub-zee Waa-laa : chuh-lo aap-ko baa-ees rüp-uh-yay kilo day doȯ-gaa. Yeh lo.

Graa-huk : Awr Tum-aa-Ter kai-say di-yay? Ayk kilo Tum-aa-Ter bhee day-naa awr daam Theek lug-aa-naa. Saath maẏ her-ay dh-un-i-yay ka guch-Chaa, doe-chaar her-ee mirch awr ayk ud-ruck kaa Tük-rDaa bhee Daal day-naa.

Sub-zee Waa-laa : Yay lo beh-hen jee, ayk kilo Tum-aa-Ter p-uch-chees rüp-uh-yay kay, yay dh-un-iyay kaa güch-Chaa, yey her-ee mirch awr ud-ruck.

Graa-huk : Kül kit-nay hü-ay?

Sub-zee Waa-laa : In sub-kay mil-aa-kay p-uch-aas rüp-yay day doe.

Graa-huk : Sw kay khül-lay hain?

Sub-zee Waa-laa : Haȧ beh-hen jee, yay lo-aap-kay baa-qee kay p-uch-aas rüp-uh-yay.

Translation

Vegetable Vendor : Come and get cauliflower, spinach, carrots, peas, eggplants, and radish.

Customer : Listen *sabzi wale* (vegetable vendor), wait for a while. What do you have today?

Vegetable Vendor : I have fresh cabbage, cauliflower, carrots, tomatoes, cilantro and capsicum (bell pepper). What do you need?

Customer : What is the price for cauliflower?

Vegetable Vendor : Madam, it is 25 rupees per kilo.

Customer : So expensive! Say the right price. In the vegetable market, it is 20 rupees per kilo.

Vegetable Vendor : 20 rupees per kilo is the price five days ago, Madam. Today vegetables have become very expensive. Tell me, how much should I give?

Customer : If you will give me 20 rupees per kilo, then I will buy.

Vegetable Vendor : OK I will give in at 22. Here you go. (Here, take this.)

Customer	:	All right and how much are you selling the tomatoes? Give me one kilo tomatoes and set the right price (don't charge too much). Add a bunch of cilantro, a few green chilies and a piece of ginger.
Vegetable Vendor	:	Madam, here is your one kilo tomatoes for 25 rupees, a bunch of cilantro, green chilies, and ginger.
Customer	:	How much is the total?
Vegetable Vendor	:	50 rupees total for all of these.
Customer	:	Do you have change for 100?
Vegetable Vendor	:	Yes, here is your change.

4.2 At the Grocery Store   किराने की दुकान पर।

Objectives

By the end of this lesson, you will be able to:

1. Pronounce the names of some common spices, dried fruits, and grains, and use adjectives in the perfective participle form such as *whole*, *washed*, and *dried*.
2. Ask if the things that you need are available.
3. Buy small household items using compound verbs with देना.

> 📖 **Culture Note**
>
> In India the concept of a supermarket has been picking up fast and many companies have already established their retail grocery stores everywhere; however smaller cities, towns or villages still have the same traditional grocery shops, where you can find only dry goods.
>
> Milk and dairy products are generally not available in these grocery stores. Some stores do keep cheese, ice cream and milk in tetra packs or plastic packets if they have refrigerators. Otherwise it is Indian tradition to buy fresh milk everyday and use it by the end of the day. Some people buy milk directly from a milkman. Milk, ice cream, yogurt, and cheese are also available at the state-run dairy booths. In India, yogurt is usually made at home or is generally available at a sweet maker's shop.
>
> When you buy milk in India, remember to boil it first before consuming it. By boiling it any bacteria present in the milk will be killed even if it is pasteurized. No one in India drinks milk without first boiling it. If you like cold milk, refrigerate it after boiling it so you won't get sick.

Vocabulary

Nouns

मंजन	(mun-jun)	*masc.*	toothpaste/tooth powder
साबुन की बट्टी	(saa-bün kee buT-Tee)	*fem.*	soap bar
झाड़ू	(jhaa-rDoo)	*fem.*	broom
नमक	(n-um-uk)	*masc.*	salt
चीनी	(chee-nee)	*fem.*	sugar
चाय की पत्ती	(chai kee p-ut-tee)	*fem.*	tea leaves
गेहूँ का आटा	(gain-hū kaa aa-Taa)	*masc.*	wheat flour
मैदा	(mai-daa)	*fem.*	all-purpose flour
दाल	(daal)	*fem.*	pulse, legume
चावल	(chaa-v-ul)	*masc.*	rice
पिसी लाल मिर्च	(pi-see laal mir-ch)	*fem.*	red chili powder
पिसा सूखा धनिया	(pi-saa soo-khaa dh-un-iyaa)	*masc.*	ground coriander
हल्दी	(h-ul-dee)	*fem.*	turmeric
जीरा	(jee-raa)	*masc.*	cumin
काली मिर्च	(kaa-lee mir-ch)	*fem.*	black pepper
इलायची	(il-aay-chee)	*fem.*	cardamom
बादाम	(baa-daam)	*masc.*	almond
पिस्ता	(pis-taa)	*masc.*	pistachio
काजू	(kaa-joo)	*masc.*	cashew
दालचीनी	(daal-chee-nee)	*fem.*	cinnamon
बिस्कुट	(bis-cüT)	*masc.*	biscuit
तेल	(tayl)	*masc.*	oil
किशमिश	(kish-mish)	*fem.*	raisin
जैतून	(jai-toon)	*masc.*	olive
डबलरोटी	(double ro-Tee)	*fem.*	bread
मूँगफली	(moong-ph-ulee)	*fem.*	peanut
छोले	(Cho-lay)	*masc. pl.*	chickpeas
राजमा	(raaj-maa)	*masc.*	kidney beans

Adjectives

पिसा हुआ	(pi-saa hüaa)	*masc.*	ground (powdered)
पिसी हुयी	(pi-see hüee)	*fem.*	ground (powdered)
पिसे हुए	(pi-say hü-ay)	*masc. pl.*	ground (powdered)
छिलके वाली	(Chil-kay waa-lee)	*fem.*	with husk (pulse)
साबुत	(saa-büt)	*unmarked*	whole
धुली हुयी	(dhü-lee hüee)	*fem.*	washed (without husk)
सूखा	(soo-khaa)	*masc.*	dried
सूखी	(soo-khee)	*fem.*	dried
सूखे	(soo-khay)	*masc. pl.*	dried
छिली	(Chi-lee)	*fem.*	peeled

Verbs

देना	(day-naa)	*v.t.*	to give
बोलना	(bowl-naa)	*v.t.*	to speak
बनाना	(bun-aa-naa)	*v.t.*	to make
आना	(aa-naa)	*v.i.*	to come
होना	(ho-naa)	*v.i.*	to be
बनना	(bun-naa)	*v.i.*	to become
दे देना	(day-day-naa)	*comp. v.t.*	to give (away)
डाल देना	(Daal day-naa)	*comp. v.t.*	to put/to pour
निकाल देना	(nik-aal day-naa)	*comp. v.t.*	to take out (from inside of X)
बना देना	(bun-aa day-naa)	*comp. v.t.*	to make
ख़त्म हो जाना	(khuh-tum ho jaa-naa)	*comp. v.i.*	to end/to finish

Grammar

Perfective Participle (Adjective)

The perfective participle is a form of verb that is used to specify a past or present action; it can be used as an adjective as well as an adverb in Hindi. Here the focus is only upon the perfective and adjectival aspects of the participle. The adjectival perfective participle represents a completed action that resulted in a state of being. Similar to this in English are the verbs that have the suffixes *-ed* and *-en* in words such as "cook<u>ed</u>," "ripen<u>ed</u>," "brok<u>en</u>," "dri<u>ed</u>," and "powder<u>ed</u>."

To simplify the concept, use a verb in the perfective form and add a noun to it; the verb that precedes the noun acts as an adjective. In fact all verbs in the simple perfect form are adjectives, modified by the gender of the noun and number that it precedes. The addition to this form is the perfective form होना ho-naa, which also agrees in gender and number.

Examples:

Infinitive form of verb	Verb root	Perfective suffixes या, यी/ई, and ये/ए or ा, ी, and े	Full form simple perfect, also an adjective	Verb in perfect tense with participle हुआ, हुये, and हुई (adjective)
खाना to eat	खा	या, यी, ये	खाया, खायी, खाये	खाया हुआ, खायी हुयी, खाये हुये (eaten)
सूखना to dry	सूख	ा, ी, े	सूखा, सूखी, सूखे	सूखा हुआ, सूखी हुयी, सूखे हुये (dried)
सड़ना to rot	सड़	ा, ी, े	सड़ा, सड़ी, सड़े	सड़ा हुआ, सड़ी हुयी, सड़े हुये (rotten)

Infinitive form of verb	Verb root	Perfective suffixes या, यी/ई, and ये/ए or ा, ी, and े	Full form simple perfect, also an adjective	Verb in perfect tense with participle हुआ, हुये, and हुई (adjective)
गलना to soften	गल	ा, ी, े	गला, गली, गले	गला हुआ, गली हुयी, गले हुये (over-ripe, soft)

NOTE The suffixes या yaa, यी/ई yee/ee, and ये/ए yaa/ay are added to most transitive verb roots and some of the intransitive verb roots in perfect tense, such as आना, जाना, सोना, लाना, and सीना. The dependent vowels ा, ी, and े are added mostly to the intransitive verb roots. To identify the transitive and the intransitive verb, look for a dependent "ा" vowel attached to the root of a transitive verb, such as बनाना, दिखाना, and पकाना. Intransitive verb roots do not have any dependent vowel with them (बनना, पकना, and दिखना) except for those mentioned above.

Practice 1

Conjugate the verbs in the first column in the table below. Follow the examples as shown above.

Infinitive form of the verb	Verb root	Perfective suffixes या, यी, and ये or ा, ी, and े	Full form simple perfect, also an adjective	Perfective participle (adjective) with हुआ, हुये, and हुई
धुलना				
छिलना				
पिसना				

Practice 2 Vocabulary-Building Exercise
Label the pictures below in Hindi.

1. broom

2. soap

3. toothpaste/ toothpowder

4. oil

_____   _____   _____   _____

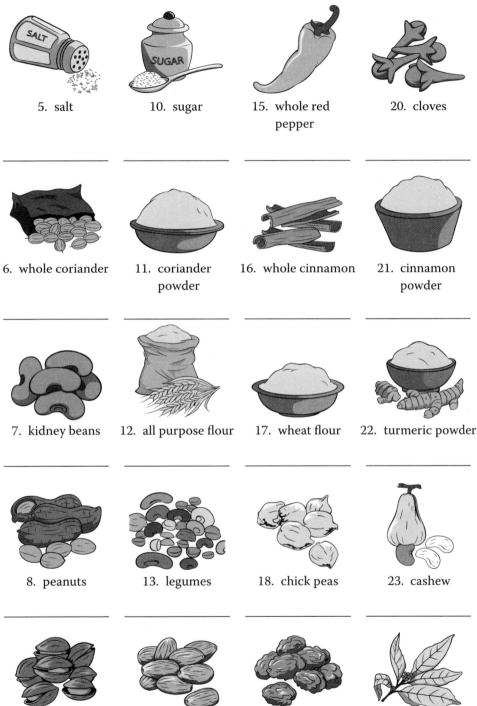

5. salt

10. sugar

15. whole red pepper

20. cloves

6. whole coriander

11. coriander powder

16. whole cinnamon

21. cinnamon powder

7. kidney beans

12. all purpose flour

17. wheat flour

22. turmeric powder

8. peanuts

13. legumes

18. chick peas

23. cashew

9. pistachio

14. almond

19. raisin

24. bay leaf

Practice 3

Match the English words on the right with the Hindi equivalents on the left.

<u>Group 1</u>
1. नमक   turmeric
2. चीनी   wheat flour
3. आटा   all-purpose flour
4. मैदा   sugar
5. हल्दी   salt

<u>Group 5</u>
1. मूँगफली   almond
2. इलायची   pistachio
3. बादाम   cashew
4. पिस्ता   raisin
5. काजू   peanut
6. किशमिश   cardamom

<u>Group 2</u>
1. मंजन   soap
2. झाड़ू   toothpaste
3. साबुन   broom

<u>Group 6</u>
1. तेल   peanut oil
2. जैतून का तेल   oil
3. मूँगफली का तेल   olive oil

<u>Group 3</u>
1. दाल   chickpeas
2. चावल   pulse
3. छोले   kidney beans
4. राजमा   rice

<u>Group 7</u>
1. डबलरोटी   butter
2. मक्खन   biscuit
3. बिस्कुट   bread

<u>Group 4</u>
1. जीरा   cinnamon
2. काली मिर्च   cumin
3. दालचीनी   black pepper

Practice 4

Listen to this conversation between a customer and a grocer, and provide the vocabulary from the conversation for each category below.

Script 1

दुकानदार : आइये बहन जी क्या दूँ आज आपको?

ग्राहक : भइया मुझे राशन लेना है, ज़रा यह-यह सामान निकाल दो।

दुकानदार : हाँ जी बोलिए।

ग्राहक : एक किलो चीनी, आधा किलो चाय की पत्ती, नमक का एक डिब्बा, पिसी लाल मिर्च, हल्दी का ढाई सौ ग्राम का पैकेट,और डेढ़ किलो राजमा।

दुकानदार : हाँ जी और कुछ?

ग्राहक : हाँ और छिली मूँगफली का क्या दाम है?

दुकानदार : छिली मूंगफली का दाम एक सौ अस्सी रुपये किलो है।

ग्राहक : अच्छा आधा किलो मूंगफली निकाल दो। एक तेल का डिब्बा भी दे दो बड़ा वाला।

Nouns

1. _____ 4. _____ 7. _____ 10. _____ 13. _____

2. _____ 5. _____ 8. _____ 11. _____ 14. _____

3. _____ 6. _____ 9. _____ 12. _____

Adjectives

1. _____ 3. _____ 5. _____ 7. _____ 9. _____

2. _____ 4. _____ 6. _____ 8. _____

Verbs

1. _____ 2. _____ 3. _____ 4. _____ 5. _____ 6. _____

Measurements/Weights

1. _____ 3. _____ 5. _____ 7. _____

2. _____ 4. _____ 6. _____

Practice 5 Comprehension

Listen again and this time answer the following questions.

1. What verbs were used in the dialogue? Write them down.

   _____ _____ _____ _____ _____

2. How did the customer and the shopkeeper address each other?

   Shopkeeper: _____

   Customer: _____

Romanization 1

Dü-kaan-daar : Aa-iyay beh-hen jee, kyaa doȯ aaj aap-ko?

Graah-uk : Bhai-yaa mü-Jhay raa-sh-un lay-naa hai, zer-aa yeh-yeh saa-maan nik-aal-doe.

dü-kaan-daar : Haȧ jee bo-li-yay.

Graah-uk	:	Ayk kilo chee-nee, aa-dhaa kilo chai kee p-ut-tee, num-uk kaa ayk Dib-baa, pisi laal mirch, Hul-dee kaa Dhaa-ee saw graam kaa packet aw-r Day-rDh kilo raaj-maa.
dü-kaan-daar	:	Haȧ jee kuCh aw-r?
Graah-uk	:	Haȧ Chi-lee moong-ph-ul-ee kaa kyaa daam hai?
dü-kaan-daar	:	Chi-lee moong-ph-ul-ee kaa daam ayk saw us-see rüp-yay kilo hai.
Graah-uk	:	Uch-Chaa ayk kilo moong-ph-ul-ee nik-aal doe. Ayk tay-l kaa Dib-baa bhee day doe ber-Daa vaa-laa.

Translation

Shopkeeper	:	Please come Madam, what would you like to have today?
Customer	:	Brother, I need to take groceries, please take these things out for me.
Shopkeeper	:	Yes, please tell me what you need.
Customer	:	One kilo sugar, half kilo tea leaves, a box of salt, ground red chili powder, a 250 gram packet of turmeric and one and half a kilo kidney beans.
Shopkeeper	:	OK. And anything else?
Customer	:	Oh yes, how much is cleaned/peeled peanuts?
Shopkeeper	:	The peeled peanuts are hundred and eighty rupees per kilo.
Customer	:	All right then, get me half a kilo peanuts and one big tin of oil as well.

Practice 6 [04-06]

Listen to Part 2 of the conversation. Then answer the questions that follow.

Script 2

ग्राहक	:	आपके पास ताज़ी डबलरोटी है?
दुकानदार	:	जी है, आज सुबह ही आयी है । कितनी दे दूँ?
ग्राहक	:	बस एक डबलरोटी, बड़ी वाली देना, साथ ही अमूल मक्खन का एक पैकेट भी दे देना । आपके पास जैतून का तेल है?
दुकानदार	:	जैतून का तेल तो नहीं, वैजीटेबिल तेल है?
ग्राहक	:	हाँ चलो ठीक है । मुझे एक झाड़ू, नहाने के साबुन की दो बट्टियाँ और निरमा वाशिंग पाउडर का एक छोटा पैकेट और कॉलगेट का मंजन भी देना ।
दुकानदार	:	पेस्ट दूँ या पाउडर?
ग्राहक	:	पेस्ट देना । अच्छा … और पाव-पाव भर के पैकेट किशमिश, काजू, बादाम और पिस्ते के भी डाल देना ।
दुकानदार	:	बादाम तो अभी नहीं हैं, ख़त्म हो गये हैं । कोई कोल्ड ड्रिंक नहीं लेंगी आज?
ग्राहक	:	अच्छा एक कोक की बोतल दे दो, बड़ी ।
दुकानदार	:	यह लीजिए । साबुत मसाले नहीं चाहिए आज?
ग्राहक	:	नहीं साबुत मसाले अभी नहीं चाहिएँ । यह बोतल कितने की है?
दुकानदार	:	ये पचपन की है ।
ग्राहक	:	अच्छा अब मेरा बिल बना दो । कितने का बना?
दुकानदार	:	यह रहा आपका बिल, कुल मिलाकर डेढ़ हज़ार रुपये हुए ।

Romanization 2

Graa-h-uk	:	Aap-kay paas taa-zee double ro-Tee hai?
dü-kaan-daar	:	Jee hai, aaj süb-uh hee aa-ee hai. Kit-nee day doȯ.
Graa-h-uk	:	Bus ayk double ro-Tee, berD-ee waa-lee day-naa, saath hee Um-ool mukh-khun bhee day day-naa. Aap-kay paas jai-toon kaa tail hai?
dü-kaan-daar	:	Jai-toon kaa tail toe nuh-heȧ hai, vegetable tail hai.
Graa-h-uk	:	Haȧ ch-ulo Theek hai. Mü-Jhay ayk jhaa-rDoo, nuh-haa-nay ki doe saa-bün ki buT-yaȧ aur nir-maa washing powder kaa ayk Cho-Taa packet bh-ee Daal day-naa. Aur colgate kaa mun-jun bh-ee day day-naa.
dü-kaan-daar	:	Paste doȯ yaa powder?
Graa-h-uk	:	Paste day-naa. Uch-Chaa … aur paav paav bh-er kay packet kish-mish, kaa-joo, baa-daam aur pis-tay kay bh-ee Daal day-naa.
dü-kaan-daar	:	Baa-daam toe ubh-ee nuh-heȧ hain, kh-utm ho guh-yay hain. Ko-ee cold drink nuh-heȧ layn-gee aaj?
Graa-h-uk	:	Uch-Chaa ayk coke kee bo-t-ul day doe, berD-ee.
dü-kaan-daar	:	Yeh lee-ji-yay. Saa-büt mus-aa-lay nuh-heȧ chaa-hi-yay aaj?
Graa-h-uk	:	Nuh-heȧ saa-büt mus-aa-lay ubh-ee nuh-heȧ chaa-hi-yaẏ. Yeh bo-t-ul kit-nay kee hai?
dü-kaan-daar	:	Yay p-uch-pun kee hai.
Graa-h-uk	:	Uch-Chaa may-raa bill bun-aa doe. Kit-nay kaa bun-aa?
dü-kaan-daar	:	Yeh ruh-haa aap-kaa bill, kül mil-aa-ker Day-rDh huz-aar rüp-yay hü-ay.

Translation 2

Customer	:	Do you have fresh bread?
Shopkeeper	:	Yes sir, it has just come this morning. How much should I give you?
Customer	:	Just one loaf of bread, give me the big one, and also a packet of Amul butter. Do you have olive oil?
Shopkeeper	:	No, I don't have olive oil, but I do have vegetable oil.
Customer	:	Ok then. Also give me a broom, two soap bars for bathing, a small packet of Nirma washing powder and a Colgate.
Shopkeeper	:	Do you want paste or powder?
Customer	:	Give me the paste. And . . . a quarter kilo packet each of raisins, cashews, almonds and pistachios.
Shopkeeper	:	We don't have almonds right now. We are out of it. Are you not going to buy any cold drinks today?
Customer	:	All right then, give me a big bottle of Coke.
Shopkeeper	:	Here you go. Are you not going to buy whole spices today?
Customer	:	No, I don't need whole spices right now. How much is the bottle?
Shopkeeper	:	This is 55 rupees.
Customer	:	Ok, prepare my bill now. How much is it?
Shopkeeper	:	Here is your bill; your total is 1,500 rupees.

*Refer to page 171 for the grammar details on the sentence structure using सकना "can/could have/cannot/will be able to."

Practice 7 Comprehension Check

1. Write the sentences in Hindi that show the unavailability of a product.

    _____

    _____

2. Write the phrases that directly translate to "should I give," and "may I give."

    _____

3. Write the sentences in which the customer asked for the bill.

    _____

    _____

Practice 8

Fill in the blanks below the Hindi words for the English words in parentheses:

आपके पास ताज़ी _____ है?
                    1. (bread)

एक अमूल _____ का एक पैकेट भी दे देना ।
              2. (butter)

मुझे एक _____, नहाने के _____ की दो _____ और कॉलगेट का _____ भी देना
         3. (broom)   4. (soap)   5. (bars)   6. (toothpaste/tooth powder)

पाव-_____ के पैकेट _____, काजू, _____ और पिस्ते के भी _____
      7. (quarter of a kilo)   8. (raisins)   9. (almonds)   10. (to put, *comp. v.t*)

बादाम तो अभी नहीं हैं, _____ ।
                        11. (have finished)

_____ मसाले नहीं _____ आज?
12. (whole)   13. (need)

मेरा बिल _____ ।
        14. (to make, *comp. v.t.*)

4.3 Shopping for Clothes कपड़ों की खरीददारी करना ।

Objectives

By the end of this lesson, you will be able to:

1. Use the following vocabulary in context: *sari, salwar kurta, chunni, chudidar pajama*, as well as some verbs, colors, and adjectives.
2. Ask questions about clothing size, color, style, texture, and price.
3. Practice refusing and agreeing to purchase an item after bargaining with the storeowner or with a salesperson.

> ### 📖 Culture Note
>
> India is a shopping paradise. Having the most dynamic retail industry in the world, it exports approximately $89B worth of ready-made clothes globally. India is a big producer of a variety of raw silk, cotton clothes, and ready-made garments. Tourists who visit India want to buy silk *saris*, silk and cotton skirts, shirts, scarfs, *salwar*, *kurta* and other native garments. Due to India's diverse culture, each state has its own specialty.
>
> If you are visiting Rajasthan, you may want to buy tie-dye clothes known as Bandhej or Bandhni, silk and cotton *lehngas* (traditional long skirts), and handmade shoes called *mojari*.
>
> Gujrat is famous for its mirror work and tie-dye garments, while Luknow is famous for a special type of embroidery called *chikankari*, a type of embroidery on muslin, silk, chiffon organza, and net cloth. It is one of Lucknow's most well-known textile decoration styles. If you want to buy silk *saris*, go for Banarasi *saris* from Banaras (Varanasi).
>
> Chanderi *saris* from the Chanderi town of Madhya Pradesh are made of handwoven and very lightweight silk, considered to be the choice of royalty because of its intricate designs. If you are traveling toward the south, Banglori *saris* from Banglore, Chennai *saris* from Chennai, and many other varieties are available in the entire south India region.

Vocabulary

Nouns

सलवार	(suh-ul-waar)	*fem.*	baggy Indian pants for men and women
कुर्ता	(kür-taa)	*masc.*	tunic
चुन्नी	(chün-nee)	*fem.*	long scarf
चूड़ीदार पजामा	(choo-rDee-daar)	*fem.*	wrinkled ankle tight pajama

Adjectives

सूती	(soo-tee)	*unmarked masc./fem.*	cotton
रेशमी	(ray-sh-me)	*unmarked masc./fem.*	silken
सादा	(saa-daa)	*masc.*	plain
हल्का	(huh-ul-kaa)	*masc.*	light
लाल	(laal)	*unmarked masc./fem.*	red
हरा	(her-aa)	*masc.*	green
नीला	(nee-laa)	*masc.*	blue
पीला	(pee-laa)	*masc.*	yellow
सफ़ेद	(suh-uf-aid)	*unmarked masc./fem.*	white
लख़नवी काम का	(Lukh-nuv-ee kaam kaa)	*masc.*	with Lukhnawi work

Verbs

पसंद करना	(pus-und ker-naa)	*conj. v.t.*	to like
अच्छा लगना	(uch-Chaa lug-naa)	*conj. v.i.*	to like
दिखाना	(dikh-aa-naa)	*v.t.*	to show

Grammar

Polite and Extra-Polite Imperatives

As mentioned earlier, at bigger stores such as showrooms, clothing stores, bookstores, most people in India use polite and extra-polite imperatives. Occasionally they will use neutral and informal imperatives as well, but that all depends on personal choice and regional usage. Remember that the polite imperative is not a command, rather it is used to request someone, mainly with a person older in age, higher in status, or with an unfamiliar person. To form a polite imperative, Hindi uses इए **iyè**, polite and for extra-polite imperatives, it uses इएगा **iyegā** as a suffix to the root of a verb. Note that there are five irregular verbs in Hindi, which has a somewhat different way of forming a polite imperative; those verbs are करना ker-naa, देना day-naa, लेना lay-naa, पीना pee-naa and सीना see-naa.

NOTE Colloquially, the polite form of कर ker is used as करिए/करिये kee-i-ay/ kee-i-yay as well.

Here are some examples:

Verb	Root	Polite	Extra Polite
करना (ker-naa)	कर (ker)	कीजिए/ कीजिये (kee-ji-ay/ kee-ji-yay)	कीजिएगा/ कीजियेगा (kee-ji-ay-gaa/ kee-ji-yay-gaa)

Verb	Root	Polite	Extra Polite
लेना (lay-naa)	ले (lay)	लीजिए/ लीजिये (lee-ji-ay/ lee-ji-yay)	लीजिएगा/लीजियेगा (lee-ji-ay-gaa/ lee-ji-yay-gaa)
देना (day-naa)	दे (day)	दीजिए/ दीजिये (dee-ji-ay/ dee-ji-yay)	दीजिएगा/ दीजियेगा (dee-ji-ay-gaa/ dee-ji-yay-gaa)
आना (aa-naa)	आ (aa)	आइए/ आइये (aa-i-ay/aa-i-yay)	आइएगा/ आइयेगा (aa-i-ay-gaa/ aa-i-yay-gaa)
दिखाना (di-kh-aa-naa)	दिखा (di-kh-aa)	दिखाइए/दिखाइये (di-kh-aa-yay/ di-kh-aa-i-yay)	दिखाइएगा/दिखाइयेगा (di-kh-aa-i-ay-gaa/ di-kh-aa-i-yay-gaa)

Subjunctives in first person: "। मैं" for asking questions such as: *Can I,* *may I, Should I*

Verb	Root	Subjunctive suffix	Subject-verb agreement
दिखाना (di-khaa-naa)	दिखा (di-khaa)	ऊँ (oon)	दिखाऊँ? (di-khaa-oon?)
बनाना (bun-aa-naa)	बना (bun-aa)	ऊँ (oon)	बनाऊँ? (bun-aa-oon?)
बना देना (*comp. v.*) (bun-aa day-naa)	बना दे (ay)	ूँ + ँ (oon)	बना दूँ? (bun-aa-doò?)
लेना (lay-naa)	ले (lay)	ूँ + ँ (oon)	लूँ (loon?)

Practice 1

In the following sentences, change the neutral into polite imperatives, and the polite imperatives into extra-polite imperatives.

Examples: यह दुकान अभी बंद है, आप कल आना । (neutral imperative)
यह दुकान अभी बंद है, आप कल आइये । (polite imperative)
यह दुकान अभी बंद है, आप कल आइयेगा । (extra-polite imperative)

1. मुझे सूती सलवार-कुर्ता दिखाना!

Polite: _____

Extra-polite: _____

2.   एक पगड़ी भी निकाल देना!

Polite: _____

Extra-polite: _____

3.   डिज़ाइन वाला नहीं सादा निकालना!

Polite: _____

Extra-polite: _____

4.   आप कुर्ता ट्राई कर लेना!

Polite: _____

Extra-polite: _____

Practice 2
Translate the English sentences using the subjunctive form of verbs in Hindi.

1.   What can I show you today?

_____

2.   Would you like it in cotton or in silk? (Can I show you in cotton or silk?)

_____

3.   Sir, would you like to see the tunic and pants in your size? (Can I show you the tunic and pants in your size?)

_____

Practice 3
Below is a conversation between a female shopper and the shop owner or salesperson. Fill in the blanks with the appropriate polite and extra-polite imperative form of the verb given in parenthesis.

दुकानदार :   आइये मैडम, आइये सर क्या दिखाऊँ?

औरत   :   मुझे सलवार-कुर्ते चाहिएँ?

दुकानदार : किस साइज़ के?

औरत   : मेरे साइज़ के, मीडियम।

दुकानदार : सूती में _____ ("to take," extra-polite imperative) या रेश्मी में?
                        (1)

औरत   : सूती में भी _____ ("to show," polite imperative) और रेश्मी में भी।
                        (2)

दुकानदार : यह _____ ("to see," polite imperative), हमारे पास बहुत से डिज़ाइन में मिलेंगे।
                (3)

         आप कैसा पसंद करेंगीं?

औरत   : सूती में मुझे सादे और हल्के रंग में _____ । ("to show," extra-polite imperative)
                                        (4)

दुकानदार : यह _____ ("to see," polite imperative)
                (5)

औरत   : यह नीले-पीले कॉम्बीनेशन वाला _____ ("to show," polite imperative)
                                        (6)

दुकानदार : यह _____ ("to see," polite imperative) मैडम। ये दोनों ही रंग आप पर अच्छे
                (7)

         लगेंगे।

औरत   : कितने का है यह?

दुकानदार : यह पन्द्रह सौ रुपये का है। ये दे दूँ ? _____ _____ ("to take out," polite
                                            (8)

         imperative)। अच्छा... और आदमियों के लिए एक लखनवी काम का चिकन का कुर्ता और

         चूढ़ीदार पजामा भी _____ ("to show," polite imperative)
                        (9)

At a Garment Store 1 परिधान की दुकान पर

Practice 4 🎧 04-08

Listen to the conversation and fill in the missing words.

दुकानदार : आइये मैडम, आइये सर क्या _____?
                                (1)

औरत   : मुझे _____ _____ चाहिएँ।
                (2)   (3)

दुकानदार : किस साइज़ के?

औरत : मेरे साइज़ के, मीडियम ।

दुकानदार : _____ में लीजिएगा या _____ में?
(4)   (5)

औरत : सूती में भी _____ और रेशमी भी ।
(6)

दुकानदार : यह देखिए, हमारे पास बहुत से डिज़ाइन में _____ । आप कैसा _____
(7)   (8)

करेंगीं?

औरत : सूती में मुझे _____ और _____ _____ में दिखाइयेगा ।
(9)   (10)   (11)

दुकानदार : यह देखिए, ये एक डिज़ाइन है _____ _____ इसमें और भी रंग हैं । यह दूसरा
(12)   (13)

है _____ और _____ कॉम्बीनेशन में । इसके साथ जॉर्जेट की एक ढाई
(14)   (15)

मीटर की _____ भी है ।
(16)

औरत : यह नीले-पीले कॉम्बीनेशन वाला दिखाइये ।

दुकानदार : यह देखिए मैडम । ये दोनों ही रंग आप पर अच्छे लगेंगे ।

औरत : _____ _____ है यह?
(17)   (18)

दुकानदार : यह _____ _____ _____ का है । ये _____ _____?
(19)   (20)   (21)   (22)   (23)

औरत : हाँ, यह नीला वाला _____ _____ ।
(24)   (25)

Script 1
दुकानदार : आइये मैडम, आइये सर क्या दिखाऊँ?
औरत : मुझे सलवार-कुर्ते चाहिएँ ।
दुकानदार : किस साइज़ के?
औरत : मेरे साइज़ के, मीडियम ।
दुकानदार : सूती में लीजिएगा या रेशमी में?
औरत : सूती में भी दिखाइये और रेशमी भी ।
दुकानदार : यह देखिए, हमारे पास बहुत से डिज़ाइन में मिलेंगे । आप कैसा पसंद करेंगीं?
औरत : सूती में मुझे सादे और हल्के रंग में दिखाइयेगा ।
दुकानदार : यह देखिए, ये एक डिज़ाइन है फूलों वाला इसमें और भी रंग हैं । यह दूसरा है नीले और पीले कॉम्बीनेशन
में । इसके साथ जॉर्जेट की एक ढाई मीटर की चुन्नी भी है ।
औरत : यह नीले-पीले कॉम्बीनेशन वाला दिखाइये ।
दुकानदार : यह देखिए मैडम । ये दोनों ही रंग आप पर अच्छे लगेंगे ।
औरत : कितने का है यह?

दुकानदार : यह पन्द्रह सौ रुपये का है। ये दे दूँ ?
औरत   : हाँ, यह नीला वाला निकाल दीजिए।

Romanization 1

dü-kaan-daar	:	Aa-iyay Madam, aa-iyay sir kyaa dikh-aa-oȯ?
Au-rut	:	Mü-jhay sul-waar-kür-tay chaa-hi-yaẏ.
dü-kaan-daar	:	Kis size kay?
Au-rut	:	May ray size kay, medium.
dü-kaan-daar	:	Soo-tee may lee-ji-yay-gaa yaa ray-sh-mee maẏ?
Au-rut	:	Soo-tee maẏ bhee dikh-aa-iyay aur ray-sh-mee bhee.
dü-kaan-daar	:	Yeh day-khi-yay hum-aa-ray paas buh-hüt say design maẏ mil-aẏ-gay. Aap kai-saa pus-und ker-ayn-gee?
Au-rut	:	Soo-tee maẏ müjh-ay saa-day aur hul-kay rung maẏ dikh-aa-iyay-gaa.
dü-kaan-daar	:	Yeh day-khi-yay, yay ayk design hai phoo-lȯ waa-laa; is-maẏ aur bhee rung hain. Yeh doos-raa hai Nee-lay pee-lay combination maẏ. Is-kay saath georgette kee ayk dhaa-ee meter kee chu-nee bhee hai.
Au-rut	:	Yeh nee-lay pee-lay combination waa-laa di-khaa-iyay.
dü-kaan-daar	:	Yeh day-khi-yay Madam, yay doe-no hee rung aap per uch-Chay lug-aẏ-gay.
Au-rut	:	Kit-nay kaa hai yeh?
dü-kaan-daar	:	Yeh pun-dr-uh saw rüp-uh-yay kaa hai, day doȯ?
Au-rut	:	Haȧ, yeh nee-laa waa-laa nik-aal dee-ji-yay.

Translation 1

Shopkeeper	:	Ma'm, please come into our shop. What can I show you today?
Woman	:	I want a *salwar-kurta*.
Shopkeeper	:	In what size?
Woman	:	My size, medium.
Shopkeeper	:	Would you like it in cotton or in silk?
Woman	:	Show me the cotton as well as the silk.
Shopkeeper	:	Here, look at this, you can get many designs in this. What kind do you prefer?
Woman	:	In cotton, please. Show me simple designs and in light colors.
Shopkeeper	:	Here, look at these. This is one design with flowers in it; I have more colors in it. Here is the other one in a blue and yellow combination. It will come with a two-and-a-half meter georgette scarf.
Woman	:	Can you please show me this in the blue and yellow combination?
Shopkeeper	:	Here ma'm. Both colors will suit you.
Woman	:	How much is it?
Shopkeeper	:	This will cost 1,500 rupees. Would you like me to pack this one?
Woman	:	Yes, set this blue one aside/take this blue one out.

Practice 5

In this conversation (Part 2), you will listen to a dialogue between a male customer and a shop owner. Listen and compare the two conversations. Find out similarities in the grammar structure and vocabularies.

At a Garment Store 2 रेडीमेड कपड़ों की दुकान पर

दुकानदार : सर आपके साइज़ का कुर्ता-पजामा दिखाऊँ?
आदमी   : हाँ मेरे साइज़ का रेशमी दिखाइयेगा, पार्टी लायक। सूती नहीं चाहिए।
दुकानदार : यह लीजिए, यह है काला वाला आर्टीफ़ीशियल सिल्क में है, यह मरून वाला रॉ सिल्क में है और यह क्रीम वाला प्योर सिल्क में है। इनके साथ कॉन्ट्रास्ट में रेशमी चुन्नी भी आएगी।
आदमी   : क्या मैं यह ट्राई कर लूँ?
दुकानदार : हाँ मेरे साथ आइये। यह ट्रायल रूम है, यहाँ आप ट्राई कर लीजिए।
आदमी   : यह रॉ सिल्क वाला मरून और क्रीम वाला निकाल दीजिए। इसके साथ क्रीम रंग की चुन्नी भी।
दुकानदार : अच्छा कुछ और भी दिखाऊँ, हमारे पास बनी-बनायी पगड़ी भी है।
आदमी   : नहीं, आज बस यही। बिल बना दीजिए, कुल कितना हुआ?
दुकानदार : दोनों का कुल साढ़े चार हज़ार बना। पन्द्रह सौ का मैडम का, और तीन हज़ार के आपके पजामे कुर्ते।
आदमी   : भई ठीक दाम लगाओ। यह तो बहुत ज़्यादा है।
दुकानदार : नहीं सर, हमारी दुकान पर चीज़ों का दाम फ़िक्सड है।
आदमी   : अच्छा यह लीजिए साढ़े चार हज़ार रुपये।
दुकानदार : बहुत-बहुत धन्यवाद सर, फिर हमारी दुकान पर आइयेगा। नमस्ते।

Romanization 2

dü-kaan-daar : Sir aap-kay size kaa kür-taa-puj-aa-maa dikh-aa-oȯ?

Aad-mee   : Haȧ may-ray size kaa ray-sh-mee dikh-aa-iyay-gaa, party laa-yuk. Soo-tee nuh-heȧ chaa-hi-yay.

dü-kaan-daar : Yeh lee-ji-yay, yeh hai kaa-laa waa-laa artificial silk maẏ hai, yeh mar-oon waa-laa raw silk maẏ hain. In-kay saath contrast maẏ ray-sh-mee chü-nee bhee aa-yay-gee.

Aad-mee   : Kyaa main yeh try ker loȯ?

dü-kaan-daar : Haȧ may-ray saath aa-ee-yay. Yeh trial room hai, yuh-haȧ aap try ker li-ji-yay.

Aad-mee   : Yeh raw silk waa-laa maroon cream waa-laa nik-aal di-ji-yay. Is-kay saath cream kee chün-nee bhee.

dü-kaan-daar : Uch-Chaa küch aur bhee dikh-aa-oȯ, hum-aa-ray paas bunee-bun-aa-ee pug-rDee bhee hai.

Aad-mee   : Nuh-heȧ, aaj bus yuh-hee. Bill bun-aa dee-ji-yay, kül kit-naa huaa?

dü-kaan-daar : doe-no kaa kül saa-rDhay chaar huz-aar bun-aa. Pun-druh saw kaa madam kaa, aur teen huzaar kay aap-kay puj-aa-may kür-tay.

Aad-mee   : Bhaa-ee Theek daam lug-aa-o. Yeh toe buh-hüt zyaa-daa hai.

dü-kaan-daar : Nuh-heȧ sir hum-aa-ree dü-kaan per chee-zȯ kaa daam fixed hai.

Aad-mee   : Uch-Chaa yeh lee-ji-yay saa-rDhay chaar huz-aar rüp-uh-yay.

dü-kaan-daar : Buh-hüt buh-hüt dhun-yaa-vaad sir, phir hum-aa-ree dü-kaan per aa-iyay-gaa. num-us-tay.

Translation 2

Shopkeeper : Sir, would you like to see the tunic and pants in your size?

Man : Yes, please show it to me in my size, party wear in silk. I don't want cotton.

Shopkeeper : Here you go, this black one is in artificial silk; this maroon one is in raw silk, and this cream one is in pure silk. There will be a contrasting silk scarf along with it.

Man : Can I try this?

Shopkeeper : Yes sir, please come with me. This is the fitting room. You can try them here.

Man : Please set the maroon one in raw silk aside. And also this cream scarf as well.

Shopkeeper : OK, would you like to see anything else? We also have ready-made turbans.

Man : No, that's all for today. Please prepare my bill, how much is it?

Shopkeeper : It is 4,500 rupees for both of them. 1,500 is for Madam's clothes and 3,000 for your tunic and pants.

Man : Brother, say the right price, this is too much.

Shopkeeper : No sir, we have fixed price for things in our shop.

Man : Ok then, please take these 4,500 rupees.

Shopkeeper : Thank you very much sir, please visit us again. Goodbye.

Practice 6

Listen to the second part of the conversation and fill in the grid with the appropriate Hindi words and cognates* from the conversation.

Nouns	Cognates	Adjectives	Adverbs	Verbs

---

* Cognates are the loan words that have their origin in languages other than your own, and are used as they are in your language. Examples: *guru, pundit,* pajama (of Hindi origin, used in English or other languages); *kitab, kamal, Shukriya* (Arabic words used in Hindi); school, station, car (English origin, used in other languages).

Practice 7 Comprehension Check

Now listen to the second part of the conversation again, and this time answer the comprehension questions in Hindi. Follow the pattern of questions in Question 1, and replace the question word with your answer. Keep the remaining part of the sentence as it is.

1. What kind of material does the man want for the *Kurta-Pajama*?
   आदमी को <u>किस कपड़े का</u> कुर्ता-पजामा चाहिए?

   _____

2. Where did the shop owner take the customer?
   दुकानदार, आदमी को <u>कहाँ</u> ले गया?

   _____

3. What is included in the set of *Kurta-Pajama*?
   कुर्ते-पजामे के साथ <u>और क्या</u> आयेगा?

   _____

4. What else is the shop owner trying to sell to the man?
   दुकानदार आदमी को <u>और क्या</u> बेचने की कोशिश कर रहा है?

   _____

5. What is the total amount that the male customer has to pay?
   आदमी को दुकानदार को <u>कितने</u> रुपये देने हैं?

   _____

4.4 At a Sari Emporium साड़ी एम्पोरियम पर

Objectives

By the end of this lesson, you will be able to:

1. Use the following vocabulary in contexts related to clothing: *blouse, skirt, pajama, salwar, churidar, kurta,* and *lehnga.*
2. Ask questions about clothing size, style, and price using के पास (to have), and show your like or dislike using अच्छी/अच्छा लगना (to like).
3. Refuse or agree to buy an item of clothing after discussing the purchase with a salesperson.

📖 **Culture Note**

The *sari* is the traditional and elegant attire of millions of Indian women across the globe. It is a five-and-a-half-meter long cloth made of a variety of materials such as cotton, silk, georgette, chiffon, muslin, nylon, and synthetic fabric. The *sari* comes in various colors and may be embroidered, printed, handprinted, and handwoven. Every state has its own textile and specialty.

These *saris* range from a couple of hundred rupees to thousands of rupees, depending on the cloth and the workmanship. Stores are laden with colorful *saris* that attract everyone, not only Indian women. Many tourists also purchase *saris* and wear them on different occasions.

Vocabulary

Nouns

साड़ी	(sari)	*fem.*	sari
ज़री	(zer-ee)	*fem.*	gold/silver thread
बहन	(beh-hen)	*fem.*	sister
सेवा	(say-waa)	*fem.*	service
मौक़ा	(mau-qaa)	*masc.*	opportunity
राज्य	(raa-jyuh)	*masc.*	state

Adjectives

कुछ	(küch)		some
सब तरह की	(sub ter-eh kee)	*fem.*	of all types
गुलाबी	(gül-aa-bee)		pink
बनारसी	(bun-aar-see)		from Banaras
भागलपुरी	(bha-gul-pü-ree)		from Bhagalpur
सम्बलपुरी	(sumb-ul-pü-ree)		from Sambalpur
बढ़िया	(berDh-i-yaa)		very good
अच्छी	(uch-Chee)	*fem.*	good
एक से एक बढ़िया	(ayk-say ayk berDh-iyaa)		one that is better than the other

Verbs

देखना	(day-kh-naa)	*v.t.*	to see
दिखाना	(di-khaa-naa)	*v.t.*	to show
लेना	(lay-naa)	*v.t.*	to take
कहना	(keh-naa)	*v.t.*	to say, to tell
बोलना	(bowl-naa)	*v.t.*	to speak, to say, to tell
चाहना	(chaah-naa)	*v.t.*	to want, to desire
कर लेना	(ker-lay-naa)	*comp. v.t.*	to do
निकाल देना	(nik-aal day-naa)	*comp. v.t.*	to take out

मौक़ा देना	(mau-qaa day-naa)	*conj. v.t.*	to give opportunity
आना	(aa-naa)	*v.i.*	to come
अच्छा लगना	(uch-Chaa luh-ug-na)	*v.i.*	to like
मिलना	(mil-naa)	*v.i.*	to get, to obtain
चाहिए	(chaa-hi-yay)	auxiliary	need

Grammar

These are explained in more details on 172.

to have	के पास
from X to Y	से लेकर
to like	अच्छी लगना

Practice 1

Read the sentences aloud, and then translate them into English to practice internal compulsion. Remember that this structure is used to show that the subject(s) "has/ have/had to" do something as an internal obligation (not forced).

Reviewing Internal Compulsion

| Subject + को + object | + | verb in infinitive form + auxiliary | है/ हैं / था/ थी / थे |
| मैं | + को = मुझे (to me) | (according to gender or number) | (*present/past*) |

1. मुझे/ मुझको साड़ी खरीदनी है/थी।
   (müJh-ay/müJh-ko sari kher-eed-nee hai/thee.)
       I have/had to buy a *sari.*

2. इसे/ इसको जूते खरीदने हैं/थे।
   (is-say/isko joo-tay kher-eed-nay hain/thay.)
       He/she has/had to buy shoes.

3. उसे/ उसको बाज़ार जाना है/ था।
   (üsay/üs-ko baa-zaar jaa-naa hai/thaa.)
       He/she has/had to go to the market.

4. इन्हें/ इनको सब कुछ खरीदना है/था।
   (in-hain/in-ko sub kuCh kher-eed-naa hai/thaa.)
       He/she has, they have/had to buy everything

5. उन्हें/ उनको बनारसी साड़ी खरीदनी है/थी।
   (ün-hain/ün-ko bun-aar-see sari kher-eed-nee hai/thee.)
       He/she has, they have/had to buy a Banarasi *sari.*

6. आपको क्या लेना है/था?
   (aap-ko kyaa lay-naa hao/thaa?)
       What do you have to take?/What did you have to take?

7. तुम्हें/ तुमको कौनसी साड़ी लेनी है/ थी?
   (tümhain/tüm-ko kawn-see sari lay-nee hai/thee?)
       Which *sari* do you have to buy?/ Which *sari* did you have to buy?

8. औरत को ज़री की साड़ी नहीं खरीदनी ।
   (Aw-rut ko zer-ee kee sari nuh-heen
   kher-eed-nee.)

   The woman doesn't have to buy a Zari *sari*.

9. दुकानदार को साड़ियाँ बेचनी हैं ।
   (dükaan-daar ko saarDi-yaan bay-ch-
   neein hain.)

   The shopkeeper has to sell *saris*.

10. लड़कियों को बढ़िया साड़ियाँ खरीदनी हैं ।
    (lerDki-yon ko berDhiyaa sarDiyaan
    kher-eed-neein hain.)

    Girls have to buy very good *saris*.

Reviewing Subjunctives for Asking Questions: "Should/Can I _____?"

Structure

Subject	+	indirect object	+	direct object	+	verb in
(in direct case)		(to you/for you)		(a noun)		subjunctive form
मैं		आज आपको		क्या		दिखाऊँ?

(main aaj aap-ko kyaa di-khaa-oò?)
What can I show you today?

मैं		आपके लिए		क्या		लाऊँ?

(main aap-kay li-yay kyaa laa-oò?)
What can I get for you?

Practice 2

Translate the following sentences into Hindi based on the structure given above.

1. What can I show you today?

   _____

2. What kind of *sari* should I show you?

   _____

3. What range of *saris* can I get for you?

   _____

4. What can I do for you today?

   _____

सकना suk-naa *can/could have/cannot/will be able to*

Subject (direct) + verb root + सकना (in required gender, number or tense) + present/past tense auxiliary verb

Example: I can come tomorrow.
मैं कल आ सकता/सकती हूँ |
(main kuh-ul aa suk-taa/suk-tee hoȯ)

NOTE To change the above sentence to a negative one, place नहीं right before the root of the main verb आ. Placing the past tense auxiliary verb at the end of a sentence changes the meaning to a "could have" construction; replacing the infinitive of सकना with a future auxiliary गा, गी, गे changes the sentence to a "will be able to" construction.

Examples:
I **can** come tomorrow.
मैं कल आ सकता/सकती हूँ।
(main kuh-ul aa suk-taa/suk-tee hoȯ)

I **cannot** come tomorrow.
मैं कल नहीं आ सकता/सकती हूँ।
(main kuh-ul nuh-heė aa suk-taa/suk-tee hoȯ)

I **could have** come yesterday.
मैं कल आ सकता था/सकती थी ।
(main kuh-ul aa suk-taa thaa/suk-tee thee)

I **will be able** to come tomorrow.
मैं कल आ सकूँगा/सकूँगी ।
(main kuh-ul aa suk-oȯ-gaa/suk-oȯ-gee)

NOTE The structure for "will not be able to" uses the verb पाना (paa-naa) in the same manner as the verb सकना; it is used to show inability.

I **will not be able** to come tomorrow.
मैं कल आ नहीं आ पाऊँगा/पाऊँगी ।
(main kuh-ul aa paa-oȯ-gaa/paa-oȯ-gee)

चाहना chaah-naa *want to/wanted to/would like to* to show desire

Subject (direct) + object + verb infinitive + चाहना (in required gender, number or tense) + present/past tense auxiliary verb

Example: We **want** to sit outside.
हम बाहर बैठना चाहते/चाहतीं हैं।
(Hum baa-her baiTh-naa chaah-tay/chaah-teė hain.)

NOTE To change the above sentence to a negative one, add नहीं right before the main verb बैठना. Placing the past tense auxiliary verb at the end of a sentence changes the meaning to a "wanted to" construction; replacing the infinitive of चाहना with a future auxiliary गा, गी, गे changes it to a "would like to" construction.

Examples:
We **want** to sit outside.
हम बाहर बैठना चाहते हैं/चाहतीं हैं।
(Hum baa-her baiTh-naa chaah-tay hain/chaah-teė hain.)

We **don't want** to sit outside.
हम बाहर नहीं बैठना चाहते हैं/चाहतीं हैं।
(Hum baa-her nuh-heė baiTh-naa chaah-tay hain/chaah-teė hain.)

We **wanted** to sit outside.
हम बाहर बैठना चाहते थे/चाहतीं थीं।
(Hum baa-her baiTh-naa chaah-tay thay/chaah-teė theė.)

We **would like** to sit outside.
हम बाहर बैठना चाहेंगे/चाहेंगी।
(Hum baa-her baiTh-naa chaah-haẏ-gay/chaah-haẏ gee.)

चाहिए chaah-i-yay to indicate need or desire

NOTE Remember when using चाहिए always add "को" after the subject and change the pronouns to their oblique form मुझे/मुझको, आपको, तुम्हें/तुमको, इसे/इसको, उसे/उसको, इन्हें/इनको, उन्हें/उनको.

Subject + को+ object (sing.) + चाहहि (sing.)
He needs a maid.
उसे नौकरानी चाहिए।
(Üsay nauk-raa-nee chaa-hi-yay.)

Subject + को + object (*pl.*) + चाहिएँ (*pl.*)
Meera wants/needs new clothes.
मीरा को नये कपड़े चाहिएँ ।
(Meera ko nuh-yay kup-rDay chaa-hi-yaẏ)

NOTE To change the above sentences to negative sentences, add नहीं right before चाहिए.

"To have" के पास

As an English speaker, you must be accustomed to using " to have" to indicate possession of a thing, an object, or to indicate a relationship with family members. However, in Hindi "to have" is used differently. In the first chapter, you have learned to use "to have" to describe a relationship between two individuals using possessive personal pronouns "मेरा" and "आपकी." It is also used in the same way for one's own body part. However, when it is used to show possession of an inanimate object(s), Hindi uses the compound postposition के पास.

NOTE When you use a proper noun for a subject, place the name + के पास = जॉन के पास. When you use a pronoun for a subject, use the contracted forms मेरे, तुम्हारे, हमारे, इसके, उसके + पास. When you use a singular marked masculine noun, use the singular oblique लड़का + के पास = लड़के के पास. When you use a plural marked masculine noun, use the plural oblique लड़के + के पास = लड़कों के पास.

Language Structure for के पास

Subject +	के पास +	Object +	Negation + (if any)	Auxiliary verb (agree in number)
I	have	one good *sari.*		
मैं +	के पास +	एक अच्छी साड़ी		है I (with personal pron.)
मेरे	पास	एक अच्छी साड़ी		है I
(may-ray paas ayk uch-Chee saa-rDee hai.)				
Sara	has	a lot of shoes.		
सैरा +	के पास +	बहुत से जूते		हैं (With names/proper nouns)
(Sai-raa kay paas buh-hüt say joo-tay hain.)				
The boy	does not have	a bicycle.		
लड़का +	के पास +	साइकिल	नहीं	है I (with marked masc. nouns)
लड़के	के पास	साइकिल	नहीं	है I (changes to sing. oblique
(lerD-kay kay paas cycle nuh-heè hain.)				to के पास)

Practice 3
Translate the following sentences into Hindi using the appropriate form of " to have."

(तुम्हारे पास   आपके पास   हमारे पास   इसके पास **उसके पास**   इनके पास   उनके पास)

1. Do you have silk *saris*? (*informal*)

_____

2. We don't have silk *saris*. (*first person, pl.*)

_____

3. She has many good *saris*. (*third person, sing.*)

_____

4. They have some good *saris*. (*third person, pl.*)

_____

The form से लेकर-तक "from-to" can be used with adverbs of time and place, direction, amount, and the like.

Practice 4
Read the sentence to get acquainted with this form.

from here to there	यहाँ से लेकर वहाँ तक	(with locations)
from north to south	उत्तर से लेकर दक्षिण तक	(with directions)
from Delhi to Mumbai	दिल्ली से लेकर मुंबई तक	(with places)
from two to ten	दो से लेकर दस तक	(with numbers)
from top to bottom	ऊपर से लेकर नीचे तक	(with adverbs)

Lagna लगना (to feel/seem) with adjectives अच्छा/अच्छी (good)

Structure
Subject + को + object + adjective (*masc./fem., pl.*) + लगना + auxiliary verb
(in required tense)

आपको	साड़ियाँ *(fem., pl)*	अच्छी *(fem.)*	लगतीं *(fem., pl.)*	हैं *(pl.)*?
(aap-ko	saa-rDi-yaã	uch-Chee	lug-tee	hain?)

Do you like *saris*?

When used with adjectives such as "good" and "bad," लगना conveys the feelings of a person toward something or someone.

Practice 5

Listen to the sentences and translate them into English.

1. मुझे भारतीय कपड़े अच्छे लगते हैं। (present habitual)

_____

2. उसे यह अच्छा लगेगा। (future)

_____

3. मुझे यह साड़ी अच्छी लग रही है। (present progressive)

_____

4. तुम्हें/आपको क्या अच्छा लगा था? (past perfect)

_____

5. उन्हें वह क़मीज़ अच्छी नहीं लगी। (simple perfect)

_____

Practice 6   Pre-Listening Activity

Fill in the blanks with the correct word from the choices given:

1. मुझे _____ साड़ियाँ लेनी हैं। (some)
   a. कई   b. कुछ   c. कोई

2. हमारे _____ सब तरह की साड़ियों की वैराइटी है। (have)
   a. पास   b. साथ   c. के पास

3. आप कैसी देखना _____? (would like [*fem.* formal])
   a. चाहोगे   b. चाहेगी   c. चाहेंगी

4. मुझे बढ़िया सिल्क की साड़ी _____ (need [*sing.*])
   a. चाहिएँ   b. चाहिए   c. चाहूँगी

5. हमारे पास तीन हज़ार _____ _____ एक लाख तक की साड़ियाँ हैं। (from...to)
   a. से देकर   b. से लेकर   c. से होकर

6. इनके _____ ब्लाउज़ भी हैं क्या? (with)
   a. पास.   b. साथ   c. बाद

7. हाँ, _____ एक से एक बढ़िया डिज़ाइनर ब्लाउज़ आते हैं। (these days)
   a. आजकल   b. कलआज   c. आज और कल

8. मुझे यह गुलाबी वाली _____ _____ _____ _____ । (like [*fem.*])
   a. अच्छी लग रही है   b. अच्छा लग रहा है   c. अच्छे लग रहे हैं

Practice 7 Script 1 04-12

Listen to the conversation and complete the activities that follow.

दुकानदार	: नमस्ते बहनजी, आइये आज आपको क्या दिखाऊँ?
औरत	: नमस्ते, मुझे कुछ साड़ियाँ लेनी हैं।
दुकानदार	: हाँ कहिए, हमारे पास सब तरह की साड़ियों की वैराइटी है, आप कैसी देखना चाहेंगी?
औरत	: मुझे ज़री बॉर्डर की, बढ़िया सिल्क की साड़ी चाहिए। आपके पास किस रेंज की साड़ियाँ हैं?
दुकानदार	: हमारे पास तीन हज़ार से लेकर एक लाख तक की साड़ियाँ हैं।
औरत	: हमें तीन चार हज़ार से आठ हज़ार तक की साड़ियाँ दिखाइये।

Romanization 1

dü-kaan-daar	: Num-us-tay be-hen jee, aa-iyay aaj aap-ko kyaa dikh-aa-oȯ?
Au-rut	: Num-us-tay, mü-jh-ay küch saa-rDee-yaȧ lay-neȯ hain.
dü-kaan-daar	: Haȧ kuh-hi-yay hum-aa-ray paas sub ter-uh kee saa-rDi-yȯ kee variety hai, aap kaisee day-kh-naa chaa-haẏ-gee.
Au-rut	: Müjh-ay zer-ee border kee, berDh-iyaa silk kee saarDee chaa-hi-yay. Aap-kay paas kis range kee saarD-iyaȧ hain?
dü-kaan-daar	: Hum-aa-ray paas teen huz-aar say lay-ker ayk laa-kh tuk kee saarD-iyaȧ hain.
Au-rut	: hum-ain teen huz-aar say aaTh huz-aar tuk kee saarD-iyaȧ dikh-aa-iyay.

Translation 1

Shop Owner	: Welcome Madam, what can I show you today?
Female Customer	: *Namaste*, I need to buy some *saris*.
Shop Owner	: Please tell me, what kind of *sari* would you prefer? We have all kinds of *saris*.
Female Customer	: I need a good silk *sari* with a *zari* border. What is the price range of your *saris*?
Shop Owner	: We have *saris* from 3,000 to 100,000 rupees.
Female Customer	: Show us those from 3,000 to 8,000.

Post-Listening Exercise

A. *Write down the sentences from the conversation that convey "need," "desire," and "request." Then translate them into English.*

1. Hindi: _____

   English: _____

2. Hindi: _____

   English: _____

3. Hindi: _____

   English: _____

B. *Write down the Hindi sentences that best match the translation for "from ... to." Then translate them into English.*

1. Hindi: _____

   English: _____

2. Hindi: _____

   English: _____

C. *Write down the Hindi sentences containing the expression "to have." Then translate them into English.*

1. Hindi: _____

   English: _____

2. Hindi: _____

   English: _____

Practice 8 🎧 04-13

Read along as you listen to the second part of the conversation and complete the activities that follow.

Script 2

दुकानदार : ये देखिए ये है पोचमपल्ली है साउथ सिलक में, ये पटोला में है, यह मैसूर सिल्क में, यह बनारसी सिल्क में है। यह मैसूर जॉर्जेट है, यह उड़ीसा का सम्बलपुरी सिल्क, यह बिहार का भागलपुरी सिल्क है। अब देखिये इसमें से आपको किस तरह की दिखाऊँ?

औरत : भैया, इन सबके साथ ब्लाउज़ भी हैं क्या?

दुकानदार : हाँ, आजकल सबके साथ एक से एक बढ़िया डिज़ाइनर ब्लाउज़ आते हैं।

औरत : यह मैसूर जॉर्जेट दिखाइये, इसमें और कौन-कौन से रंग है?

दुकानदार : यह देखिए, यह गुलाबी-ग्रे कॉम्बीनेशन में, यह हरे और नारंगी कॉम्बीनेशन में, सलैक्ट कर लीजिए।

औरत : मुझे यह गुलाबी-ग्रे कॉम्बीनेशन वाली अच्छी लग रही है। यह निकाल दीजिए। कितने की है यह?

दुकानदार : यह बहनजी सात हज़ार की है। इसके साथ यह ब्लाउज़ का कपड़ा भी है।

औरत : ठीक बोलिए।

दुकानदार : जी हमारी दुकान पर फ़िक्सड दाम पर ही साड़ियाँ मिलती हैं।

औरत : ठीक है, यह साड़ी दे दीजिए। यह लीजिए सात हज़ार रुपये।

दुकानदार : बहुत-बहुत धन्यवाद, फिर सेवा का मौक़ा दीजिएगा।

Romanization 2

dü-kaan-daar : Yay day-khi-yay, yay hai Po-chum-p-ul-lee, south silk maẏ, yay P-uT-olaa maẏ hai, yeh Mysore silk maẏ, yeh Bun-aa-rusee silk maẏ hai. Yeh Mysore georgette hai, yeh Orri-saa kaa sum-bul-püree silk, yeh Bihar kaa bhaag-ul püree silk hai. Ub aap day-khi-yay is-maẏ say aap-ko kis ter-uh kee dikh-aa-oȯ?

Au-rut : Bh-ai-yaa, in sub-kay saath blouse bhee hain kyaa?

dü-kaan-daar : Haä aaj-k-ul sub-kay saath ayk say ayk berDh-iyaa designer blouse aa-tay hain.

Au-rut : Yeh Mysore georgette dikh-aa-iyay, is-maẏ aur kawn-kawn say rung hain?

dü-kaan-daar : Yeh day-khi-yay, yeh gül-aa-bee-grey combination maẏ, yeh her-ay aur naa-rungee combination maẏ, select ker lee-ji-yay.

Au-rut : Mü-jhay yeh gül-aa-bee grey combination waa-lee uch-Chee l-ug ruh-hee hai, yeh nik-aal dee-ji-yay? Kit-nay kee hai?

dü-kaan-daar : Yeh beh-hen jee saat huz-aar kee hai. Is-kay saath yeh blouse kaa kup-erDaa bhee hai.

Au-rut : Theek bo-li-yay.

dü-kaan-daar : Jee hum-aa-ree dü-kaan per fixed daam per hee saa-rDi-yaȧ mil-tee hain.

Au-rut : Theek hai, yeh saa-rDee day-dee-ji-yay. Yeh lee-ji-yay saat huz-aar rü-puh-yay.

dü-kaan-daar : Buh-hüt- buh-hüt dh-unya-vaad, phir say-waa kaa maw-quaa dee-ji-yay-gaa.

Translation 2

Shop Owner	:	Look at this Pochumpalli in south silk, this in Patola, this in Mysore Silk, and this in Banarasi silk. This is Mysore georgette, this is Sambalpuri silk from Orrisa, and this is Bhagalpuri silk from Bihar. Tell me, out of these, what type would you like to see?
Female Customer	:	Brother, does a blouse come with it?
Shop Owner	:	Yes, these days a very good designer blouse comes with it.
Female Customer	:	Show me this Mysore georgette—what other colors do you have?
Shop Owner	:	Here, look at this one. This is in pink and gray combination, and this one is in orange and green combination: you can choose from these.
Female Customer	:	I like this pink and gray combination. Take this one out. How much is it?
Shop Owner	:	Sister, its cost is 7,000 rupees. A blouse will come with it.
Female Customer	:	Please price it right.
Shop Owner	:	Madam, we sell *saris* at a fixed price.
Female Customer	:	OK, please give me this *sari*, and here is 7,000 rupees.
Shop Owner	:	Thank you very much. Please come again.

Practice 9 Comprehension Check

Answer the comprehension questions below in Hindi.

1. दुकानदार के पास किस रेंज की साड़ियाँ हैं?

   _____

2. भागलपुरी साड़ी किस राज्य की है?

   _____

3. दुकानदार के पास मैसूर जॉर्जेट में कितने रंग की साड़ियाँ है?

   _____

4. क्या साड़ी के साथ ब्लाउज़ भी आता है?

   _____

Practice 10

*Based on your notes, recreate a dialogue between yourself and a sari salesman, then compare your version of the text with the original. The salesman's part is already given in the activity; you simply have to create your own lines (as the customer). Remember that in the context of shopping, polite imperatives, internal compulsion, need (*चाहिए*), or the compound verbs* ले लेना *and* दे देना *are generally used.*

दुकानदार : आइये बहन जी, आपको क्या दिखाऊँ?

आप : _____

दुकानदार : किस कपड़े/ मटीरियल में दिखाऊँ?

आप : _____

दुकानदार : किस रेंज में दिखाऊँ?

आप : _____

दुकानदार : हमारे पास दो हज़ार से लेकर एक लाख तक की साड़ियाँ हैं।

आप : _____

दुकानदार : यह देखिए, यह मैसूर सिल्क में है।

आप : _____

दुकानदार : इसमें चार-पाँच रंग आयेंगे। बैंगनी, पीला, हरा और गुलाबी। पसंद कर लीजिए

आप : _____

दुकानदार: यह सात हज़ार की है।

आप : _____

दुकानदार: हाँ, इसके साथ यह ब्लाउज़ का कपड़ा भी है।

आप : _____

दुकानदार : बस एक ही लेंगीं?

आप : _____

दुकानदार : धन्यवाद, फिर आइयेगा।

*Read the full dialogue on page 193.

CHAPTER

5

Eating in India

5.1 Eating at A Roadside Restaurant ढाबे पर खाना खाना

Objectives

By the end of this lesson, you will be able to:

1. Use vocabulary in food-related contexts in India: *perantha, roti, cholay, bhaturay, lassi, gobhi, aloo,* and *pani.*
2. Ask questions about the taste of food and style of cooking using various adjectives such as *roasted, fried, spicy, hot,* and *cold* in Hindi.
3. Order food and indicate your seating preference.
4. Ask for the bill and pay it.
5. State whether you liked the food or not.

> 📖 **Culture Note**
>
> As a traveler, you would enjoy the local delicacy on the go. As anywhere in the world, enjoying the real taste of a particular region can be done at roadside restaurants. In India these roadside restaurants are called *dhaba.* These *dhabas* serve fresh, value-for-money, and tasty food. Many *dhabas* serve mainly vegetarian food items for breakfast, lunch and dinner, and beverages. Some of them also serve non-vegetarian food that includes chicken, goat, fish and seafood based on the local cuisine and availability of the food items.

Vocabulary 05-01

Nouns

Breads

रोटी, चपाती	(ro-Tee, ch-up-aa-tee)	*fem.*	a type of Indian flatbread, cooked on an iron skillet
मिस्सी रोटी	(miss-see ro-Tee)	*fem.*	bread made from gram flour and whole wheat flour
सादा नान	(saa-daa naan)	*masc.*	plain *naan*

पराँठा	(per-aàTh-aa)	*masc.*	Indian bread made of wheat flour, filled with a spicy blend of vegetables, cheese or plain, cooked on a skillet.

Rice

सादे चावल	(saa-day chaa-vuh-ul)	*masc.*	plain rice
जीरा चावल	(jee-raa chaa-vuh-ul)	*masc.*	rice with cumin
वेज पुलाव	(veg pull-ao)	*masc.*	vegetable *pulao*/rice
मसाला पुलाव	(mus-aa-laa pull-ao)	*masc.*	masala *pulao*/rice
पनीर पुलाव	(pun-eer pull-ao)	*masc.*	cheese *pulao*/rice
मटर पुलाव	(mutter pull-ao)	*masc.*	pea *pulao*/rice

Salad/vegetables

प्याज़	(pyaa-z)	*fem.*	onion
टमाटर	(Tum-aa-ter)	*masc.*	tomato
गाजर	(gaa-jer)	*fem.*	carrot
ककड़ी	(kuk-rDee)	*fem.*	Indian cucumber
खीरा	(khee-raa)	*masc.*	cucumber
आलू	(aa-loo)	*masc.*	potato

Dishes

पालक-पनीर	(paa-luck pun-eer)	spinach and Indian cheese
दम आलू	(d-um aa-loo)	steamed potato simmered in spicy sauce
गोभी	(go-bhee)	cauliflower
दाल-मसाला	(daal mus-aa-laa)	legumes in spicy sauce
छोले-भटूरे	(Cho-lay bhuh-Too-ray)	chick peas and fried bread

Breakfast and Snacks

पकौड़ा	(puck-orDaa)	*masc.*	*pakoda* is deep fried vegetables or cheese (*paneer*) fritters, battered in gram flour
पाव-भाजी	(Paav-bhaa-jee)	*fem.*	bun and vegetables
भाजी	(bhaa-jee)	*fem.*	*bhaji-litterly* meaning "vegetable"; however, this is a concoction of potatoes, bell pepper, peas, and tomatoes

Beverages

पानी/जल	(paa-nee)	*masc.*	water
चाय	(chaa-yuh)	*fem.*	tea
दूध	(doo-dh)	*masc.*	milk
लस्सी	(luhs-see)	*fem.*	yogurt shake
जीरा छाछ	(Jee-raa Chaa-Ch)	*fem.*	cumin buttermilk

Utensils

गिलास	(gil-aas)	*masc*	glass
चम्मच	(chum-uch)	*fem.*	spoon
काँटा	(kaȧ-Taa)	*masc.*	fork
छुरी	(Chü-ree)	*fem.*	knife
थाली	(Thaa-lee)	*fem.*	steel plate
कटोरी	(cuT-oree)	*fem.*	bowl

Other

हवा	(huh-uv-aa)	*fem.*	air

Adjectives

सादा	(saa-daa)	*masc.*	plain
सादी	(saa-dee)	*fem.*	plain
सादे	(saa-day)	*masc. pl.*	plain
दम	(duh-um)	*unmarked*	steamed
मज़ेदार/स्वादिष्ट	(muz-ay-daar/swaa-dish-T)	*unmarked*	tasty
बढ़िया	(berDh-iyaa)	*unmarked*	good
ज़्यादा	(zyaa-daa)	*unmarked*	lots
कम	(kuh-um)	*unmarked*	less
लिखा	(likh-aa)	*masc.*	written
तला	(tuh-ul-aa)	*masc.*	fried
तली	(tuh-ul-ee)	*fem.*	fried
तले	(tuh-ul-ay)	*masc. pl.*	fried
भुना	(bhü-naa)	*masc.*	roasted
भुनी	(bhü-nee)	*fem.*	roasted
भुने	(bhü-nay)	*masc. pl.*	roasted
ताज़ी	(taa-zee)	*fem.*	fresh
ताज़ी-ताज़ी	(taa-zee-taa-zee)	*fem.*	very fresh

Adverbs

खुले में	(khü-lay may)		in the open
यहाँ	(yuh-haȧ)		here
पहले	(peh-lay)		first
बाद में	(baad-maẏ)		later on
अभी	(ub-hee)		right away, right now
जल्दी से	(j-ul-dee say)		quickly

Verbs

बोलना	(bol-naa)	*v.t.*	to speak
रुकना	(rük-naa)	*v.i.*	to wait, to stop
बताना	(but-aa-naa)	*v.t.*	to tell
ले आना	(lay aa-naa)	*comp. participle*	to bring

देख लेना	(day-kh lay-naa)	*comp. v.t.*	to look at
देखकर	(day-kh-ker)	*conj. participle*	after looking, upon checking
पसंद करना	(puh-us-und ker-naa)	*conj. v.t.*	to like (Usage: मैं पसंद करूँगा, हम पसंद करेंगे "I would like to, we would like to")

Grammar: Review Future Tense

Structure

Subject	+	Object	+	Verb root	+ suffix ऊँगा, ऊँगी, एँगे, एगी, एँगीं, ओगे
मैं		खाना		खाऊँगा/खाऊँगी ।	

(main   khaa-naa   khaa-oȯ-gaa/khaa-oȯ-gee.)
I will eat food. (First person)

हम/आप   पानी   पिएँगे ।
(hum   paa-nee   pi-yaẏ-gay.)
We/you will drink water. (*First person, pl./formal*)

तुम   क्या   खाओगे?
(tüm   kyaa   khaa-o-gay.)
What will you eat? (Informal)

यह/वह   नान   लेगा/लेगी ।
(yeh/veh   naan   lay-gaa/lay-gee.)
He/she will take *naan*. (*Third person, sing.*)

ये/वे   चाय   पियेंगे/पियेंगीं ।
(yay/vay   chai   pi-yaẏain-gay/pi-yaẏ-gee.)
He/she will drink tea. (*Third person, pl./formal/honorific*)

Brainstorming

Scenario: You are on your way to Ajmer from Jaipur in Rajasthan. It is almost lunchtime and you are hungry. You see a roadside restaurant and plan to make a stop to eat there. You see some pictures of food items with words written on the board. They don't have any menu to give to you except for what is posted on the board. Make a list of what you would like to order. Remember that this *dhaba* is a vegetarian one.

Kadai Se		
Veg. Kadai	90.00	वेज कड़ाई
Mushroom Curry	90.00	मशरूम करी
Mushroom Peas Curry	90.00	मशरूम पीस करी
Kadai Paneer	110.00	कड़ाई पनीर
Kadai Mushroom	110.00	कड़ाई मशरूम
Mushroom Butter Masala	120.00	मशरूम बटर मसाला
Kaju Curry	140.00	काजू करी

Dal		
Dal Fry	40.00	दाल फ्राई
Dal Palak	40.00	दाल पालक
Dal Tadka (with Cream)	50.00	दाल तड़का (क्रीम)
Dal Butter	60.00	दाल बटर
Dal Makhani	70.00	दाल मक्खानी
Dal Handi	70.00	दाल हांडी
Dal Panjabi Tadka Special	75.00	दाल पंजाबी तड़का स्पेशल

Salad		
Onion Salad	10.00	ओनियन सलाद
Green Salad	20.00	ग्रीन सलाद
Sirca Salad	25.00	सिरका सलाद
Kuchumber Salad	35.00	कचुम्बर सलाद

Dahi Se		
Butter Milk	15.00	बटर मिल्क (छाछ)
Sweet Lassi	25.00	लस्सी
Plain Curd	30.00	प्लेन दही
Bundi Raita	40.00	बूंदी रायता
Veg. Raita	50.00	वेज रायता
Aloo Raita	50.00	आलू रायता
Fruit Raita	70.00	फ्रूट रायता

Basmati Se		
Steam Rice	35.00	स्टीम राईस
Jira Rice	50.00	जीरा राईस
Veg. Pulao	60.00	वेज पुलाव
Peas Pulao	60.00	पीस पुलाव
Veg. Biryani	60.00	वेज बिरयानी
Hydrabadi Biryani	70.00	हैदराबादी बिरयानी
Paneer Pulao	75.00	पनीर पुलाव
Paneer Biryani	80.00	पनीर बिरयानी
Kashmiri Pulao	90.00	कश्मीरी पुलाव

Papad		
Roasted Papad	10.00	रोस्टेड पापड़
Papad Fry	20.00	पापड़ फ्राई
Masala Papad	30.00	मसाला पापड़
Masala Papad Fry	30.00	मसाला पापड़ फ्राई

Practice 1 Vocabulary-Building Exercise

Match the adjectives and adverbs on the left with their corresponding antonyms on the right.

1. अच्छा   बाद में
2. अन्दर   वहाँ
3. अभी   बुरा
4. पहले   ज़्यादा

5. मज़ेदार   बाहर
6. कम   के बाद
7. सादा   बेस्वाद
8. यहाँ   तला-भुना

Practice 2
Based on the list, categorize each Hindi word in the respective columns.

(दे देना, ककड़ी, छाछ, अन्दर, चपाती, सादा, चावल, चम्मच, प्याज़, यहाँ, छोला, पकौड़ा, कटोरी, पराँठा, पानी, टमाटर, मटर, दम, मिस्सी रोटी, जीरा, पाव-भाजी, देखकर, पनीर पराँठा, बाहर, काँटा, ले आना)

Bread	Breakfast/Snacks	Beverages	Vegetables	Adjectives/Verbs/Adverbs
Utensils				

Practice 3
Now read the following Hindi phrases and sentences that might be used by a customer at a restaurant. Translate them into English.

हम यहाँ बाहर बैठकर खायेंगे।

1. _____

सबसे पहले एक प्लेट प्याज़ पकौड़ा दे दो।

2. _____

पाँच मिनट रुको।

3. _____

एक गिलास पानी भी ले आना।

4. _____

मैं देखकर बताता हूँ।

5. _____

कितनी देर लगेगी?

6. _____

बिल ले आओ। कितने हुए?   बस और कुछ नहीं चाहिए।

7. _____   9. _____

काँटे-चम्मच भी ले आना।   मिनरल वॉटर की बोतल देना।

8. _____   10. _____

Practice 4 🎧 05-02

Listen to the conversation and answer the questions that follow in Hindi.

Script 1
लड़का   : आओ मैडम, आओ साहब कहाँ बैठोगे, अन्दर या बाहर?
आदमी   : हम यहाँ बाहर खाट पर बैठकर खाना खायेंगे।
लड़का   : अच्छा साहब तो बोलो क्या लोगे?
आदमी   : लंच में क्या-क्या है?
लड़का   : साहब, मैन्यू सब यहाँ बोर्ड पर लिखा है, वैसे लंच में पालक-पनीर है, दम आलू हैं, गोभी है, दाल मसाला
           है, छोले-भटूरे हैं, आप क्या लोगे?
आदमी   : अच्छा,पाँच मिनट रुको, मैं अभी देखकर बताता हूँ।

Romanization 1
LerD-kaa   : Aao Madam, aao saa-hub kuh-haȧ baiTho-gay, under yaa baa-her?
Aad-me   : Hum yuh-haȧ baa-her khaaT per baiTh-ker khaa-naa khaa-yaẏ-gay.
LerD-kaa   : Uch-Chaa saa-hub toe bo-lo kyaa lo-gay?
Aad-me   : Lunch maẏ kyaa-kyaa hai?
LerD-kaa   : Saa-hub menu sub yuh-haȧ board per likh-aa hai. Vai-say lunch maẏ paa-
              luck pun-eer hai, dum-aa-loo hain, go-bhee hai, daal mus-aa-laa hai, Cho-lay-
              bhuT-oo-ray hain. Aap kyaa lo-gay?
Aad-me   : Uch-Chaa paȧ-ch min-uT rü-ko, main ub-hee day-kh-ker but-aa-taa hoȯ.

Translation 1
Boy   : Welcome madam, welcome sir. Where would you like to sit: inside or outside?
Man   : We will sit here, and eat outside on the bed.
Boy   : OK sir, what would you like to have?
Man   : What is there on the lunch menu?
Boy   : Sir, the menu is written here on the board; however, we have a cheese and
          spinach dish, steamed potatoes, cauliflower, masala legume, chickpeas and fried
          bread. What would you like to order?
Man   : OK, wait for five minutes. Let me decide and I will tell you shortly.

Comprehension Check

1. ग्राहक कहाँ बैठना चाहते हैं?

   Where would the customer like to sit? _____

2. खाने का मैन्यू कहाँ लिखा है?

   Where is the menu written? _____

Practice 5

Listen to the second part of the conversation. Then do the Post-Listening Exercise.

Script 2

लड़का : हाँ साहब तो बोलो, क्या लाऊँ?

आदमी : सबसे पहले मुझे एक प्लेट प्याज़ पकौड़ा दे दो। और खाने में एक प्लेट दम आलू, एक प्लेट गोभी, दो सादी चपातियाँ, एक मटर पुलाव। अच्छा! सलाद खाने के साथ ही होगा?

लड़का : हाँ साहब सलाद खाने के साथ होगा। खाने से पहले कुछ पीने के लिए?

आदमी : एक गिलास लस्सी भी ले आना।

लड़का : ठीक है साहब, कुछ और?

आदमी : कितनी देर लगेगी?

लड़का : यही कोई दो-चार मिनट।

आदमी : ठीक है।

Romanization 2

LerD-kaa : Haȧ saa-hub toe bolo kyaa laa-oȯ?

Aad-me : Sub-say peh-lay mü-jhay ayk plate puck-orDaa day doe. Aur khaa-nay mein ayk plate dum aa-loo, ayk plate go-bhee, doe saa-dee chup-aa-ti-yȧ, ayk mutter pül-ao. Uch-Chaa! Suh-ul-aad khaa-nay kay saath hee ho-gaa?

LerD-kaa : Haȧ saa-hub sul-aad, khaa-nay kay saa-th ho-gaa. Khaa-nay say peh-lay küCh-pee-nay kay li-yay?

Aad-me : Ayk gil-aas luss-see bhee lay aa-naa.

LerD-kaa : Theek hai saa-hub, kuCh aur?

Aad-me : Kit-nee day-r lug-ay-gee?

LerD-kaa : Yuh-he ko-ee doe-chaar min-ut.

Aad-me : Theek hai.

Post-Listening Exercise

1. आदमी को पीने के लिए क्या चाहिए?

   What does the man want to drink? _____

2. आदमी ने सबसे पहले क्या मँगाया?

   What was the first item he ordered? _____

3.   खाने में आदमी ने क्या-क्या चीज़ें मँगवायीं?
     What did the customer order for lunch? _____

Translation 2

Waiter : OK sir! So what should I get for you?

Man   : So, first of all, get me some onion *pakoda*. Then for lunch: one plate of *dum-aloo*, one plate of *gobhi*, two plain *chapatis*, and one plate of *matar-pulao*. And will the salad be included with the meal?

Waiter : Yes sir, the salad comes with the food. Would you like to drink something before the food arrives?

Man   : Get me a glass of *lassi* as well.

Waiter : OK sir, anything else?

Man   : How long is it going to take?

Waiter : Just a few minutes.

Man   : OK.

5.2 Dining in a Fine Restaurant
एक अच्छे रेस्तराँ में खाना खाना ।

Objectives

By the end of this lesson, you will be able to:

1.   Order food and indicate your seating preference.
2.   Ask for the bill and pay it.
3.   State whether you liked the food or not using पसंद आना and अच्छा लगना.

📖 **Culture Note**

An unexpected guest is called *atithi*, अतिथि, which is translated as "an unannounced guest." It is believed that all guests are like God "अतिथि देवो भव:," therefore, those who set foot at your doorstep, are offered water, food, and a place to sit.

Offering hospitality is essential to Indian culture. Whether you are a family member, a friend, a stranger, or a foreigner, people in India treat everyone with great respect. Especially in the fine food and hotel industry, the moment a guest steps into the hotel (to eat or stay), the staff will welcome him/her by applying *teeka* (wet red vermillion powder) on the guest's forehead and presenting a fresh flower garland. When the guest leaves, they remain at his/her service.

Grammar
पसंद आना (Puh-sund aa-naa) or
अच्छा लगना (Uch-Chaa l-ug-naa) (to like)

पसंद आना is most commonly used in response to something you liked after you've experienced it, whereas अच्छा लगना can be used for all tenses. In this construction the subject is always indirect because the "liking comes to a person" and the verb agrees in number and gender. So remember to change a pronoun into the oblique or indirect case in these types of sentences.

Structure
Subject + को + Object (*masc./fem./pl.*) + पसंद + आना/ अच्छा लगना (in perfect tense)

Example:
मुझे   खाना   बहुत पसंद आया/ अच्छा लगा।
(müJh-ay   khaa-naa buh-hüt   pus-und aa-yaa/uch-Chaa lug-aa.)
I liked the food a lot.

उस   स्ट्रॉबैरी आइसक्रीम   पसंद आयी/ अच्छी लगी।
(üsay   is-traw-berry ice-cream   pus-und aa-yee/uch-Chaa lug-ee.)
She liked the strawberry ice cream.

Practice 1 Pre-Listening Activity
Fill in the spaces with the appropriate words for the pictures, and complete the dialogue.

होटल मैनेजर: वैलकम सर, _____  कितने लोगों के लिए? (please come)
                              (1)

आदमी: हम _____  हैं। (people)
                         (2)

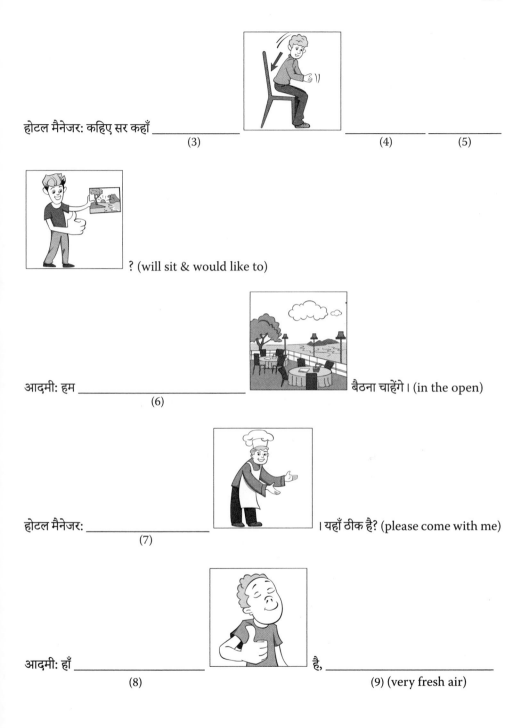

होटल मैनेजर: कहिए सर कहाँ _____ (3) _____ (4) _____ (5)

? (will sit & would like to)

आदमी: हम _____ (6) बैठना चाहेंगे । (in the open)

होटल मैनेजर: _____ (7) । यहाँ ठीक है? (please come with me)

आदमी: हाँ _____ (8) है, _____ (9) (very fresh air)

रही है। रही है। (Ok here)

बैरा: मैन्यू सर, _____  , मैं फिर आता हूँ। (please take a look)

(10)

Practice 2 Seating in the Restaurant 🎧 05-04

Now listen to the audio and match the words that you have just filled in, in the pre-listening activity with the audio and script.

Script 1

होटल मैनेजर	: वैलकम सर, आइये, कितने लोगों के लिए?
आदमी	: हम चार जने हैं।
होटल मैनेजर	: कहिए सर कहाँ बैठना पसंद करेंगे?
आदमी	: हम खुले में बैठना चाहेंगे।
होटल मैनेजर	: मेरे साथ आइये। यहाँ ठीक है?
आदमी	: हाँ यहाँ अच्छा है, ताज़ी-ताज़ी हवा आ रही है।
बैरा	: मैन्यू सर, आप देख लीजिए, मैं फिर आता हूँ।

Romanization 1

Hotel Manager	: Welcome sir, aa-i-yay, kit-nay low-g hain?
Aad-me	: H-um chaar j-un-ay hain.
Hotel Manager	: Kuh-hi-yay sir kuh-haȧ baiTh-naa pus-und ker-aẏ-gay?
Aad-me	: Huh-um khül-ay maẏ baiTh-naa chaa-haẏ-gay.
Hotel Manager	: May-ray saath aa-i-yay, Yuh-haȧ Theek hai?
Aad-me	: Haȧ yuh-haȧ uch-Chaa hai, taa-zee taa-zee h-uw-aa aa ruh-hee hai.
Hotel Manager	: Menu sir, aap day-kh lee-ji-yay, main phir aa-taa hoȯ.

Practice 3

How would you say these phrases in Hindi?

1. We would like to sit out in the open. _____

2. There are four people in our party. _____

3.   Yes, this place is good. We would like to sit out in the open. _____

_____

Translation 1

Hotel Manager : Welcome sir, please come in. For how many people?

Man   : We are four in our party.

Hotel Manager : Yes sir. Please tell me where you would like to sit.

Man   : We would like to sit out in the open.

Hotel Manager : Please follow me. Is it OK here?

Man   : Yes, it's fine here; there is a fresh breeze blowing here.

Hotel Manager : Menu sir, please take a look. I'll be right back.

Ordering खाना मंगवाना

Practice 1

Read the dialogue and then listen to it.

Script 2

बैरा   : सर आप ऑर्डर देने के लिए तैयार हैं? एपीटाइज़र में क्या लेंगे?

आदमी   : एपीटाइज़र में.....दो ऑर्डर पनीर टिक्का, दो सिज़लर्स। सिज़लर में क्या-क्या आयेगा?

बैरा   : सर इसमें, चिकन टिक्का, झींगा, रेश्मी क़बाब, सींक क़बाब और मछली आयेगी।

आदमी   : ठीक है तो दो जगह सिज़लर्स भी ले आना।

बैरा   : ओके सर, पीने के लिए कुछ?

आदमी   : चार ग्लास विहस्की, बढ़िया वाली। साथ में बर्फ़ भी ले आना।

बैरा   : ओके सर, खाना बाद में ऑर्डर करेंगे?

आदमी   : हाँ, पहले ये सब चीज़ें ले आओ।

बैरा   : ठीक है सर।

Romanization 2

Bai-raa : Sir aap order day-nay kay li-yay tai-yaar hain? Appetizer maẏ kyaa laẏ-gay?

Aad-me : Appetizer maẏ … doe order Paneer Tikka, doe sizzlers. Sizzler maẏ kyaa-kyaa aa-yay-gaa?

Bai-raa : Sir is-maẏ chicken Tikka, Jheė-gaa, ray-shmee kub-aab, seėk kub-aab aur muCh-lee aa-yay-gee.

Aad-me : Theek hai toe doe jug-uh sizzlers bhee lay aa-naa.

Bai-raa : OK sir, pee-nay kay li-yay kuCh?

Aad-me : chaar glaas Whisky, berDh-iyaa waa-lee. Saath maẏ berf bhee lay aa-naa.

Bai-raa : OK sir, khaa-naa baad maẏ order ker-aẏ-gay?

Aad-me : Haa, peh-lay yay sub cheez-aẏ lay aao.

Bai-raa : Theek hai sir.

Vocabulary

पनीर-टिक्का	(pun-eer Tik-kaa)	marinated, grilled/roasted Indian cheese cubes
चिकन-टिक्का	(chi-ckin Tik-kaa)	marinated, grilled/roasted chicken cubes
झींगा	(Jheen-gaa)	prawns
रेशमी क़बाब	(ray-sh-mee kabab)	marinated ground meat, skewered and grilled
सींक क़बाब	(seenk kabab)	marinated ground meat, skewered and grilled
मछली	(muh-Ch-lee)	fish
बर्फ़	(berf)	ice

Practice 2 Post-Listening Exercise

1. Write the phrase that suggests "taking orders in a restaurant" and translate it into English.

   _____

2. Write the phrase that suggests "giving order for the food" and translate it into English.

   _____

3. Write the sentences where the compound verbs are used. What do those constructions convey in terms of the tone?

   _____

   _____

Translation 2

Waiter : Sir, are you ready to order? What would you like for appetizer?

Man : For appetizer, two orders of *Paneer Tikka* and two sizzlers. What is in the sizzlers?

Waiter : Sir, it comes with chicken *Tikka*, prawns, *Rashmi Kabab, Seenk kabab* and fish.

Man : OK then, get us two orders of sizzlers as well.

Waiter : OK sir, anything to drink?

Man : Get us four glasses of whiskey, the good one along with ice.

Waiter : OK sir, are you going to order food later?

Man : Yes, get us these things first.

Waiter : OK sir.

5.3 Paying the Bill बिल चुकाना

Objectives

By the end of this lesson, you will be able to ask for a bill and pay it at any restaurant in India.

> 📖 **Culture Note**
>
> If you are being taken out to dinner by a formal host, i.e. a grandparent or boss, always let them pay for the bill. If you interject and refuse their offer to pay, it is considered impolite.
>
> For tipping and gratuities, 20-50 rupees is considered ideal for roadside or *dhaba*-like restaurants. For a higher-end restaurant, a 10% service charge is applied to the overall bill, but if you wish to tip because you enjoyed the service from your server, it's completely welcome to leave a little extra on the table or to hand it directly to him/her.

Preview the thematic vocabulary below and then complete the activity.

लेना   कुछ और   खाना पसंद आना   ले आना   सिर्फ़   रसीद   कर देना   फिर आना   बिल

Practice 1 Pre-Listening Activity

Create your part of the dialogue. It may be a question or a reply. We will provide you with the waiter's response. Remember that this is the follow-up dialogue, after you have finished lunch or dinner. Think of what a customer might say and ask in such a situation before writing your dialogue.

आप : _____

बैरा : सर कुछ और लेंगे? आपको खाना पसंद आया?

आप : _____

बैरा : अच्छा सर, यह लीजिए आपका बिल।

आप : _____

बैरा : हाँ सर हम क्रैडिट कार्ड भी लेते हैं।

आप : _____

बैरा : यह लीजिए सर, आपकी रसीद, आप यहाँ साइन कर दीजिए।

आप : _____

Practice 2 🎧 05-06

Now compare your dialogue with that in the script. Find the similarities and differences. Then do the activity that follows.

Script

बैरा	:	सर कुछ और लेंगे? आपको खाना पसंद आया?
ग्राहक	:	खाना बहुत अच्छा था। हम और कुछ नहीं लेंगे, तुम हमारा बिल ले आओ।
बैरा	:	अच्छा सर, यह लीजिए आपका बिल।
ग्राहक	:	यहाँ क्रैडिट कार्ड लेते हैं या सिर्फ़ कैश ही लेते हैं?
बैरा	:	हाँ सर हम क्रैडिट कार्ड भी लेते हैं।
ग्राहक	:	ठीक है, यह लो।
बैरा	:	यह लीजिए सर, आपकी रसीद, आप यहाँ साइन कर दीजिए।
ग्राहक	:	यह लो, क्या इस में टिप भी शामिल है?
बैरा	:	हाँ सर टिप इसमें शामिल है। थैंक्यू सर, फिर आइयेगा।

Romanization

Bai-raa	:	Sir kuCh aur laẏ-gay? Aap-ko khaa-naa pus-und aa-yaa?
Graa-h-uk	:	Khaa-naa buh-hüt uch-Chaa thaa. H-um aur kuCh nuh-heė laẏ-gay, tüm h-um-aa-raa bill lay aao.
Bai-raa	:	Uch-Chaa sir, yeh lee-ji-yay aap-kaa bill.
Graa-h-uk	:	Yuh-haȧ credit card lay-tay hain yaa sirf cash he lay-tay hain?
Bai-raa	:	Haȧ sir h-um credit card bhee lay-tay hain.
Graa-h-uk	:	Theek hai, yeh lo.
Bai-raa	:	Yeh lee-ji-yay sir, aap-kee rus-eed, aap yuh-haa sign ker dee-ji-yay.
Graa-h-uk	:	Yeh lo kyaa is-may/tip bhee shaa-mil hai?
Bai-raa	:	Haȧ sir, tip is-may shaa-mil hai. Thank you sir, phir aa-i-yay gaa.

Translation

Waiter	:	Sir, would you like to have something else? Did you enjoy the food?
Customer	:	The food was very good. We don't want anything else, just bring us the bill.
Waiter	:	OK sir, here is your bill.
Customer	:	Do you also take credit cards or just cash?
Waiter	:	We also take credit cards.
Customer	:	OK then take this.
Waiter	:	Here is your receipt sir, please sign here.
Customer	:	Here, is the tip included in this bill?
Waiter	:	Yes sir, the tip is included in the bill. Thank you sir, please come again.

Listening Activity

Listen to the conversation again and repeat it for practice.

Practice 3 Post-Listening Activity

3.1 Write down the sentences from the conversation that express "hospitality or courtesy" and translate them into English.

1. Hindi: _____

   English: _____

2. Hindi: _____

   English: _____

3.2 Write down the sentences that best match the translation for "Here is your receipt sir," and "Please sign here."

1. _____   2. _____

3.3 Write down the sentences containing the compound verbs in the imperative form, and translate them into English.

1. Hindi: _____

   English: _____

2. Hindi: _____

   English: _____

Practice saying the following phrases in Hindi.

1. Please bring the bill.

   _____

2. We have enjoyed the food a lot.

   _____

3. Is the tip included in the bill?

   _____

4. Do you take credit cards?

   _____

*Read the full dialogue on page 222.

CHAPTER

Interacting With Locals

6.1 Hiring a Washerman धोबी रखना।

Objectives

By the end of this lesson, you will be able to:

1. Converse with a washerman/washerwoman, and ask him/her whether he/she can wash your clothes, starch and iron them, using the habitual present, internal compulsion, and causative forms of verbs.
2. Confirm the washerman's/washerwoman's availability to wash and iron your clothes, which needs to be done urgently.

> 📖 **Culture Note**
> You must be curious: Who is this washerman/washerwoman? In India, this is a person, who washes people's clothes, starch them if needed, and irons them as a job. He/She is known as a *dhobi/dhobin* and usually comes from the Dhobi clan, whose family business is to wash other people's clothes or dryclean them, and iron them. Once you hire one, he/she will come to your home and collect your dirty clothes, and return them washed and ironed.

Vocabulary

Nouns

परिवार	(per-i-waar)	*masc.*	family
बेटा	(bay-Taa)	*masc.*	son
बेटी	(bay-Tee)	*fem.*	daughter
तालाब	(taa-laab)	*masc.*	pond
कपड़े	(kup-rDay)	*masc., pl.*	clothes
धोबी	(dho-be)	*masc.*	washerman
इस्त्री	(is-tree)	*fem.*	iron (press)
कलफ़	(k-ul-uf)	*masc.*	starch
काम	(kaam)	*masc.*	work
हिसाब	(his-aab)	*masc.*	payment, calculation

किनारा	(kin-aa-raa)	*masc.*	banks, shore
महीना	(muh-he-naa)	*masc.*	month

Adjectives

छोटा	(Cho-taa)	*masc., sing.*	younger, small
दोनों	(doe-nȯ)		both
सूती	(soo-tee)		cotton
गंदा	(gun-daa)	*masc., sing.*	dirty
गंदे	(gun-day)	*masc., pl.*	dirty
ज़रूरी	(zer-oo-re)		important
पिछला	(piCh-laa)	*masc., sing*	last, previous

Adverbs

पीछे ही	(pee-chay he)		right behind
अब	(ub)		now
अभी	(ub-he)		right now
सिर्फ़	(sirf)		only
आज	(aaj)		today
कल	(k-ul)		tomorrow, yesterday

Compound Postpositions

के पीछे	(kay pee-chay)		behind of *X*
के किनारे	(kay kin-aa-ray)		on the banks of *X*

Verbs

रहना	(reh-naa)	*v.i.*	to live
करना	(ker-naa)	*v.t.*	to do
कर देना	(ker day-naa)	*comp. v.t.*	to do
करवाना	(ker-waa-naa)	*comp. v.t.*	to have done
धोना	(dho-naa)	*v.t.*	to wash
धुलवाना	(dhül-waa-naa)	*caus. v.t.*	to have washed
लगवाना	(lug-waa-naa)	*caus. v.t.*	to have applied (starch on clothes)
ले जाना	(lay jaa-naa)	*v.i.*	to take away
ले आना	(lay-aa-naa)	*v.i.*	to bring
माँगना	(maȧg-naa)	*v.t.*	to ask for

Grammar Review

In this lesson you will be able to review:

1. **Present Habitual Tense** (to indicate what one does everyday in the present time]
   Subject + object + verb root + suffix ता, ती, ते + auxiliary है/ हैं /हो
   (direct–*masc./fem./pl.*)

2. **Future Tense** (to indicate what one will do in the future/next hour/day]

    Subject   + object + verb root + suffix ऊँगा/ऊँगी/ओगे/ओगी/एगा/एगी/एँगे/एँगी (direct–*masc./fem./pl.*)

3. **Internal Compulsion** (to indicate one's internal desire to do something or something one has to do)

    Subject with को + object (*masc./fem./pl.*) + infinitive of the main verb (*masc./fem./ pl.*) + auxiliary (present/past)

4. **Causatives** (used in types of sentences where the subject has the work done by an agent)

5. **Imperative: Polite and Neutral** (used to request with the pronoun आप and to suggest something using the infinitive form with all the pronouns)

    Subject + object + verb root + suffix इये/ इए (polite)
    Subject + object + verb (infinitive form — to suggest)

Practice 1 Pre-Listening Activity

You are in India and need someone to take care of your laundry and iron clothes as you don't have time to do so yourself. You need to hire a washerman/washerwoman to do this job.

Look at the illustration and predict the words and expressions which are likely to appear in the following conversation.

1. _____   2. _____   3. _____

4. _____   6. _____   8. _____

5. _____   7. _____   9. _____

Practice 2 Listening Exercise [06-02]

Listen to the conversation and take notes. Write down familiar words or grammatical structures that you hear. Go over your list and listen to the conversation one more time. Then answer the comprehension questions.

Script 1

शीला : तुम्हारा नाम क्या है?

धोबी : जी मेरा नाम माधव है।

शीला : तुम कहाँ रहते हो?

धोबी : मैं आप के घर के पीछे ही तालाब के किनारे रहता हूँ।

शीला : तुम रघुवीर के छोटे भाई हो?

धोबी : जी, मैं रघुवीर धोबी का भाई हूँ।

शीला : तुम्हे परिवार में कौन कौन है?

धोबी : मेरे परिवार में मैं, मेरी पत्नी, मेरे दो बेटे और दो बेटियाँ हैं।

शीला : तुम कितने घरों में कपड़े धोते हो?

धोबी : जी मैं ५ घरों में कपड़े धोता हूँ और मेरी पत्नी २ घरों में कपड़े धोती है।

शीला : देखो माधव, रघुवीर ने हमारे कपड़े धोना अब छोड़ दिया है, क्या तुम ये काम करोगे?

धोबी : क्या आपको सिर्फ़ कपड़े धुलवाने हैं या इस्त्री भी करवानी है?

शीला : मुझे दोनों ही काम करवाने हैं। तुम हर दो दिन बाद गंदे कपड़े ले जाना और उन्हें धोकर, उन पर इस्ली करके दूसरे दिन ले आना।

धोबी : सूती साड़ियों पर कलफ़ भी लगवाएँगी या नहीं?

शीला : हाँ सूती साड़ियों, क्रमीज़ों और पजामों- कुर्तों पर कलफ़ भी लगवाना है।

धोबी : ठीक है बहनजी, आपका काम कर दूँगा।

Familiar words: _____

Grammatical structures: _____

Romanization 1

Sheela : tüm-haa-raa naam kyaa hai?

dho-be : Jee may-raa naam Maa-dh-uv hai.

Sheela : tüm kuh-haȧ reh-tay ho?

dho-be : Maiṅ app-kay gher kay pee-Chay he taa-lab kay kin-aa-ray reh-taa hoȯ.

Sheela : tüm Rug-hü-veer kay Cho-Tay bhaa-ee ho?

dho-be : Jee main Rug-hü-veer dho-be kaa Cho-Taa bhaa-ee hoȯ.

Sheela : tüm-haa-ray per-i-waar maẏ kawn-kawn hai?

dho-be : May-ray per-i-waar maẏ, may-re p-ut-nee, may-ray doe bay-Tay aur doe bay-Ti-yaȧ hain.

Sheela : tüm kit-nay gher-ȯ maẏ kup-rDay dho-tay ho?

dho-be : Jee main paanch gher maẏ kup-rDay dho-taa hoȯ aur may-re p-ut-nee doe ghar mein kup-rDay dho-tee hai.

Sheela : day-kho Maa-dh-uv, Rug-hü-veer nay hum-aa-ray kup-rDay dho-naa ChorD di-yaa hai, kyaa tüm yay kaam ker-o-gay?

dho-be : Kyaa app-ko sirf kup-rDay dhül-waa-nay hain, yaa is-tree bhee ker-waa-nee hai?

Sheela : Mü-jhay do-nȯ hee kaam ker-waa-nay hain, tum her doe din baad gun-day kup-rDay lay jaa-naa aur ün-haẏ dho-ker, un-per is-tree ker-kay doos-ray din lay aa-naa.

dho-be : Soo-tee saa-rDi-yȯ per k-ul-uf bhee l-ug-waa-aẏ-gee yaa nuh-heȯ?

Sheela : Haȧ soo-tee saa-rDi-yȯ, kum-ee-zȯ, p-uj-aa-mȯ kür-tȯ per k-ul-uf bhee l-ug-waa-naa hai.

dho-be : Theek hai beh-hen jee, aap-kaa kaam ker doȯ-gaa.

Translation 1

Sheila	: What is your name?
Washerman	: Ma'am, my name is Madhav.
Sheila	: Where do you live?
Washerman	: I live right behind your house near the pond.
Sheila	: Aren't you Raghuveer's younger brother?
Washerman	: Yes, I am Raghuveer-dhobi's younger brother.
Sheila	: How many people are in your family?
Washerman	: In my family I have a wife, two sons, and two daughters.

Sheila	: For how many families do you wash clothes?
Washerman	: I wash clothes for five families. And my wife washes for two families.
Sheila	: Listen, Raghuveer doesn't wash our clothes anymore. Would you like to work for us?
Washerman	: Do you want me to just wash the clothes or iron them as well?
Sheila	: I need both things done. Every two days take the dirty clothes and then bring them back ironed the next day.
Washerman	: Would you like me to starch the cotton *saris*?
Sheila	: Yes, use starch on the cotton *saris*, the shirts, and the *kurta-pajama*.
Washerman	: No problem ma'am, consider it done.

Practice 3 Post-Listening Exercise

Fill in the blanks with the correct Hindi word from the choices given.

1. मैं आप के घर _____ रहता हूँ। (behind)

   a. के किनारे   b. के पीछे

2. जी,मैं रघुवीर धोबी का _____ हूँ। (brother)

   a. बेटी   b. भाई

3. तुम कितने _____ में कपड़े धोते हो? (homes)

   a. तालाबों   b. घरों

4. क्या तुम यह काम _____ ? (will do)

   a. करोगे   b. देखोगे

5. क्या आपको कपड़े _____ हैं? (to cause to be washed)

   a. धुलवाने   b. लगवाने

6. तुम हर दो दिन बाद कपड़े _____ । (take away)

   a. ले जाना   b. ले आना

Practice 4 Comprehension Check
Answer the following questions.

1. रघुवीर कौन है?
   Who is Raghuveer?

   _____

2. माधव क्या काम करता है?
   What does Madhav do?

   _____

3. शीला को माधव से क्या-क्या करवाना है?
   What work does Sheela have Madhav do?

   _____

4. शीला को साड़ियों पर क्या लगवाना है?
   What does Sheela like to have put on the *saris*?

   _____

Practice 5

Listen to the second part of the conversation and do the exercises that follow.

Script 2

शीला : तो ठीक है, मुझे दो दिन में दिल्ली जाना है इसलिए मुझे कुछ ज़रूरी कपड़े धुलवाने है।

धोबी : आप को कपड़े कब चाहिए ?

शीला : मुझे परसों रात को जाना है इसलिए मुझे कपड़े कल शाम तक चाहिएँ। तुम आज मेरे कपड़े ले जाओ और इन्हें धोकर कल ले आना। सुनो कपड़े ठीक से धोना।

धोबी : लाइये, धुलने वाले कपड़े दे दीजिए।

शीला : यह लो, ये चार सूती साड़ियाँ हैं, इन पर कलफ़ लगाकर इस्त्री करवानी है और ये चार जोड़ी सलवार-कुर्ते हैं। इन्हें धोकर सिर्फ़ इस्त्री कर देना।

धोबी : ठीक है बहनजी और हाँ, भाई ने पिछले महीने का हिसाब माँगा है।

शीला : असल में माँ अभी घर पर नहीं हैं। हिसाब कल शाम को ले जाना।

धोबी : जी अच्छा नमस्ते।

Then answer the following comprehension questions in Hindi.

1. शीला को कपड़े कब चाहिएँ?
   When does Sheela need her clothes?

   _____

2. शीला को साड़ियों पर क्या लगवाना है?
   What does Sheela need on her *saris*?

   _____

3. धोबी ने शीला से क्या माँगा?
   What did the washerman ask Sheela?

   _____

Practice 6

Below are a few sentences. Read and determine the speaker of each sentence.

1. मुझे कुछ जरूरी कपड़े धुलवाने हैं।

   _____

2. लाइये, धुलने वाले कपड़े दे दीजिए।

   _____

3. मुझे दो दिन में दिल्ली जाना है।

   _____

4. आप को कपड़े कब चाहिएँ?

   _____

5. ये आपकी चार सूती साड़ियाँ, इन पर कलफ़ लगाकर इस्त्री कर दी है।

   _____

6. मेरा हिसाब दे दीजिए।

   _____

7. सुनो कपड़े ठीक से धोना!

_____

8. हिसाब कल शाम को ले जाना।

_____

Romanization 2

Sheila   : toe Theek hai, mü-jhay doe din maẏ dil-lee jaa-naa hai is-li-yay mü-jhay kuCh zer-oo-ree kup-rDay dhül-waa-nay hain.

dho-be : Aap-ko kup-rDay kub chaa-hi-yaẏ?

Sheila   : Mü-jhay per-só raat ko jaa-naa hai, is-li-yay mü-jhay kup-rDay k-ul shaam tuk chaa-hi-yaẏ. tüm aaj may-ray kup-rDay lay jaa-o aur in-haẏ dho-ker k-ul lay aa-naa. Sü-no kup-rDay Theek say dho-naa.

dho-be : Laa-iyay, dhül-nay waa-lay kup-rDay day di-ji-yay.

Sheila   : Yeh lo, yay chaar soo-tee saa-rD-iyà hain, in per kul-uf l-ug-aa-ker is-tree ker-waa-nee hai. Aur yay chaar jorDee sul-waar-kür-tay hai. In-haẏ dho-ker sirf is-tree ker day-naa.

dho-be : Theek hai beh-hen jee, aur haà bhaa-ee nay pi-Cha-lay muh-hi-nay kaa his-aab maà-gaa hai.

Sheila   : Us-ul maẏ mummy ub-he gh-er per nuh-heè hain. His-aab k-ul sham ko lay jaa-naa.

dho-be : Jee uch-Chaa num-us-tay.

Translation 2

Sheila   : All right then. Listen, I have to go to Delhi in two days, so I need to have these clothes washed.

Washerman : When do you want them?

Sheila   : I have to leave the night after tomorrow, so I need them by tomorrow evening.

Washerman : OK, why don't you go and get them?

Sheila   : Here are four cotton _saris_. Just iron them, with starch. And here are four pairs of _salvaar-kurtas_. Wash and iron them.

Washerman : No problem ma'am. My brother asked about his payment for last month.

Sheila   : Actually, mom isn't home right now. Come and collect the payment tomorrow night.

Washerman : All right ma'am. Bye.

6.2 Reporting a Theft चोरी की रिपोर्ट करना ।

Objectives

By the end of this lesson you will be able to:

1. Call the police.
2. Report a theft, using vocabulary such as *to get stolen, to report, cash, things* and present and past perfect tense to indicate whether the theft was a recent incident or otherwise.
3. Show concern about the incident.
4. Review the use of perfect tense for reporting an incident.

> 📖 **Culture Note**
>
> One must always be cautious when traveling. The easiest mistake one can make is being too trustworthy. Even locals have to deal with looters and con artists on a daily basis. Keep the essentials (money, passport, etc.) close to you. Accept that not everyone in uniform will be of valuable help. And most importantly, try to keep yourself safe from harm. India is a vast country with both good and bad people, so please be cautious to avoid being taken advantage of.

Vocabulary 06-04

Nouns

चोरी	(cho-ree)	*fem.*	theft
जानकारी	(jaan-kaa-ree)	*fem.*	information
कार्रवाई	(kaar-rvaa-ee)	*fem.*	action
सामान	(saa-maan)	*masc.*	stuff, things, luggage
नक़द	(na-q-ud)	*masc.*	cash
विदेश	(vi-day-sh)	*masc.*	foreign country
दूतावास	(doo-taa-vaas)	*masc.*	embassy
थाना	(thaa-naa)	*masc.*	police station
पता	(p-ut-aa)	*masc.*	address
संपर्क	(sum-perk)	*masc.*	contact

Verbs

लगना	(lug-naa)	*v.i.*	to feel, to seem
ठहरना	(Theh-herna)	*v.i.*	to stay
निकलना	(nik-ul-naa)	*v.i.*	to leave, to depart
रिपोर्ट मिलना	(report mil-naa)	*v.i.*	to receive a report
रिपोर्ट करना	(report ker-naa)	*v.t.*	to file a report
लिखवाना	(likh-waa-naa)	*caus. v.t.*	to cause to write
चोरी होना	(cho-ree ho-naa)	*v.i.*	to be stolen

चोरी जाना	(cho-ree jaa-naa)	*v.i.*	to be stolen
पता लगना	(puh-ut-aa lug-naa)	*v.i.*	to find out, to become aware about
पता चलना	(puh-ut-aa chuh-ul-naa)	*v.i.*	to find out, to become aware about
चला जाना	(ch-ul-aa jaa-naa)	*comp. v.i*	to be stolen
वापस आना	(vaap-us aa-naa)	*v.i.*	to come back
ग़ायब होना	(gaa-yub ho-naa)	*v.i.*	to disappear
शक़ होना	(shuh-uq ho-naa)	*v.i.*	to be doubtful/to suspect
बात करवाना	(baat ker-waa-naa)	*caus. v.t.*	to have connected with X
कार्रवाई करना	(kaar-rvaa-ee ker-naa)	*v.t.*	to take action
संपर्क करना	(sum-perk ker-naa)	*conj. v.t.*	to contact
दे देना	(day day-naa)	*comp. v.t.*	to give away

Miscellaneous

जब	(juh-ub)	*relative clause*	when
के बारे में	(kay baa-ray maẏ)	*comp. postposition*	about X
उसी समय	(ü-see sum-ay)	*adv.*	right away, right at the moment
परसों	(per-só)	*adv.*	day before, day after
तुरंत	(tür-unt)	*adv.*	immediately
किसी (कोई + का, की, के, को)	(ki-see)	*adj*	someone (to, of)

Grammar

Perfect Tense (Present and Past)

Structure 1: Transitive verbs with ने

• Subject + ने + object + verb root + या, यी, ये (simple perfect with transitive verbs)

आदमी ने काम किया।

(aad-mee nay kaam ki-yaa.)

The man did the work.

• Subject + ने + object + verb root + या, यी, ये + है, हैं (present perfect tense with transitive verbs)

लड़की ने आइसक्रीम खायी है।

(lerD-kee nay ice-cream khaa-yee hai.)

The girl has eaten the ice cream.

- Subject + ने + object + verb root + या, यी, ये + था, थी, थे (past perfect tense with
transitive verbs)

उसने   पैसे   लिये   थे।
(üs-nay paise li-yay thay.)
He had taken the money.

Structure 2: Intransitive verbs without ने
- Subject + verb root + या, यी, ये (simple perfect with intransitive verbs)
वह भारत गया।
(veh bhaa-rut guh-yaa.)
He went to India.

- Subject + verb root + या, यी, ये + है, हैं, हो (present perfect tense with intransitive verbs)
वह भारत गया है।
(veh bhaa-rut guh-yaa hai.)
He has gone to India.

- Subject + verb root + या, यी, ये + था, थी, थे (past perfect tense with intransitive verbs)
वह भारत गया था।
(veh bhaa-rut guh-yaa thaa.)
He had gone to India.

Practice 1 Vocabulary-Building Exercise
Match the words in the left column with their synonyms on the right.

1. ग़ायब होना   रहने की जगह की जानकारी
2. वापस आना   मालूम होना
3. पता   खो जाना
4. पता लगना   रुकना
5. ठहरना   बताना
6. रिपोर्ट करना   लौटना

Practice 2
Match the words in the left column with their corresponding antonyms on the right.

1. निकलना   उधार
2. ग़ायब हो जाना   स्वदेश
3. चले जाना   आना
4. विदेश   चलना
5. नक़द   आ जाना
6. ठहरना   मिल जाना

Practice 3 🎧 06-05

Listen to the conversation and complete the activities that follow.

Script 1

पुलिस : इस होटल से हमें चोरी की रिपोर्ट मिली है।
मोनिका : हाँ, मैंने रिपोर्ट की है।
पुलिस : हाँ बताइये मैडम, आप का क्या क्या सामान चोरी हुआ है और कहाँ से चोरी हुआ है?
मोनिका : होटल एम्बेसेडर के कमरा नंबर चार सौ दो से। मैं वहाँ दो दिन से ठहरी हुई हूँ।
पुलिस : आपका क्या क्या सामान चोरी हुआ है और ये आपको कब पता लगा?
मोनिका : जी मेरे ऑफ़िस का कंप्यूटर, मेरा सूटकेस, जिसमें मेरे कपड़े, मेरा टिकट, मेरा पासपोर्ट और कुछ नकद, सब कुछ चला गया।
पुलिस : चोरी के समय आप कहाँ थी?
मोनिका : उस समय मैं नहा रही थी। नहाकर जब मैं वापस आयी तो देखा कि मेरा सामान ग़ायब है।
पुलिस : आपने होटल मैनेजर को चोरी के बारे में कब बताया?
मोनिका : मैंने होटल मैनेजर को उसी समय बता दिया था।
पुलिस : आप को किसी पर शक़ है।
मोनिका : जी, मुझे लगता है होटल के ही किसी आदमी ने यह काम किया है।

Romanization 1

Pü-lis : Is hotel say h-um-aẏ cho-re kee report mil-ee hai.

Monica : Main-ay report ki hai.

Pü-lis : Haȧ but-aa-iyay madam, aap kaa kyaa-kyaa saa-maan cho-re hüaa hai aur kuh-haȧ say cho-re hüaa hai?

Monica : Hotel Ambassador kay kum-raa number chaar saw doe say. Main vuh-haȧ doe din say Theh-ree hu-ee hoȯ.

Pü-lis : Aap-kaa kyaa-kyaa saa-maan cho-re hüaa hai, aur yay aap-ko kub p-ut-aa l-ug-aa?

Monica : Jee may-ray office kaa computer, may-raa suitcase, jis-maẏ may-ray kup-rDay, may-raa Tick-uT, may raa passport aur küCh n-uq-ud sub küCh chuh-ul-aa guh-yaa.

Pü-lis : cho-re kay sum-uh-yuh aap kuh-haȧ theȧ.

Monica : Üs sum-uh-yuh main nuh-haa ruh-hee thee. nuh-haa ker j-ub main vaa-puh-us aa-yee toe day-khaa ki may-raa saa-maan guh-aa-yub hai.

Pü-lis : Aap-nay hotel manager ko cho-re kay baa-ray maẏ kub but-aa-yaa?

Monica : Main-ay hotel manager ko cho-re kay baa-ray maẏ üs-see sum-uh-yuh but-aa di-yaa thaa.

Pü-lis : Aap-ko ki-see per sh-ucq hai?

Monica : Jee mü-jhay l-ug-taa hai hotel kay he ki-see aad-me nay yeh kaam ki-yaa hai.

Comprehension Check

Answer the following comprehension questions.

1. List the things that are missing from the room.
   कमरे से चोरी हुए सामान की सूचि बनाइये।

2. When was the theft reported?
    चोरी की जानकारी कब दी गई?

    _____

3. Whom does Monica suspect for the theft?
    मोनिका को किस पर शक़ है?

    _____

4. Where was Monica at the time of the theft?
    चोरी के समय मोनिका कहाँ थी?

    _____

Practice 4

Choose the correct word, and fill in the blank. Hints are given in English for you to choose the right word for the blank.

1. इस होटल से हमें _____ की रिपोर्ट मिली है। (theft)
    a. छोरी   b. चोरी

2. मुझे चोरी की रिपोर्ट _____ है। (to cause to be written)
    a. दिखवानी   b. लिखवानी

3. होटल _____ किसी आदमी ने यह काम किया है। (hotel's only [*masc. pl.*])
    a. के ही   b. की ही

4. मेरा पासपोर्ट और कुछ नकद _____ चल गया। (everything)
    a. कुछ भी   b. सब कुछ

5. आपका क्या _____ चोरी हुआ है? (things/luggage)
    a. समान   b. सामान

Translation 1

Policeman : We received a report of a theft from this hotel.
Monica   : Yes, I reported it.
Policeman : Yes ma'am. Now tell me, what belongings of yours have been taken and
            where did it happen?
Monica   : Here at the hotel. Room number 402 is where it happened. I have been
            staying here for two days.
Policeman : What has been stolen? And when exactly did you find out?

Monica	:	My work computer, my mobile phone, and my suitcase which had all my clothes, my tickets, my passport, and some cash. They're all gone now.
Policeman	:	Where were you at the time of the theft?
Monica	:	At that time I was taking a bath. After I finished taking the bath, I saw that everything was gone.
Policeman	:	When did you report the theft to the hotel manager?
Monica	:	I reported it right away.
Policeman	:	Do you suspect anyone?
Monica	:	I'm not exactly sure, but I suspect that maybe someone from the hotel did it.

Practice 5 Vocabulary-Building Exercise

Match the words on the left column with their corresponding synonyms on the right.

1.	कब तक	जल्द ही
2.	वापस निकलना	मालूम होना
3.	ठहरना	कितने दिनों तक
4.	बात करवाना	रुकना
5.	जानकारी देना	संपर्क करवाना
6.	तुरंत	लौटना
7.	पता चलना	किसी के बारे में बताना

Practice 6 🎧 06-06

Listen to the second half of the conversation and complete the activity that follows.

Script 2

पुलिस	:	अच्छा आप यहाँ कब तक ठहरेंगी?
मोनिका	:	मुझे तो कल ही वापस निकलना था।
पुलिस	:	कहाँ के लिए?
मोनिका	:	दिल्ली के लिए। परसों मेरी अमरीका वापस जाने की उड़ान है।
पुलिस	:	अच्छा मैडम आप हमारे साथ पुलिस थाने चलिए। वहाँ हम आपके दूतावास से आपकी बात करवाएँगे, आप अपने पासपोर्ट चोरी होने की जानकारी उन्हें दे दीजिएगा। आपके सामान को ढूँढने की कार्रवाई हम तुरंत शुरू कर रहे हैं। पता चलते ही आपसे संपर्क करेंगे।
मोनिका	:	ठीक है।
पुलिस	:	आप अपना पता और फोन नम्बर हमें लिखवा दें।

Romanization 2

Pü-lis	:	Uch-Chaa aap yuh-haä kub t-uk Theh-raẏ-gee?
Monica	:	Mü-jhay to k-ul hee vaap-us nik-ul-naa thaa.
Pü-lis	:	Kuh-haä kay li-yay?
Monica	:	Dil-lee kay li-yay. Per-sȯ may-re Um-ree-kaa vaap-us jaa-nay kee urDaan hai.

Pü-lis : Uch-Chaa madam aap h-um-aa-ray saa-th pü-lis thaa-nay ch-ul-i-yay vuh-haȧ h-um aap-kay doo-taa-vaas say aap-kee baat ker-waa-yaẏ-gay, aap up-naa passport cho-re ho-nay kee jaan-kaa-ree un-haẏ day-dee-ji-yay-gaa. Aap-kay saa-maan ko Dhoȯ-dh-nay kee kaar-r-vaa-yee hum tü-runt shü-roo ker ruh-hay hain. P-ut-aa ch-ul-tay he aap-say sum-perk ker-aẏ-gay.

Monica : Theek hai.

Pü-lis : Aap up-naa p-ut-aa aur phone number hum-aẏ likh-waa daẏ.

Write down the sentences from the conversation in which instructions were given, and translate them into English.

1. Hindi sentence: _____

    English translation: _____

2. Hindi sentence: _____

    English translation: _____

Write down the sentences that have causative verbs. In what context are they used?

1. _____

2. _____

Practice 7
Answer the following comprehension questions in Hindi.

1. What is Monica's plan for the next day?

    _____

2. Where did the police go to investigate the theft report?

    _____

How would you say these phrases in Hindi?

1. I need to file a report.

    _____

2. My things have been stolen.

   _____

3. I was at the restaurant downstairs.

   _____

4. What should I do now?

   _____

5. I have to return home tomorrow.

   _____

6. Can you connect me to my embassy?

   _____

Translation 2

Policeman : OK, how many more days are you planning to stay here at the hotel?
Monica   : I am supposed to leave tomorrow.
Policeman : For where?
Monica   : I have a flight back to my home country the next day.
Policeman : OK ma'am, come with us to the police station and we'll get in touch with your embassy to file a stolen passport report. As for your belongings we will get right to it, and we will contact you if we find anything.
Monica   : Ok.
Policeman : Please give us your contact information.

6.3 At the Doctor's डॉक्टर के यहाँ।

Objectives

By the end of this lesson, you will be able to:
1. Talk to a doctor in Hindi.
2. State your symptoms using the verbs hona होना and lagna लगना to express physical and mental states of being in the present progressive tense.
3. State your concern about your health.

> 📖 **Culture Note**
>
> Health insurance is a rather new concept in India, and only a few can afford it. For the common person, all medical businesses are run on a cash basis. If you are a foreigner, doctors in India may not accept the insurance that you have for medical treatment in your country. It does not mean that you will not get good treatment. It's just how the Indian health infrastructure works. Most doctors own a practice and run the entire facility or a clinic. They may or may not be affiliated with a hospital. So use your discretion when getting your treatment. As for filling a prescription, take your prescription to any pharmacy, pay cash, and it will be filled right away. In fact all these privately owned medical facilities also run a pharmacy; however, you are not bound to buy from them.

Vocabulary 06-07

Nouns

तक़लीफ़	(tuq-leaf)	*fem.*	problem, pain
ज़ुकाम	(zü-kaam)	*masc.*	head cold
बुख़ार	(bü-khaar)	*masc.*	fever
खाँसी	(khaȧ-see)	*fem.*	coughing
कमज़ोरी	(kum-zo-ree)	*fem.*	weakness
ठंड	(Th-unD)	*fem.*	cold
दवाई/दवा	(d-uv-aa/ee)	*fem.*	medicine
मुँह	(müh)	*masc.*	mouth, face
गला	(g-ul-aa)	*masc.*	throat
तबियत	(tub-i-yut)	*fem.*	condition (when sick)
दर्द	(derd)	*masc.*	pain
फ़ायदा	(faay-daa)	*masc.*	benefit
ख़ून	(khoon)	*masc.*	blood
पर्ची	(per-chee)	*fem.*	prescription, a piece of paper
जाँच	(jaȧ-ch)	*fem.*	test

Adjectives

बहुत	(buh-hüt)		very, a lot
तेज़	(tay-z)		high (temperature)
कोई	(ko-ee)		any, someone
कुछ	(küCh)		some, few
कितना	(kit-naa)	*masc. sing.*	how many, how much
कितने	(kit-nay)	*masc. pl.*	how many, how much
ख़ूब सारा	(khoob saa-raa)	*masc. sing.*	lots of
अपना	(up-naa)	*masc. sing.*	yours, my, his, her, their

Adverbs

सुबह	(süb-uh)	*fem.*	morning
शाम	(shaam)	*fem.*	evening

Verbs

होना	(ho-naa)	*v.i.*	to be
देखना	(day-kh-naa)	*v.t.*	to see, to look
दिखाना	(dikh-aa-naa)	*v.t.*	to show
उतर जाना	(üter jaa-naa)	*comp. v.i.*	to come down
घबराना	(gh-ub-raa-naa)	*v.i.*	to be anxious, worried
लगना	(l-ug-naa)	*v.i.*	to seem, to look, to appear
हो जाना	(ho jaa-naa)	*comp. v.i.*	to become, to happen
लेते रहना	(lay-tay reh-naa)	*conj. v.t.*	to continue to take

Grammar

होना (**hona** "to be") and लगना (**lagna** "to feel") are used to express physical and mental states of being, and होना as a final auxiliary verb.

Progressive Tense

The progressive tense indicates an action that is taking place in the present time, or was in progress at a certain time in the past. Hindi progressive tense is made up of five parts: the subject (direct); the object; the verb root/stem; the progressive endings रहा (*masc.*) रही (*fem.*) and रहे (*pl.*) which agree with the subject in gender and number; and the final part is the auxiliary verb based on the time frame: for present auxiliary है (is), हैं or हो (are) or past auxiliary था, थी or थे is used.

Refer to the following structures:

• **Structure 1**

Subject +	Object +	Verb root +	रहा, रही, रहे +	है, है, हो/था,थी, थे	
(direct)			(*masc./fem./pl.*)	(*masc./fem./pl.*)	
मैं (*masc., sing*)	पानी	पी	रहा	हूँ/था। था।	Regular verb use

(müJh-ay khaå-see ho ruh-hee hai/thee.)

I		water		drinking	am/was

= I am/was drinking water.

• **Structure 2**

Subject + (indirect)	Object +	Verb root +	रहा, रही, रहे (*masc./fem./pl.*)	है, हैं, हो/था,थी, थे (*masc./fem./pl.*)	
मुझे	खाँसी (*fem., sing.*)	हो	रही	है/थी।	Conjunct verb use with होना

(müJh-ay khaan-see ho ruh-hee hai/thee.)

| I (to me) | cough | having (literally: is happening) | | am/was | |

= I am/was having a cough.

Use of होना as a final auxiliary verb in a direct sentence with an adjective

Read the sentences to practice the phrases:

To be sick: बीमार होना

मैं बीमार हूँ/वह बीमार है/ये बीमार हैं/वे बीमार हैं।
(main bee-maar hoȯ. veh bee-maar hai/yay bee-maar hain/vay bee-maar hain.)
I am sick./he is sick./he or she *(hon.)* is sick./he or she is sick *(hon.)*.

To be weak: कमज़ोर होना

वह कमज़ोर है/वे कमज़ोर हैं/तुम कमज़ोर हो/आप कमज़ोर हैं।
(veh kum-zor hai/vay kum-zor hain/tüm kum-zor ho/aap kum-zor hain.)
he or she is weak/he or she is weak *(hon.)*./you are weak *(fam.)*/you are weak *(hon.)*

To be tired: थका/थकी/थके होना

मैं थका हूँ/मैं थकी हूँ/तुम थके हो/थकी हो/यह, वह थका है/थकी है/ ये, वे थके हैं/थकी हैं।
(main thuk-aa hoȯ/main thuk-ee hoȯ/tüm thuk-ay ho/thuk-ee ho/yeh, veh thuk-aa hai/thuk-ee hai/yay, vay thuk-ay hain/thuk-ee hain.)
I am tired *(masc.)*/I am tired *(fem.)*/you are tired/he or she is tired/he or she, they are tired *(hon.)*

To be worried: परेशान होना

मैं परेशान हूँ/तुम क्यों परेशान हो? आप क्यों परेशान हैं?
(main per-ay-shaan hoȯ/tüm kyȯ per-ay-shaan ho? aap kyȯ per-ay-shaan hain?)
I am worried./Why are you worried? *(fam.)*/Why are you worried? *(hon.)*

Using होना as a final auxiliary verb in an indirect sentence with a noun

I have a cold.	मुझे ज़ुकाम है।	(Literally: To me the cold is)
	(müJh-ay zü-kaam hai.)	
I have a fever.	मुझे बुखार है।	
	(müJh-ay bü-khaar hai.)	
I have a cough.	मुझे खाँसी है।	
	(müJh-ay khaan-see hai.)	
I have a headache.	मेरे सिर में दर्द है।	(Literally: In my head the pain is.)
	(may-ray sir main der-d hai.)	
I have a stomachache.	मेरे पेट में दर्द है।	
	(may-ray pay-T main der-d hai.)	

All these sentences above indicate a person's state of being. Note that in Hindi, the postposition को is used to mark a direct object (a person). In the first three English examples given above, "I" is the logical subject of Hindi, which is always followed by the postposition को, literally, meaning "to" in English.

When a person is "getting sick"—showing an occurring or ongoing condition—then the verb होना will either appear in the present progressive tense or in the present perfect tense using the compound verb हो जाना. The present perfect tense shows that the action has recently occurred and still exists in the present time.

Compare the sentences below with those given earlier.

Present Progressive	**Present Perfect**
I am having a cold.	I have a cold.
मुझे ज़ुकाम हो रहा है।	मुझे ज़ुकाम हो गया है। (*comp. v.i.*)
(müJh-ay zü-kaam ho ruh-haa hai.)	(müJh-ay zü-kaam ho guh-yaa hai.)
I am having a fever.	I have a fever.
मुझे बुखार हो रहा है।	मुझे बुखार हो गया है। (*comp. v.i.*)
(müJh-ay bü-khaar ho ruh-haa hai.)	(müJh-ay bü-khaar ho guh-yaa hai.)
I am having a cough.	I have a cough.
मुझे खाँसी हो रही है।	मुझे खाँसी हो गयी है। (*comp. v.i.*)
(müJh-ay khaȧ-see ho ruh-hee hai.)	(müJh-ay khaȧ-see ho guh-yee hai.)
I am having a headache.	
मेरे सिर में दर्द हो रहा है।	
(may-ray si-r mein der-d ho ruh-haa hai.)	

I am having stomachache.
मेरे पेट में <u>दर्द</u> हो रहा है।
(may-ray pay-T mein der-d ho ruh-haa hai.)

The verb **लगना** has many usages in Hindi. One of them is to express feelings or bodily conditions. It is also used to mean "looks," "seems," and "appears to be."

With nouns

I am feeling cold.	मुझे ठंड लग रही है। (müJh-ay Th-und l-ug ruh-hee hai.)
I have a cold.	मुझे ठंड लग गयी है। (müJh-ay Th-und l-ug guh-yee hai.)
I am feeling hot.	मुझे गर्मी लग रही है। (müJh-ay ger-mee l-ug ruh-hee hai.)
I have gotten sunstroke/heatstroke.	मुझे लू लग गयी है। (müJh-ay loo l-ug guh-yee hai.)
I am feeling weak.	मुझे कमज़ोरी लग रही है। (müJh-ay k-um-zo-ree l-ug ruh-hee hai.)
I am feeling tired.	मुझे थकान लग रही है। (müJh-ay Thuk-aan l-ug ruh-hee hai.)

With adjectives

She seems to be sick.	वह बीमार लग रही है। (veh bee-maar l-ug luh-hee hai.)
He seems to be tired.	वह थका लग रहा है। (veh th-uk-aa l-ug ruh-haa hai.)
He looks worried.	वे परेशान लग रहे हैं। (vay per-ay-shaan l-ug ruh-hay hain.)

Practice 1 Vocabulary-building

Label the pictures with the appropriate Hindi words.

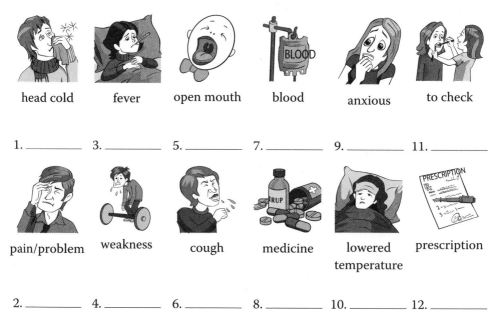

head cold   fever   open mouth   blood   anxious   to check

1. _____ 3. _____ 5. _____ 7. _____ 9. _____ 11. _____

pain/problem   weakness   cough   medicine   lowered temperature   prescription

2. _____ 4. _____ 6. _____ 8. _____ 10. _____ 12. _____

Do you remember when you last visited a doctor for a common illness such as a fever, cold, or cough? Recall the conversation that you had with your doctor and write it down on a piece of paper. Write short and simple phrases in English. Next, translate those sentences that you have just written into Hindi. If needed, refer to the vocabulary you previewed in earlier activities.

_____

_____

_____

_____

_____

_____

_____

Practice 2 🎧 06-08

Listen to the conversation and try to pronounce the vocabulary correctly as well as get used to the grammatical structure. Read along with the audio.

Script 1

मोहन   : नमस्ते डॉक्टर साहब।

डॉक्टर : कहो, क्या तक़लीफ़ है?

मोहन   : मुझे बहुत तेज़ ज़ुकाम हो रहा है और खाँसी भी हो रही है।

डॉक्टर : क्या बुखार भी हो रहा है?

मोहन   : हाँ कुछ दिनों से बुखार भी है।

डॉक्टर : कितने दिनों से बुखार है?

मोहन   : तीन-चार दिनों से।

डॉक्टर : कमज़ोरी महसूस होती है?

मोहन   : हाँ, बहुत कमज़ोरी महसूस हो रही है।

डॉक्टर : अपना गला दिखाओ, मुँह खोलो। देखूँ कितना बुखार है अभी। ऐसा लगता है कि तुम्हें कोई इन्फ़ैक्शन हो गया है।

मोहन   : कोई घबराने वाली बात तो नहीं है डॉक्टर साहब?

डॉक्टर : नहीं, नहीं तुम्हें ठंड लग गयी है और इन्फ़ैक्शन हो गया है। मैं बुखार उतारने की कुछ दवाइयाँ लिख रहा हूँ। नीचे जाकर फ़ार्मेसी से ले लो। इसे खाने के साथ एक सुबह और एक शाम को लो और खूब सारा पानी भी पियो। एक हफ़्ते बाद मुझे फिर आकर दिखाना।

Romanization 1

Mohan : Num-us-tay doctor saa-hub.

Doctor : Kuh-ho, kyaa tuq-leaf hai?

Mohan : Müj-hay buh-hüt tayz zukh-aam ho ruh-haa hai aur khà-see bhee ho ruh-hee hai.

Doctor : Kyaa bukh-aar bhee ho ruh-haa hai?

Mohan : Haà küCh din-ò say bükh-aar bhee hai.

Doctor : Kit-nay din-ò say bükh-aar hai?

Mohan : Teen-chaar din-ò say.

Doctor : Kum-zo-ree meh-soos ho-tee hai?

Mohan : Haà, buh-hüt kum-zo-ree meh-soos ho ruh-hee hai.

Doctor : up-naa gul-aa dikh-aao, mühn kho-lo, day-khoò kit-naa bü-khaar hai ub-hee. Aai-saa I-ug-taa hai ki tüm-heỳ koi infaction ho guh-yaa hai.

Mohan : Koi ghub-raa-nay vaa-lee baat tow nuh-heè hai doctor saa-hub?

Doctor : Nuh-heè, nuh-heè tüm-heỳ Th-unD lug guh-yee hai aur infaction ho guh-yaa hai. Main bü-khaar ütaar-nay ki küCh duv-aa yuh-haà likh ruh-haa hù. nee-chay jaa-ker farmacy say ay lo. Is-ay khaa-nay kay saa-th ayk süb-uh aur ayk sh-aam ko lo aur khoob saa-raa paa-nee bhee pi-yo. Ayk huf-tay baad mu-jhay phir aa-ker dikh-aanaa.

Practice 3 Post-Listening Exercise

Translate the following phrases into Hindi.

1. I am not feeling well.

_____

2. I've had a fever for the last three days.

_____

3. I am feeling cold.

_____

4. I feel very weak.

_____

5. I have a cold.

_____

6. I am coughing a lot.

_____

7. Is there anything to worry about?

_____

Practice 4
Translate the conversation and match your translation with the script.

_____

_____

_____

_____

_____

Practice 5
Then listen one more time for overall understanding, and answer the following questions in Hindi:

1. मोहन को क्या तक़लीफ़ है?
   What problem does Mohan have? _____

2. क्या मोहन घबरा रहा है?
   Is Mohan worried or anxious? _____

3. डॉक्टर को क्या लगता है, मोहन को बुखार क्यों है?
   What does the doctor think about Mohan's fever? What is the reason for his fever?

   _____

4. मोहन को दवाई कहाँ से मिलेगी?
   Where can Mohan get the medicine?

   _____

5.   डॉक्टर ने मोहन को दवा कैसे और कब लेने को कहा है?
     What instructions did the doctor give regarding the time and the manner of taking
     the medicine?

Translation 1

Mohan   :   Good day doctor.
Doctor :   Tell me what is wrong with you.
Mohan   :   I have a really bad head cold and a cough.
Doctor :   Do you have a fever as well?
Mohan   :   Yes, I've had a fever for a few days now.
Doctor :   How many days have you had the fever?
Mohan   :   3–4 days.
Doctor :   Do you feel weak?
Mohan   :   Yes, very weak.
Doctor :   Let me see your throat, open your mouth. It seems like you have contracted a
            virus.
Mohan   :   Is it serious?
Doctor :   No. I am prescribing you some medication that will relieve your fever. Go get
            it from the pharmacy downstairs. Take it twice a day: once in the morning,
            and once at night with food and plenty of water. Come back in a week for a
            follow-up.

Practice 6

Follow-up Appointment
Listen to the dialogue of Mohan's next visit with the doctor.

Script 2

डॉक्टर :   तो अब कैसी तबियत है तुम्हारी? क्या दवा से बुखार उतरा?
मोहन   :   हाँ डॉक्टर साहब, बुखार तो उतर गया है, लेकिन मेरे सिर और गले में अभी भी बहुत दर्द है।
डॉक्टर :   क्या निगलने में तक़लीफ़ हो रही है?
मोहन   :   हाँ, कुछ भी खाने-पीने में बहुत दर्द होता है।
डॉक्टर :   बुखार कब उतरा?
मोहन   :   चार दिन हो गये हैं।
डॉक्टर :   मैं तुम्हारे लिए एक ब्लड टैस्ट लिख रहा हूँ। नीचे लैब में जाकर टैस्ट करवा लेना। और अपनी दवाइयाँ
            लेते रहना, हो सकता है कि उससे कुछ और फ़ायदा हो।
मोहन   :   ठीक है डॉक्टर साहब।
डॉक्टर :   यह रही खून के जाँच की पर्ची, आज ही जाकर करवा लेना और दो दिन बाद मुझसे आकर मिलना।

Romanization 2

Doctor : Toe ub tub-i-yut kai-see hai tüm-haa-ree? Kyaa d-uw-aa say bü-khaar üt-raa?

Mohan : Haȧ Doctor saa-hub, bü-khaar toe üter guh-yaa hai, lay-kin may-ray g-ul-ay maẏ ubhee bhee buh-hüt derd hai.

Doctor : Kyaa nig-ul-nay maẏ tuq-leaf ho ruh-hee hai?

Mohan : Haȧ küCh bhee khaa-nay pee-nay maẏ buh-hüt derd ho-taa hai.

Doctor : Bü-khaar kub üt-raa?

Mohan : chaar din ho guh-yay hain.

Doctor : Main tüm-haa-ray li-yay ayk blood test likh ruh-haa hoȯ. Nee-chay lab maẏ jaa-ker test ker-waa lay-naa, aur up-nee d-uw-aa-i-yaȧ lay-tay reh-naa, ho suk-taa hai ki üs-say küCh faay-daa ho.

Mohan : Theek hai doctor saa-hub.

Doctor : Yeh ruh-he kh-oon ki jaȧ-ch kee per-chee, aaj hi jaa-ker ker-waa lay-naa aur doe din baad mü-jh-say aa-ker mil-naa.

Practice 7 Post-Listening Exercise

Write down the sentences from the conversation that convey bodily symptoms of illness and translate them into English.

1. Hindi sentence: _____

    English translation: _____

2. Hindi sentence: _____

    English translation: _____

3. Hindi sentence: _____

    English translation: _____

Practice 8

Write down four questions that the doctor asked and translate them into English.

1. Hindi sentence: _____

    English translation: _____

2. Hindi sentence: _____

    English translation: _____

3. Hindi sentence: _____

    English translation: _____

4. Hindi sentence: _____

    English translation: _____

Practice 9

Write down the doctor's instructions to Mohan and translate them into English.

1. Hindi sentence: _____

    English translation: _____

2. Hindi sentence: _____

    English translation: _____

3. Hindi sentence: _____

    English translation: _____

4. Hindi sentence: _____

    English translation: _____

Translation 2

Doctor : So how are you feeling now? Did the medication help with the fever?
Mohan : Yes, the fever has come down, but my head and my throat still hurt considerably.
Doctor : Do you have trouble swallowing?
Mohan : Yes, whenever I drink or eat something, I feel pain.
Doctor : How long has it been since the fever went away?
Mohan : Four days ago.
Doctor : I am going to suggest that we run a blood test. There is a lab downstairs. Go get it done there and meanwhile keep taking the medication, and we'll see if that helps.
Mohan : OK.
Doctor : Here's a referral, go and get it done today, and come back for your results in two days.

6.4 Hiring a Maid नौकरानी रखना

Objectives

By the end of this lesson, you will be able to:

1. Communicate with a maid.
2. Interview a maid and hire her for the job.
3. Give the maid directions to carry out tasks, using neutral imperative and compound verbs.

> 📖 **Culture Note**
>
> Since the caste system was established in Indian society centuries ago, the people who would serve others in terms of doing low-end jobs such as cleaning dishes, washing clothes, mopping and sweeping floors, cleaning bathrooms, and the like are of the lowest caste. They are very much in demand, and the entire nation relies on them. This tradition still continues and nowadays as the families have become nuclear and both husband and wife work outside of the home, a maid is needed to do household chores every day. There are many agencies in India who contract out maids. But India is a country of billions of people and there are very many of them who need employment and are not affiliated with any agency of this sort. Due to the lack of education, money, and information, they work for daily wages. The agencies that supply maids do a background check before the maid starts working anywhere, due to the increased number of theft and other unpleasant incidents especially in metropolitan cities like Delhi. So beware, use your discretion when hiring a maid.

Vocabulary 🎧 06-11

Nouns

काम	(kaam)	*masc.*	work
बर्तन	(ber-t-un)	*masc.*	utensil
खाना	(khaa-naa)	*masc.*	food
घर	(gh-er)	*masc.*	house
समय	(sum-ay)	*masc.*	time
पिता	(pi-taa)	*masc.*	father
जगह	(jug-uh)	*fem.*	space, place
कामवाली	(kaam-vaa-lee)	*fem.*	maid

Verbs

करना	(ker-naa)	*v.t.*	to do
माँजना	(maȧ-juh-naa)	*v.t.*	to clean (a dish)
पकाना	(puk-aa-naa)	*v.t.*	to cook

शुरू करना	(shürü ker-naa)	*conj. v.t.*	to begin
देना	(day-naa)	*v.t.*	to give
करवाना	(ker-waa-naa)	*caus. v.t.*	to have done
बनवाना	(bun-vaa-naa)	*caus. v.t.*	to have made
रहना	(reh-naa)	*v.t.*	to live
कर देना	(ker day-naa)	*comp. v.t.*	to do
बना देना	(bun-aa day-naa)	*comp. v.t.*	to make
पका देना	(puk-aa day-naa)	*comp. v.t.*	to cook
ख़त्म कर देना	(kh-utm ker day-naa)	*comp. v.t.*	to finish up
धो देना	(dho day-naa)	*comp. v.t.*	to wash up

Grammar Review: Habitual Present, Causative

We have already covered the habitual present tense in an earlier chapter. This part of the conversation is very similar to the routine conversations previously covered, except that this is a conversation between the lady of the house and a maid.

Verbs, and Compound Verbs with देना

Remember the compound verb in chapter 2 (page102)? The compound verb लेना gives the benefit of the action to its doer, while the compound verb देना benefits someone other than the doer. The compound verb जाना indicates a completed action in the present, past, and future. All these compound verbs produce shades of meaning and convey a lower intensity of expression, that is, if a command is given with a regular verb, it becomes a suggestion in a compound verb.

Practice 1

Follow the example in the first column and conjugate the following verbs.

Main verb	Habitual Present	Perfect	Future
कर लेना (example)	कर लेता/लेती/कर लेती/कर लेते	कर लिया/कर ली/ कर लिये/कर लीं	कर लेगा/कर लेगी/ कर लेंगी/कर लेंगे
1. ले लेना (to take away)			
2. आ जाना (to come back)			
3. बना देना (to make ready)			
4. पका देना (to cook)			

	Main verb	Habitual Present	Perfect	Future
5.	चले जाना (to go back)			
6.	बैठ जाना (to sit down)			
7.	कर लेना (to complete work)			
8.	माँज लेना (to wash up dishes)			
9.	कर जाना (to finish up and go)			

Practice 2

Translate the following sentences into Hindi using a compound verb and causatives.

1. Finish all the work before I come home. (Use the compound verb कर लेना in the neutral imperative.)

   _____

2. The maid has prepared the food. (Use the compound verb बना लेना in the present perfect tense)

   _____

3. Before I come home, wash all the dishes. (Use the compound verb माँज देना in the habitual present)

   _____

4. Clean up the house. (Use the compound verb साफ़ कर देना in the familiar imperative form/command)

   _____

5. You go, I will do all the work. (Use the compound verb कर लेना in the future tense.)

   _____

6. Listen, have her make the food before I come home. (Use the compound verb बनवा लेना in the causative neutral imperative form.)

_____

Practice 3
Fill in the blanks as indicated. Remember the subject-verb conjugation in your answer.

1. _____ नाम क्या है?
   (your [familiar imperative])

2. _____ नाम मीना है।
   (my)

3. तुम क्या क्या _____ _____ _____?
   (work you do)

4. मैं _____ _____ हूँ और खाना भी _____ हूँ।
   (clean the dishes)   (cook)

5. _____ _____ _____ काम करती हो?
   (in how many houses)

6. _____ _____ _____ बर्तन माँजती हूँ और _____ _____ _____ में खाना पकाती हूँ।
   (in five houses)   (in two houses)

7. _____ कितने बजे काम _____ _____ _____?
   (morning)   (begin working)

8. जी सुबह ६ बजे _____ दोपहर के २ बजे _____ काम करती हूँ।
              (from)   (till)

9. क्या _____ _____ भी काम करती हो ?
   (in the evening)

Practice 4 🎧 06-12
Listen to the conversation and complete the exercise that follows.

Script 1
मालिकन   : तुम्हारा नाम क्या है?
कामवाली : जी मेरा नाम मीना है।

मालकिन : तुम क्या क्या काम करती हो?
कामवाली : जी मैं बर्तन माँजती हूँ और खाना भी पकाती हूँ।
मालकिन : कितने घरों में काम करती हो?
कामवाली : पाँच घरों में बर्तन माँजती हूँ और २ घरों में खाना पकाती हूँ।
मालकिन : सुबह कितने बजे काम शुरू करती हो?
कामवाली : जी सुबह ६ बजे से दोपहर के २ बजे तक काम करती हूँ।
मालकिन : क्या शाम को भी काम करती हो ?
कामवाली : जी शाम को एक घर में खाना पकाती हूँ।

Romanization 1

Maal-kin : tüm-haa-raa naam kyaa hai?
Kaam vaa-lee : Ji may-raa naam mee-naa hai.
Maal-kin : tüm kyaa kyaa kaam ker-tee ho?
Kaam-vaa-lee : Ji maiṅ bert-un maanj-tee hṅ aur khaa-naa bhee puk-aatee hoṅ.
Maal-kin : Kit-nay gharȯ meiṅ kaam ker-tee ho?
Kaam-vaa-lee : Paȧ-ch gharȯ meiṅ bert-un maanj-tee hoṅ aur though gharȯ meiṅ khaa-naa
puk-aatee hoṅ.
Maal-kiṅ : Süb-uh kit-nay buj-ay kaam shü-roo ker-tee ho?
Kaam-vaa-lee : Ji süb-uh 6 buj-ay say dow-pah-er kay though buj-ay tuk kaam ker-tee hoṅ.
Malkin : Kyaa shaam ko bhee kaam ker-tee ho?
Kaam-vaa-lee : Ji shaam ko ayk gher meiṅ khaa-naa puk-aatee hoṅ.

Post-Listening Exercise

Guess the meaning of each bold word in the sentences. Then translate the sentences.

1. तुम कल **दोपहर** में आना।

   Meaning: _____

   Translation: _____

2. मुझे रहने के लिए **जगह** भी चाहिए।

   Meaning: _____

   Translation: _____

3. क्या तुम **खाना पकाना** जानती हो?

   Meaning: _____

   Translation: _____

4.   **बर्तन माँजने** का कितना लोगी?

Meaning: _____

Translation: _____

5.   काम कब **से शुरु करना** है?

Meaning: _____

Translation: _____

Comprehension Questions [06-13]

Listen to the conversation and answer the following questions in Hindi.

1.   मीना क्या-क्या काम करती है?
     What types of work does Meena do?

     _____

2.   वह कितने बजे से कितने बजे तक काम करती है?
     What are her working hours?

     _____

3.   वह शाम को क्या करती है?
     What does she do in the evening?

     _____

Practice 5 Vocabulary-Building Exercise

1.   *Provide the Hindi meaning to the following words.*

1.   both times   _____   5.   place to live   _____

2.   utensils   _____   6.   date   _____

3.   to have made   _____   7.   to begin   _____

4.   work   _____   8.   to clean dishes   _____

2. *As a future employer list a few questions or statements that you may ask a maid.*

_____

_____

_____

Translation 1

Mistress : What is your name?
Meena   : My name is Meena.
Mistress : What work do you do?
Meena   : I wash utensils and cook food.
Mistress : How many houses do you work for?
Meena   : In five homes I clean utensils, and I cook for two houses.
Mistress : What time do you start working?
Meena   : I work from 6 a.m. to 2 p.m.
Mistress : Do you work in the evening?
Meena   : I cook the meal in the evening for one house.

Practice 6

Before attempting to listen to the conversation below (script 2), complete your part of the dialogue, whether it is a question or a response. The maid's part in the dialogue is given. Remember that this is the follow-up dialogue, which took place after you have finished talking to her about her routine. Think of what a maid might say and ask in such a situation.

नौकरानी: आपको क्या काम करवाना है?

आप: _____

नौकरानी: खाना कितने समय का बनवाना है?

आप: _____

नौकरानी: कितने पैसे देंगीं?

आप: _____

नौकरानी: कुछ और भी करवाना है?

आप: _____

नौकरानी: सफ़ाई के पैसे अलग से लूँगी।

आप: _____

नौकरानी: इन सबके तीन हज़ार रुपये महीना लूँगी।

आप: _____

Practice 7 🎧 06-14

Now listen to the following sentences and translate them. Also determine whether the speaker of each sentence is the employer or the maid.

1. मुझे बरतन करवाने हैं। _____

2. आपको खाना बनवाना है? _____

3. आपके यहाँ रहने की जगह है? _____

4. मैं आपके यहाँ खाना बना दूँगी। _____

5. मेरे पास समय नहीं है। _____

6. मैं अपने पति से बात करके बताऊँगी। _____

7. कितने पैसे महीना देंगीं? _____

Practice 8 🎧 06-15

Listen to the follow-up conversation and complete the activity that follows.

Script 2

मीना	:	बहनजी, आपको को क्या-क्या काम करवाना है?
मालकिन	:	मुझे दोनों समय का खाना बनवाना है, और बरतन भी करवाने हैं। करोगी?
मीना	:	नहीं, मेरे पास समय नहीं है।
मालकिन	:	मैं तुमको ज्यादा पैसा दूँगी।
मीना	:	कितने पैसे देंगी ?
मालकिन	:	दो हज़ार रूपये महीना।
मीना	:	क्या आप के यहाँ रहने की जगह होगी? क्योंकि जहाँ मैं रहती हूँ वहाँ शाम का खाना भी पकाती हूँ। आप के यहाँ रहूँगी तो आपके घर का काम भी कर दूँगी और खाना भी बना दूँगी।
मालकिन	:	तुम्हारे घर में कौन कौन है?
मीना	:	मैं और मेरे पिता जी।
मालकिन	:	ठीक है, मैं अपने पति से बात करके तुम को कल बताऊँगी। तुम कल शाम को ४ बजे आना ठीक है?

मीना : जी ठीक है, काम कब से शुरू करना होगा?
मालकिन : अगले महीने की पहली तारीख़ से।
मीना : जी ठीक है, नमस्ते।

Romanization 2

Meena : Beh-hen jee,aap-ko kyaa-kyaa kaam ker-waa-naa hai?
Maal-kin : Mü-jhay do-nȯ sum-ay kaa khaa-naa bun-waa-naa hai, aur ber-ton bhee ker-waa-nay hain, ker-o-gee?
Meena : Nuh-heė may-ray paas sum-ay nuh-heė hai.
Maal-kin : Main tüm-ko zyaa-daa pai-say doȯ-gee.
Meena : Kit-nay pai-say daẏ-gee?
Maal-kin : Doe huz-aar rüp-uh-yay muh-he-naa.
Meena : Kyaa app-kay yuh-haȧ reh-nay kay li-yay jug-uh ho-gee? Kyȯ-kee main juh-haȧ reh-tee hoȯ vuh-haȧ khaa-naa bhee puk-aa-tee hoȯ. Aap kay yuh-haȧ ruh-hoȯ-gee to aap-kay gher kaa kaam bhee ker doȯ-gee aur khaa-naa bhee bun-aa doȯ-gee.
Maal-kin : Tüm-haa-ray gher may kawn-kawn hai?
Meena : Main aur may-ray pit-aa-jee.
Maal-kin : Theek hai main up-nay p-ut-tee say baat ker-kay k-ul tüm-ko but-aa-oȯ-gee, tüm kuh-ul sham ko chaar buj-ay aa-naa. Theek hai?
Meena : Jee Theek hai, kaam kub say shü-rü ker-naa ho-gaa?
Maal-kin : Ug-lay muh-he-nay kee peh-lee taa-ree-kh say.
Meena : Jee Theek hai, num-us-tay.

Practice 9 Post-Listening Activity

1. *Write down the sentences from the conversation that used causative verbs, and translate them into English.*

1. Hindi sentence: _____

   English translation: _____

2. Hindi sentence: _____

   English translation: _____

3. Hindi sentence: _____

   English translation: _____

4. *Write down the sentence that best matches the translation for "Well, I'll discuss this with my husband and I will let you know tomorrow."*

_____

5. *Write down the sentences that contain the compound verbs and translate them into English.*

a. Hindi sentence: _____

   English translation: _____

b. Hindi sentence: _____

   English translation: _____

Translation 2

Meena   : Madam, what is the work you want done?
Mistress : I want dinner to be cooked and my utensils cleaned. Will you do it?
Meena   : No, I do not have time.
Mistress : I'll give you more money
Meena   : How much will you give?
Mistress : 2,000 rupees a month.
Meena   : Do you have a room available for me to live here? Because the place where I cook meals in the evening is also the place where I live.
Mistress : Who is there in your house?
Meena   : Me and my father.
Mistress : Well, I'll discuss this with my husband and I will let you know tomorrow. Come tomorrow in the evening at 4 p.m. Is that OK?
Meena   : When do I start working?
Mistress : The first of next month.
Meena   : All right, *namaste*.

6.5 Car Trouble गाड़ी ख़राब हो जाना।

Objectives

By the end of this lesson, you will be able to:

1. Talk to a mechanic or the repairman/owner of a shop.
2. State your car problem such as what happened to your car, what kind of help you need, and how much time it will take to do the necessary repairs, using conjunct and compound verbs.

> 📖 **Culture Note**
>
> If you were in India and driving on your own, always keep in mind that in case of car trouble, the emergency road services provided by AAA or your insurance company is not available there unless you buy the service from the manufacturer of your car. Most of the big car companies such as Maruti, Hyundai, Tata, Mahindra, Honda, and Nissan do provide roadside assistance emergency support if you have one of their cars. Their dealership is available throughout India at every 125 km. These companies provide roadside assistance 24/7. However if you have any other vehicle whose company does not provide this kind of service, then you will have to seek local assistance by conversing with locals or local mechanics in Hindi, especially in rural areas.

Vocabulary

Miscellaneous

कोई	(ko-ee)	*indef. pron.*	someone
किसी को	(ki-see ko)	*oblique indef. pron.*	to someone
के साथ	(kay saa-th)	*comp. pp.*	along with, with
के किनारे	(kay kin-aa-ray)	*comp. pp.*	on the side of...
के बीच	(kay bee-ch)	*comp. pp.*	in the middle of
ज़रूर	(zer-oor)	*adv.*	definitely
लगभग	(lug-bh-ug)	*adv.*	approximately
अचानक	(uch-aa-nuk)	*adv.*	suddenly
दूर	(door)	*adj.*	far
खाली	(khaa-lee)	*unmarked adj.*	free
किसी की	(ki-see kee)	*fem. adj.*	someone's
दूसरी	(doos-re)	*fem. adj.*	another, other
अजीब सी	(uj-eeb-see)	*fem. adj.*	rather strange
खड़ी	(kherD-ee)	*fem. adj.*	parked (car, bicycle etc.)
लेकिन	(lay-kin)	*conj.*	however, but
पास के	(paas kay)	*adj.*	nearby

Nouns

धुआँ	(dhu-aȧ)	*masc.*	smoke
तख़त	(tuh-kh-ut)	*masc.*	wooden bed
मालिक	(maa-lik)	*masc.*	owner
ख़याल	(khuh-yaal)	*masc.*	opinion

Verbs

भेजना	(bhayj-naa)	*v.t.*	to send
मिलना	(mil-naa)	*v.t.*	to get
चलाना	(ch-ul-aa-naa)	*v.t.*	to drive, to operate
आ जाना	(aa-jaa-naa)	*comp. v.t.*	to arrive, to come
खड़ी होना	(kherD-ee ho-naa)	*conj. v.i.*	to park
मालूम नहीं होना	(maa-loom nuh-heė ho-naa)	*conj. v.i.*	to be unaware of
आवाज़ करना	(aa-waaz ker-naa)	*conj. v.i.*	to make noise (engine, car)
ख़राब हो जाना	(kher-aab ho jaa-naa)	*conj. comp. v.i.*	to break down
खराबी आ जाना	(kher-aa-be aa jaa-naa)	*conj. comp. v.i.*	to have a problem
बंद हो जाना	(bund ho jaa-naa)	*conj. comp. v.i.*	to stop (as a mechanism)

Phrases

कोई बात नहीं	(ko-ee baat nuh-hee)	no problem
अभी लाता हूँ	(ub-hee laa-taa hoȯ)	I'll get it right away (male speaker)
क्यों नहीं	(kyȯ nuh-heė)	why not

Grammar

Conjunct and Compound Verbs

Conjunct verbs are formed with a noun or an adjective plus a verb. We will touch upon the conjunct verbs with आना, होना, and करना. The following are some examples and their use. Read them and practice saying them.

With a noun	Usage in various tenses	With an adjective	Usage in various tenses
आवाज़ आना (aa-waa-z aa-naa) to make noise	गाड़ी से आवाज़ आ रही है। (gaa-rDee say aa-waaz aa ruh-hee hai.) My car is making noise.	खड़ी होना (kherDee ho-naa) to park (*v.i.*)	मेरी गाड़ी <u>खड़ी है</u>। (may-ree gaa-rDee kherDee hai.) My car is parked.
इंतज़ार करना (in-te-zaar ker-naa) to wait	वह रोज़ बस का इंतज़ार करता है। (veh roz bus kaa in-te-zaar ker-taa hai.) He waits for the bus every day.	खड़ी करना (kherDee kar-naa) to park (*v.t.*)	मैं गाड़ी <u>खड़ी कर</u> रहा हूँ। (gaa-rDee main kher-aa-bee aa gayee hai.) I am parking the car.
ख़राबी आना (kher-aa-bee aa-naa) to have problems	गाड़ी में ख़राबी आ गई है। (gaa-rDee main kher-aa-bee aa gayee hai.) The car is having problems.	बंद होना (buh-und hona) to stop (*v.i.*)	मेरी गाड़ी <u>बंद हो गई है</u>। (may-ree gaa-rDee buh-und ho guh-yee hai.) My car has been stopped.

With a noun	Usage in various tenses	With an adjective	Usage in various tenses
ख़राबी होना (kher-aa-bee ho-naa) to have problems	मशीन में ख़राबी हो रही है। (m-ush-een main kher-aa-bee ho ruh hee hai.) The machine is having problems.	बंद करना (buh-und ker-naa) to shut down/turn off (*v.t.*)	गाड़ी को बंद करो। (gaa-rDee ko buh-und ker-o!) Turn off/shut down the car!
		ख़राब होना (gaa-rDee main Khee-aapbee aa gavee hai.) to break down (*v.i.*)	मेरी गाड़ी ख़राब हो गई है। (may-ree gaa-rDee kher-aab ho guh-ee hai.) My car has broken down.
		ख़राब करना (kher-aab ker-naa) to damage, to ruin (*v.t.*)	उस मैकेनिक ने मेरी गाड़ी ख़राब कर दी। (üs ma-ca-nick nay meri gaa-rDee kher-aab ker dee.) That mechanic has ruined my car.
		ठीक करना (Theek ker-naa) to repair (*v.t.*)	आप मेरी गाड़ी ठीक कर दीजिए। (aap may-ree gaa-rDee Theek ker dee-ji-yay.) Please repair my car.
		ठीक होना (Theek ho-naa) to repair (*v.i.*)	आपकी गाड़ी ठीक हो गई है। (aap-kee gaa-rDee Theek ho guh-yee.) Your car has been fixed/repaired.

Compound Verbs

As you have already learned in previous chapters, when two or more verbs are joined together, they are called compound verbs. They are made up of one main verb and an auxiliary verb, and convey a special meaning. Hindi uses many varieties of compound verbs. The verbs used with the auxiliary जाना indicate the completion of an action in the past, present, or future.

Remember:
1. Compound verbs are unique to the Hindi language.
2. Compound verbs cannot be used in a negative sentence and in the progressive tense.
3. जाना as an auxiliary verb is inflected based on gender, number, tense, or voice.
4. जाना always compounds with an intransitive verb and indicates the completion of an action.
5. Compound verbs are used frequently with verbs of motion.
6. Compound verbs have shades of meaning.
7. A simple verb when used in the simple perfect tense to narrate a past action indicates that the "thought" is not yet complete; it is completed only when a sentence ends with a compound verb, thus completing the action or the thought.
8. A simple verb in the future tense indicates the certainty of an action, while its compound use in the future tense indicates probability.
9. To master the compound verb, one has to be fully and completely immersed in the language.

Examples:

आ जाना I **aa-jaa naa** (to come back/to arrive)

1. मैकैनिक आया।   The mechanic came. (simple verb in simple perfect)
   (ma-ca-nick aa-yaa.)
2. मैकैनिक आ गया है।   The mechanic has (already) arrived. (compound
   (ma-ca-nick aa guh-yaa hai.)   verb in present perfect)
3. गाड़ी आयी।   The car came.
   (gaa-rDee aa-yee.)
4. गाड़ी आ गयी है।   The car/train has (already) arrived.
   (gaa-rDee aa-guh-yee hai.)

चला जाना I **ch-ul-aa jaa-naa** (to go back/to return)

1. आदमी गया।   The man left.
   (aa-d-mee guh-yaa.)
2. आदमी चला गया है।   The man has (already) left.
   (aa-d-mee ch-ul-aa guh-yaa hai.)

हो जाना I **ho jaa-naa** (to be/to become)

1. मेरी गाड़ी ख़राब हुई।   My car broke down.
   (may-ree gaa-rDee kher-aab hu-ee.)
2. मेरी गाड़ी ख़राब हो गई है।   My car has broken down.
   (may-ree gaa-rDee kher-aab ho guh-ee hai.)
3. मेरी गाड़ी ठीक हुई।   My car was fixed.
   (may-ree gaa-rDee Theek hu-ee.)
4. मेरी गाड़ी ठीक हो गई है।   My car has been fixed.
   (may-ree gaa-rDee Theek ho guh-ee hai.)

Practice 1

Read the story in Hindi to understand the concept of the compound verb with जाना.
This story will show you the use of simple verbs versus compound verbs in the
simple, present, past perfect, and future tenses. In the passage, the simple verbs
are in bold and the compound verbs are bold and underlined.

कल शाम को मैं अपने दोस्त के घर **गया** था। रात को घर आते समय अचानक मेरी गाड़ी रास्ते में ख़राब **हो गई**। मैंने अपनी गाड़ी सड़क के किनारे **खड़ी की** और गाड़ी का हुड/बोनट **उठाया** तो **देखा** कि इंजन से धुँआ निकल रहा है। मैंने बहुत सी गाड़ियों से मदद माँगने की **कोशिश की** लेकिन कोई भी मेरी मदद के लिए नहीं **आया**। मेरे पास अपना फ़ोन भी नहीं था क्योंकि वह मैं अपने घर <u>**भूल गया था,**</u> इसलिए मैं पैदल ही चलकर एक मील दूर एक गाड़ी ठीक करने वाले की दुकान पर पहुँचा। वहाँ पहुँचकर मैंने दुकानदार से **बात की**, लेकिन मैकैनिक पास के गाँव से गाड़ी ठीक करके **आया** नहीं था। मैंने उससे पूछा " मैकैनिक कब आयेगा?" दुकानदार ने कहा " आप बैठिये, वह थोड़ी देर में <u>**आ जायेगा**</u>"। मैं वहाँ एक तख़्त पर **बैठ गया** और मैकैनिक का इंतज़ार करने लगा।

Romanization

Kuh-ul sham ko main up-nay ayk dost kay gh-er guh-yaa thaa. Raat ko gh-er aa-tay sum-uy uch-aa-n-uk may-re gaa-rDee kher-aab ho guh-ee. Main-ay up-nee gaa-rDee serD-uk kay kin-aa-ray

Kh-erDee kee aur gaa-rDee kaa huD/bonuT üTh-aa-yaa toe day-khaa ki in-jun say dhü-aȧ nik-ul ruh-haa hai. Mai-nay buh-hüt see gaa-rD-iyȯ say mud-ud maȧg-nay kee ko-shish kee laykin ko-ee bhee may-ree mud-ud kay li-yay nuh-heȧ aa-yaa. May-ray paas up-naa phone bhee nuh-heȧ thaa kyȯ-ki veh main up-nay gh-er bhool guh-yaa thaa, is-li-yay main pai-dul hee ch-ul-ker, puh-hün-ch-ker mai-nay dü-kaan-daar say baat kee, laykin mechanic paas kay gaȧv say gaa-rDee Theek ker-kay aa-yaa nuh-heȧ thaa. Mai-nay üs-say poo-chaa "Mechanic cub aa-ay-gaa?"

dü-kaan daar nay kuh-haa "aap baiTh-iyay, veh tho-rDee day-r may aa-jaa-yay-gaa." Main vuh-haȧ ayk tukh-ut per baiTh guh-yaa aur mechanic kaa int-zaar kaer-nay lug-aa.

Translation

Yesterday I went to my friend's house. On the way home at night, my car broke down. I stopped on the side of the road, and when I looked under the hood, I saw smoke coming out of the engine. I tried to get help from other drivers, but no one stopped to help. I didn't have my phone because I had left it at home, so I walked for a mile and reached a car repair shop. There, I talked to the owner. But his mechanic had not returned from the nearby village. I asked him, "When will the mechanic return?" The shop owner said, "Please have a seat, he'll come back soon." So I sat down on a *takhat** there and waited for the mechanic.

*takhat: wooden bed

Practice 2

Write your own experience with car trouble. Use the verbs from the Vocabulary list.

_____

_____

_____

Practice 3 Vocabulary-Building Exercise

Match the words in the left column with their antonyms on the right.

1. ठीक   दूर के
2. मालिक   किनारे पर
3. खड़ी होना   अपने आप
4. ज़रूर   पास
5. क्यों नहीं   ख़राब
6. पास के   चले जाना
7. बीच में   बिल्कुल नहीं
8. के साथ   नौकर
9. दूर   क्यों
10. आ जाना   चलना

Practice 4

Listen to the conversation in two parts and complete the activity that follows.

Script 1 🎧 06-17

यात्री	:	जी नमस्ते, यहाँ कोई मैकेनिक है क्या ?
दुकानदार	:	जी बताइये, क्या काम है ?
यात्री	:	मेरी गाड़ी ख़राब हो गई है। क्या आप किसी को मेरे साथ भेज सकतें हैं?
दुकानदार	:	जी ज़रूर, क्यों नहीं लेकिन आप की गाड़ी है कहाँ?
यात्री	:	यहाँ से लगभग १ मील दूर सड़क के किनारे खड़ी है।
दुकानदार	:	गाड़ी में क्या खराबी आ गई है?
यात्री	:	मुझे नहीं मालूम, मैं गाड़ी चला रहा था कि अचानक गाड़ी से धुआँ निकलने लगा, इंजन से जलने की बदबू सी आ रही थी; गाड़ी अजीब सी आवाज़ भी कर रही थी।
दुकानदार	:	गाड़ी सड़क के किनारे है या सड़क के बीच?
यात्री	:	सड़क के किनारे।
दुकानदार	:	आप दो मिनट बैठिए, मैं किसी को आपके साथ भेजता हूँ।

Script 2 🎧 06-18

याली	:	कोई मैकैनिक खाली है?
दुकानदार	:	हमारे पास अभी दूसरा मैकैनिक नहीं है। एक मैकैनिक किसी की गाड़ी ठीक करने के लिये पास के गाँव गया है।
याली	:	वो कब तक आ जायेगा?
दुकानदार	:	मेरे ख़याल में एक घंटे में आ जायेगा।
याली	:	ठीक है, क्या मुझे एक दूसरी गाड़ी मिल सकती है?
दुकानदार	:	जी नहीं, मेरे पास कोई गाड़ी आप को देने के लिए नहीं है। क्या आप कुछ देर इंतज़ार कर सकते हैं?
याली	:	कोई बात नहीं, तो मैं उसका इंतज़ार कर लेता हूँ।
दुकानदार	:	जी अच्छा, आप यहाँ तख़त पर बैठ जाइये।
याली	:	क्या मुझे एक गिलास पानी मिल सकता है?
दुकानदार	:	जी आप बैठिये मैं अभी लाता हूँ।

Romanization 1

Yaat-re	:	Jee num-us-tay, ya-uh-haan koi ma-ca-nic hai kyaa?
dü-kaan-daar	:	Jee but-aa-iyay, kyaa kaam hai?
Yaat-re	:	May-re gaarD-ee kher-aab ho guh-ee hai. Kyaa aap ki-see ko may-ray saath bhej suk-tay hain?
dü-kaan-daar	:	Jee zer-oor kyo nuh-heė, lay-kin aap-kee gaarD-ee hai kuh-haȧ?
Yaat-re	:	Yuh haȧ say lug-bh-ug ayk meel do-oor serD-uk kay kin-aa-ray.
dü-kaan-daar	:	GaarD-ee maȧ kyaa kher-aa-be aa-guh-ee hai?
Yaat-re	:	Mü-jhay nuh-heė maa-loom, main gaarD-ee ch-ul-aa ruh-haa thaa, ki uch-aa-nuk gaarD-ee say dhü-aȧ nik-ul-nay lug-aa, in-jun say j-ul-nay kee bud-boo see aa-ruh-hee thee. GaarDee uj-eeb see aa-waaz bhee ker ruḥ hee thee.
dü-kaan-daar	:	GaarD-ee serD-uk kay kin-aa-ray hai yaa beech maȧ.
Yaat-re	:	SerD-uk kay kinaa-ray.
dü-kaan-daar	:	Aap do minuT baiTh-iyay, main aap-kay saath ki-see ko bhej-taa hoȯ.

Romanization 2

Yaat-re	:	Koi mechanic khaa-lee hai?
dü-kaan daar	:	Hum-aa-ray paas ub-hee doos-raa mechanic nuh-heė hai. Ayk mechanic ki-see ki gaarD-ee Theek ker-nay kay li-yay paas kay gaȧv guh-yaa hai.
Yaat-re	:	Vo kub t-uk aa-jaa-yay-gaa?
dü-kaan daar	:	May-ray kh-yaal may ayk gh-un-Tay mein aa-jaa-yay-gaa.
Yaat-re	:	Oh! Kyaa mü-jhay ayk doos-ree gaarD-ee mil suk-tee hai?
dü-kaan daar	:	Jee ub-hee toe ko-ee gaarD-ee nuh-heė hai. Kyaa aap küCh int-zaar ker suk-tay hain?
Yaat-re	:	Ko-ee baat nuh-heė, main uskaa int-zaar ker lay-taa hoȯ.
dü-kaan daar	:	Jee uch-Chaa, aap yuh-haȧ tukh-ut per baiTh jaa-i-yay.
Yaat-re	:	Kyaa mü-jhay ayk gi-laas paa-nee mil suk-taa hai?
dü-kaan daar	:	Jee aap baiTh-i-yay main ub-hee laa-taa hoȯ.

Match the words on the left with the corresponding sentences on the right.

1. इंतज़ार   मेरी गाड़ी _____ हो गई है। (broken down)

2. धुआँ   गाड़ी में क्या _____ आ गई है? (problem)

3. ख़राब   गाड़ी से _____ निकलने लगा। (smoke)

4. आवाज़   कोई बात नहीं तो मैं उसका _____ करता हूँ। (wait)

5. मालिक़   आप _____ _____ मेरे साथ भेज सकते हैं? (someone)

6. पास के   एक अजीब सी _____ आ रही है। (noise)

7. किसी को   गाड़ी _____ हो गई है। (stopped)

8. बंद   यहाँ _____ मैकेनिक है क्या? (any)

9. कोई   गाड़ी सड़क _____ है। (on the side)

10. ख़राबी   दरअसल मैं तो दुकान का _____ हूँ, मैकेनिक नहीं। (owner)

11. के किनारे   वह दूसरी गाड़ी ठीक करने के लिए _____ गाँव गया है। (nearby)

Practice 5

A. *Write down the sentences from the conversation that express "emergency situation," and translate them into English.*

1. Hindi sentence: _____

    English translation: _____

2. Hindi sentence: _____

    English translation: _____

3. Hindi sentence: _____

    English translation: _____

B. *Write down the sentences that best match the translation for "I will wait" and "to repair," and translate them into English.*

1. Hindi sentence: _____

    English translation: _____

2. Hindi sentence: _____

    English translation: _____

C. *Write down the sentences containing compound verbs, then translate them into English.*

1. Hindi sentence: _____

    English translation: _____

2. Hindi sentence: _____

    English translation: _____

3. Hindi sentence: _____

    English translation: _____

4. Hindi sentence: _____

    English translation: _____

Practice 6 Comprehension Check
Answer the following comprehension questions in Hindi.

1. यात्री किससे मिला और क्यों?
    Whom did the traveler meet and why?

    _____

2. यात्री की गाड़ी को क्या हुआ था, पूरी कहानी बताइये ।?
    What happened to the traveler's car?

    _____

3. दुकानदार ने मैकैनिक के बारे में यात्री को क्या बताया?

   What did the shop owner tell the traveler about the mechanic?

_____

Translation 1

Traveler : Hello, is there a mechanic nearby?

Shop Owner : Yes sir, what can I do for you?

Traveler : My car broke down. Can you send somebody with me?

Shop Owner : Of course sir. Where is your car located?

Traveler : It's about a kilometer from here, on the roadside.

Shop Owner : What's wrong with it?

Traveler : I don't know. I was driving it when I suddenly saw smoke coming from the engine. There was a strange noise and the car stopped completely.

Shop Owner : Is the car on the side or in the middle of the road?

Traveler : On the side of the road.

Shop Owner : Please have a seat, let me send someone with you.

Translation 2

Traveler : Do you have any available mechanic?

Shop Owner : We don't have any mechanic at this time. One of my mechanics has gone to a nearby village to repair someone's car.

Traveler : When will he be back?

Shop Owner : I think he'll be back in an hour.

Traveler : OK, can I get a car from you for the time being?

Shop Owner : Sir, I am afraid, we don't have any car to give to you. Can you wait for a little while?

Traveler : OK then, I'll wait for him.

Shop Owner : Sir, you can have a seat over here on this wooden bench.

Traveler : Can I get a glass of water?

Shop Owner : By all means. Please have a seat; I'll get it right away.

APPENDIX

India and Its Geography   भारत और भारत का भूगोल

Introduction

India is a vast country, situated in the Indian sub-continent of Asia. On the north are the plains of the holy river Ganga that flows through north India and irrigates its land, making it fertile and prosperous. Its embankments, also known as *ghat*, have always attracted tourists to its shores. To the west is the great desert of Thar, which holds mounds of dramatic and romantic fortresses, singing the glory of its brave sons and daughters throughout history. Its sand dunes have mesmerized travelers from across the globe, and the hospitality of its simple inhabitants is incomparable. To the north stands the great Himalaya, literally meaning "the abode of snow," safeguarding India from its enemies. India is surrounded by an ocean, a sea and a bay. Let's take you to India, the land of many cultures and faiths, for you to really appreciate its beauty, culture, land, and friendly people.

The Taj Mahal, Northern India

Practice 1 Pre-reading Exercise

Getting Familiar with India

Look at the map of India below and locate the mountain ranges, rivers, and oceans around it.

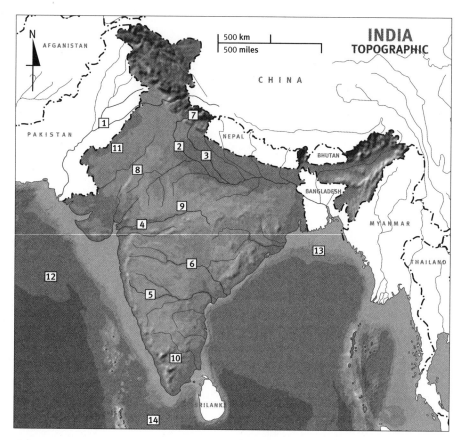

Rivers

1. _____ 4. _____ 7. _____

2. _____ 5. _____

3. _____ 6. _____

Mountains

8. _____   10. _____

9. _____   11. _____

<u>Desert</u>   <u>Sea</u>

12. _____   13. _____

Vocabulary 🎧 0A-01

Nouns

भारत	(bhaa-rut)	*masc.*	India
देश	(day-sh)	*masc.*	country
महाद्वीप	(muh-haa-dweep)	*masc.*	continent
उप महाद्वीप	(üp muh-haa-dweep)	*masc.*	sub-continent
रेगिस्तान	(ray-gis-taan)	*masc.*	desert
द्वीप	(dweep)	*masc.*	island
समूह	(sum-ooh)	*masc.*	group
राज्य/प्रदेश	(raaj-yuh/pruh-day-sh)	*masc.*	state
संघ राज्य	(sungh raaj-yuh)	*masc.*	union territory
महासागर	(muh-haa-saa-ger)	*masc.*	ocean
सागर	(saa-ger)	*masc.*	sea
मौसम	(mau-sum)	*masc.*	weather
ऋतु	(ri-tü)	*fem.*	season
पर्वत माला	(per-wut-maa-laa)	*fem.*	a mountain range
खाड़ी	(khaa-rDee)	*fem.*	bay
नदी	(nuh-ud-ee)	*fem.*	river
भाषा	(bhaa-shaa)	*fem.*	language
दिशा	(dish-aa)	*fem.*	direction
गर्मी	(ger-mee)	*fem.*	summer
सर्दी	(ser-dee)	*fem.*	winter
बारिश	(baa-rish)	*fem.*	rain

Adjectives

उत्तर	(üt-ter)	North
दक्षिण	(duk-shin)	South
पूरब/पूर्व	(poo-rub/poo-rv)	East
पश्चिम	(p-ush-chim)	West
आधिकारिक	(aa-dhi-kaa-rik)	official

Grammar

The Verb *to be* होना

The verb होना in Hindi has a variety of uses. One common use is to indicate a present condition, a fact, or a situation: Hindi uses the auxiliary verb है or हैं for the present.

The other use of होना indicates the usual occurrences and the natural quality of animate and inanimate objects. In these cases होता है (*masc.*), होती है (*fem.*), and होते है (*masc. pl.*) are used.

Stating present condition and factual information
1. It's very cold here today.   आज यहाँ बहुत ठंड है।
2. India's capital is Delhi.   भारत की राजधानी दिल्ली है।

Indicating natural and usual occurrences
1. It is usually very cold here.   यहाँ हमेशा बहुत ठंड होती है। (*fem. sing.*)
2. It is usually very hot in Africa.   अफ़्रीका में बहुत गर्मी होती है। (*fem. sing.*)

Expressing the natural quality of something
An ocean is usually very big.   महासागर बहुत बड़ा होता है।

Read the examples below and understand how the verb **होना** is used.

Factual Information using है and हैं
1. America is a big country.
   अमरीका एक बड़ा देश है।

2. America is in the North American continent.
   अमरीका, उत्तरी अमरीका महाद्वीप में है।

3. There are two oceans surrounding the United States.
   उत्तरी अमरीका की दोनों ओर दो महासागर हैं।

4. Hawaii is an island of the US; Puerto Rico and Guam are US territories.
   हवाई अमरीका का एक द्वीप है। पोर्टरीको और ग्वाम संघ राज्य हैं।

5. There are fifty states in the United States.
   अमरीका में पचास राज्य हैं।

Present weather conditions using है and हैं

1. It is very hot today.
   आज बहुत गर्मी है।

2. It is very foggy today.
   आज बहुत कोहरा है।

3. It is very cloudy today.
   आज बहुत बादल हैं।

होता है, होती है, होते हैं **for Usual and Natural Occurrences**

1. It is usually very hot in Africa.
   अफ्रीका में बहुत गर्मी होती है।

2. It usually rains a lot in Britain.
   ब्रिटेन में बहुत बारिश होती है।

3. It is usually very foggy in Shimla.
   शिमला में बहुत कोहरा होता है।

4. It is (usually) very hot in the months of June and July.
   जून और जुलाई में बहुत गर्मी होती है।

5. Spring season falls in the month of February.
   बसंत का मौसम फ़रवरी में होता है।

Practice 2

Fill in the blanks with the appropriate verb endings है (singular) and हैं (plural).

1. एन्टार्टिका एक महाद्वीप _____

2. भारत में अट्ठाईस राज्य _____

3. दुनिया में कुल सात महासागर _____

4. जापान की आधिकारिक भाषा जापानी _____

5. सहारा रेगिस्तान सबसे बड़ा रेगिस्तान _____

Practice 3

Translate the following sentences into Hindi using होना for general or usual occurrences. To write the sentences correctly, change the verb होना based on the noun preceding it. It means that the subject of your sentence will reflect its gender and number upon the verb.

1. There are usually four seasons. (*fem. pl.*) _____

2. It rains a lot in the Amazon rainforest. (*fem. sing.*) _____

3. It usually is very cold in the northern areas. (*fem. sing.*) _____

4. It is very hot in June in India. (*fem. sing.*) _____

5. It snows a lot in the Himalayas. (*fem. sing.*) _____

Practice 4

Read the passage and then fill in the map with the vocabulary of directions, terrain, and country names.

Script

इंडिया, दुनिया का सातवाँ सबसे बड़ा देश है। इंडिया को भारत भी कहते हैं। भारत एक उपमहाद्वीप है। यह एशिया महाद्वीप में दक्षिण-पूर्व दिशा में स्थित है। भारत की राजधानी नई दिल्ली है। भारत के उत्तर पश्चिम में अफ़ग़ानिस्तान और पाकिस्तान, उत्तर में भूटान और नेपाल; पूरब में म्यांमार और बाँग्लादेश और दक्षिण में श्री लंका है।

भारत में उत्तर में हिमालय पर्वत मालाएँ, पूर्व में बंगाल की खाड़ी, पश्चिम में अरब सागर तथा थार रेगिस्तान और दक्षिण में हिन्द महासागर है। भारत में बंगाल की खाड़ी में अंडमान-निकोबार द्वीप समूह हैं। भारत की मुख्य नदियाँ, गंगा, यमुना, कृष्णा, कावेरी, गोदावरी, नर्मदा, ब्रह्मपुत्र आदि हैं। भारत में उनतीस राज्य और सात संघ राज्य हैं।

यहाँ पर कुल बाईस मुख्य भाषाएँ हैं। हर प्रदेश की अलग-अलग भाषा है। हिन्दी भारत की राजभाषा है। भारत में आमतौर पर चार मौसम होते हैं, दिसम्बर से फरवरी तक सर्दियों, मार्च से जून तक गर्मियों, जून से सितम्बर तक दक्षिण पश्चिमी मानसून या बारिश का मौसम और अक्तूबर से नवम्बर तक मानसून के बाद का मौसम होता है।

Romanization

India, düni-yaa kaa saat-vaå sub-say berD-aa day-sh hai. India ko Bhaa-rut bhee keh-tay hain. Bhaa-rut ayk üp muh-haa-dweep hai. Yeh Asia muh-haa-dweep maẏ duk-shin poo-rv di-shaa maẏ sthi-t hai.Bhaa-rut kee raaj-dhaa-nee nuh-ee dil-lee hai. Bhaa-rut kay ütter-p-ush-chim maẏ Uf-ghaan-is-taan aur Paak-is-taan, ütter maẏ Bhoo-Taan aur Nepal; poo-rub maẏ Myaan-maar aur Baang-laa-daysh aur duck-shin maẏ Shree Lunk-kaa hai.

Bhaa-rut maẏ ütter maẏ Himaa-luh-ya per-vut maa-laa-aẏ, poorv maẏ bung-aal kee khaa-rDee,p-ush-chim maẏ Ur-ub saa-ger tuh-thaa thaar ray-gis-taan aur duk-shin maẏ Hind muh-haa-saa-ger hai. Bhaa-rut maẏ Bung-aal kee khaa-rDee maẏ Und-maan-Niko-baar dweep sum-ooh hain. Bhaa-rut kee mükh-yuh nud-i-yaå hain, Gung-gaa, Yum-ünaa, Krish-naa, kaa-way-re, Go-daa-ver-ee, Bruhm-püt-ruh aa-di. Bhaa-rut maẏ ün-tees raaj-yuh aur saat sungh raaj-yuh hain.

Yuh-haà per kül baa-ees mükh-yuh bhaa-shaa-aẏ hain. Her pruh-day-sh kee ul-ug ul-ug bhaa-shaa hai. Bhaa-rut maẏ aam-tawr per chaar maw-sum ho-tay hain. Di-sum-ber say Fer-veree t-uk ser-di-yò, March say June t-uk ger-mi-yò, June say si-tum-ber t-uk duk-shin p-ush-chi-mee maan-soon yaa baa-rish kaa maw-sum aur Uk-too-ber say nuv-um-ber t-uk maan-sson kay baad kaa maw-sum ho-taa hai.

Translation

India is the seventh largest country in the world. It is also called Bharat. India is a sub-continent. It is situated in the southeast region/portion/corner of the continent of Asia. India's capital city is New Delhi. Afghanistan and Pakistan are to the northeast of India; Bhutan and Nepal are to the north; to the east are Myanmar and Bangladesh; and to the south is Sri Lanka. The Himalayan Mountain ranges are in the northern part of India. The Bay of Bengal is in the east, the Arabian Sea and the Thar Desert are in the west, and the Indian Ocean is in the south. In India, the Andaman Nicobar islands are in the Bay of Bengal. The main rivers of India are Ganga, Yamuna, Krishna, Kaveri, Godavari, Narmada, and Brahmaputra. India has 29 states and 7 union territories. Hindi is India's official language. India usually has four seasons. From December to February is the winter season; from March to June is the summer season; from June to September is the rainy season or monsoon season; and from October to November is the post-monsoon season. There are 22 main languages spoken, and each state has its own language.

Practice 5 Post-Reading Exercise

Label the pictures below with the appropriate vocabulary.

1. ocean   2. mountain range   3. desert

_____   _____   _____

4. world

6. bay

8. winter season

_____

_____

_____

5. island

7. seashore

9. rainy season / weather

_____

_____

_____

Creative Writing

Write about your own country and its geographical features in Hindi. Use the "Introduction to India" as a reference, and fill in the information about your country. You can also record your information on a recording device to improve your pronunciation and reading fluency.

_____

_____

_____

_____

_____

_____

ENGLISH-HINDI WORDLIST

A

a *adj.* एक

a little bit, very little *adj.* ज़रा सा, सी, से थोड़ा सा, सी, से

a little less *adj.* थोड़ा कम

a lot *adj.* बहुत सा, सी, से बहुत ज़्यादा

a lot, too much *adj.* बहुत

a rupee and a half *masc. pl.* डेढ़ रुपये

about X *cpp.* के बारे में

above *pp.* ऊपर

above X *cpp.* के ऊपर

account *masc. sing.* ख़ाता

action *fem. sing* कार्रवाई

address *masc. sing.* पता

after looking *participle* देखकर

after that *adv.* उसके बाद

age *fem. sing.* उम्र

ahead *pp.* आगे

ahead of X *cpp.* के आगे, से आगे

all around *cpp.* चारो तरफ़

all-purpose flour *fem. sing.* मैदा

almond *masc. sing.* बादाम

along with *cpp.* के साथ

also *adv.* भी

always *adv.* हमेशा

am *aux. v.* हूँ

amount *fem. sing.* राशि

another *adj. masc./fem./pl.* दूसरा, दूसरी, दूसरे

any, someone *adj./indef. pron.* कोई

approximately *adv.* लगभग/क़रीब

around *adv./pp.* चारो तरफ़

arrival *masc. sing.* आगमन

as well *adv.* भी

at *pp.* पर

at least *adv.* कम से कम

at the back side *cpp.* पीछे की तरफ़

at the bottom *adv.* सबसे नीचे

attached to *cpp.* के साथ

auto rickshaw driver *masc. sing.* ऑटो रिक्शे वाला

B

baggy Indian pants *fem. sing.* सलवार

bank, shore *masc. sing.* किनारा

bathroom *masc. sing.* ग़ुसलख़ाना, स्नानघर

bay *fem. sing.* खाड़ी

bedroom *masc. sing.* सोने का कमरा

behind *adv.* पीछे

behind of X *cpp.* के पीछे

bell pepper, capsicum *fem. sing.* शिमला मिर्च

below *adv.* नीचे

below X *cpp.* के नीचे

benefit *masc. sing.* फ़ायदा

big *adj. masc./fem./pl.* बड़ा, बड़ी, बड़े

bigger than *comp. adj.* से बड़ा, बड़ी, बड़े

biggest of all *superl. adj.* सबसे बड़ा, बड़ी, बड़े

biscuit *masc. sing.* बिस्कुट

black pepper *fem. sing.* काली मिर्च

blood *masc. sing.* ख़ून

blue *adj. masc./fem./pl.* नीला, नीली, नीले

both *adj.* दोनों

both sides *adv.* दोनों तरफ़

boundry wall *fem. sing.* चारदीवारी

bowl *fem. sing.* कटोरी

bread *fem. sing.* डबलरोटी

brisk walk *fem. sing.* सैर

broom *fem. sing.* झाड़ू

brother *masc. sing.* भाई, भैया

bun and concoction of vegetables *fem. sing.* पाव-भाजी

bunch *masc. sing.* गुच्छा

but *conj.* लेकिन

by *pp.* से

C

cabbage *fem. sing.* पत्ता गोभी

carrot *fem. sing.* गाजर

cash *masc. sing.* नक़द

cashew *masc. sing.* काजू

cauliflower *fem. sing.* फूल गोभी

ceiling *fem. sing.* छत

change (coins) *masc. pl.* छुट्टे, खुल्ले

change (coins) *fem. sing.* रेज़गारी

cheap *adj. masc./fem./pl.* सस्ता, सस्ती, सस्ते

checking *adj.* चालू

cheese *pulao*/rice *masc. sing.* पनीर पुलाव

chick peas *masc. pl.* छोले

children *masc. pl.* बच्चे

cilantro, coriander *masc. sing.* धनिया

cinnamon *fem. sing.* दालचीनी

class *fem. sing.* श्रेणी

clay shingle *masc. sing.* केलू

climb, hike, incline *fem. sing.* चढ़ाई

clothes *masc. pl.* कपड़े

coin *masc. sing.* सिक्का

coin, money *masc. sing.* पैसा

cold *fem. sing* ठंड

color *masc. sing.* रंग

complete, entire *adj.* पूरा

condition *fem. sing.* तबियत

contact *masc. sing.* संपर्क

continent *masc. sing.* महाद्वीप

coriander powder *masc. sing.* पिसा सूखा धनिया

cotton *adj.* सूती

coughing *fem. sing.* खाँसी

country *masc. sing.* देश

courtyard *masc. sing.* आँगन

cucumber *masc. sing.* खीरा

cumin *masc. sing* जीरा

cumin rice *masc. sing* जीरा चावल

currency *fem. sing.* मुद्रा

D

date *masc. sing.* तारीख़ दिनाँक

daughter *fem. sing.* बेटी

day after tomorrow, yesterday *adv.* परसों

definitely *adv.* ज़रूर

departure *masc. sing.* प्रस्थान

desert *masc. sing.* रेगिस्तान

destination *masc. sing.* गंतव्य

detail *masc. sing.* विवरण

dining room *masc. sing.* खाने का कमरा

direction *fem. sing.* दिशा

dirty *adj.* गंदा, गंदी, गंदे

doctor *masc./fem. sing.* चिकित्सक

documents *masc. pl.* काग़ज़ात

door *masc. sing.* दरवाज़ा

double *fem. sing.* तक़लीफ़

dozen *adj.* दर्जन

drawing room *fem. sing.* बैठक

dried *adj. masc./fem./pl.* सूखा, सूखी, सूखे

E

east *adj.* पूरब/ पूर्व

eight *adj.* आठ

embassy *masc. sing.* दूतावास

empty *adj.* खाली

evening *fem. sing.* शाम

expensive *adj. masc./fem./pl.* महंगा, महँगी, महंगे

F

face *masc. sing.* मुँह, चेहरा

family *masc. sing.* परिवार

far *adv.* दूर

fare *masc. sing.* किराया

father *masc. sing.* पिता जी

fever *masc. sing.* बुखार

few, a little *indef. pron.* कुछ

fifteen minutes after (time) *adj.* सवा

fifty five *adj.* पचपन

fifty *pasie*, half rupee *masc. pl.* पचास पैसे

first *adv.* पहले

first of all *superl. adv.* सबसे पहले

five *adj.* पाँच

floor *masc. sing.* फ़र्श

flower *masc. sing.* फूल

food *masc. sing.* खाना

for *cpp.* के लिए

for a while/for some time *adv.* थोड़ी देर

foreign country *masc. sing.* विदेश

four *adj.* चार

free *adj.* खाली

fresh *adj. masc./fem./pl.* ताज़ा, ताजी, ताज़े

fried *adj. masc./fem./pl.* तला, तली, तले

fritters *masc. sing.* पकौड़ा

from *pp.* से

from Banaras *adj.* बनारसी

from Bhagalpur *adj.* भागलपुरी

from here *cpp.* यहाँ से

from Sambalpur *adj.* सम्बलपुरी

from where *question word* कहाँ से?

front of X *cpp.* के आगे

fruit *masc. sing.* फल

G

garden *masc. sing.* बाग़, बग़ीचा

gender *masc. sing.* लिंग

ginger *fem. sing.* अदरक

give me your best price *phrase* ठीक बोलो!

glass *masc. sing.* काँच

gold/silver thread *fem. sing.* ज़री

good *adj.* बढ़िया

grade *fem. sing.* श्रेणी

gram (flour) *masc. sing.* बेसन

gram flour bread *fem. sing.* मिस्सी रोटी

green *adj. masc./fem./pl.* हरा, हरी, हरे

green chili *fem. sing.* हरी मिर्च

ground (powdered) *adj. masc./fem./pl.* पिसा हुआ, पिसी हुयी, पिसे हुये

group *masc. sing* समूह

H

half kilo *masc. sing.* आधा किलो

hand *masc. sing.* हाथ

head cold *masc. sing.* जुकाम

here *adv.* यहाँ

hey! *interj.* अरे!

high (temperature) *adj.* तेज़

home *masc. sing.* घर

hour *masc. sing.* घंटा

hours *masc. pl.* घंटे

house *masc. sing.* मकान, घर

housewife *fem. sing.* गृहिणी

how many *adj. masc./fem./pl.* कितना, कितनी, कितने

how much *adj. masc./fem./pl.* कितना, कितनी, कितने

how much is it for? *phrase* कितने का दिया?, कैसी दी?, कैसी दीं?, कैसे दिये?, क्या भाव दिया?, क्या भाव दी?, क्या भाव दीं?

how much is the total? *phrase* कुल कितने पैसे हुये?

however *conj.* लेकिन

hundred *adj.* सौ

husband *masc. sing.* पति

I

I *pron.* मैं

I will get it right away *phrase* अभी लाता हूँ, अभी लाती हूँ

identification card *masc. sing.* पहचान पत्र

if *conj.* अगर, यदि

if you want to go *phrase* अगर तुम जाना चाहते हो...

immediately *adv.* तुरंत, फ़ौरन

in *pp.* में

in front of X *cpp.* X के सामने

in the front *pp.* सामने, आगे

in the middle of *cpp.* बीच में

in the open *cpp.* खुले में

indeed *adv.* ज़रूर

India *masc. sing* भारत

Indian flat bread *fem. sing.* रोटी, चपाती

Indian cucumber *fem. sing.* ककड़ी

information *fem. sing.* जानकारी

introduction *masc. sing* परिचय

iron *fem. sing.* इस्त्री

is *aux. v.* है

island *masc. sing.* द्वीप

J

job *fem. sing.* नौकरी

journey *masc. sing./fem. sing.* सफ़र, यात्रा

just *adj.* सिर्फ़ बस

K

kidney beans *masc. sing.* राजमा

kilo *masc. sing.* किलो

kitchen *fem. sing.* रसोई

knife *fem. sing.* छुरी

L

ladder *fem. sing.* सीढ़ी

language *fem. sing.* भाषा

last *adj.* पिछला, पिछली, पिछले

later on *cpp.* बाद में

lawyer *masc. sing.* वकील

less *adj.* कम

let's go *suggestion* चलो, चलिए, चल

letter of proof, certificate *masc. sing* प्रमाण पत्र

light (color) *adj.* हल्का

little *adj.* ज़रा, थोड़ा

living room *fem. sing.* बैठक

long scarf *fem. sing.* चुन्नी

lots *adj.* ज़्यादा

lots of *adj. masc./fem./pl.* खूब सारा, बहुत सारा, सारी, सारे

lower *adj.* निचला, निचली, निचले

M

maid *fem. sing.* कामवाली, नौकरानी

main *adj.* मुख्य

male teacher *masc. sing.* शिक्षक

man *masc. sing.* आदमी

many *adj.* कई

married *adj.* शादी शुदा
medicine *fem. sing.* दवाई, दवा
metal plate *fem. sing.* थाली
milk *masc. sing.* दूध
mirror *masc. sing.* काँच
month *masc. sing.* महीना
more *adj.* और
morning *fem. sing.* सुबह
mother *fem. sing.* माँ, माता
mountain range *fem. sing.* पर्वत माला
mouth *masc. sing.* मुँह
my *adj. masc./fem./pl.* मेरा, मेरी, मेरे

N

name *masc. sing.* नाम
near *pp.* पास
near by *cpp.* पास में, के पास, पास के
need *v. fem. sing.* ज़रूरत, चाहिए
newspaper *masc. sing.* अख़बार
next to X *cpp.* की बगल में
night *fem. sing.* रात
no problem *phrase* कोई बात नही
non-vegetarian *adj.* माँसाहारी
north *adj.* उत्तर
now *adv.* अब

O

ocean *masc. sing.* महासागर
o'clock *adv.* बजे
of *pp.* का, की, के
of all *adj. masc./fem./pl.* सब का, की, के
of all types *adj. masc./fem./pl.* सब तरह का, की, के
office *masc. sing.* दफ़्तर
official *adj.* आधिकारिक
oil *masc. sing.* तेल
older *adj. masc./fem./pl.* बड़ा, बड़ी, बड़े
olive *masc. sing.* जैतून
on *pp.* पर
on the banks of *cpp.* के किनारे
on the side of *cpp.* के किनारे
on the top *superl. adv.* सबसे ऊपर
one *adj.* एक
one and one quarter kilo *masc. sing.* सवा किलो
one that is better than other *adj.* एक से एक बढ़िया
onion *fem. sing.* प्याज़
only *adv.* सिर्फ़

opinion *masc. sing.* ख़याल, विचार
opportunity *masc. sing.* मौक़ा
other *adj. masc./fem./pl.* दूसरा, दूसरी, दूसरे
over-ripe, soft *adj. masc./fem./pl.* गला हुआ, गली हुयी, गले हुये
owner *masc. sing.* मालिक

P

pain *masc. sing.* दर्द
palce *fem. sing.* जगह
parked *adj.* खड़ी
passenger *fem. sing.* यात्री, सवारी
path *masc. sing* रास्ता, पथ, मार्ग
payment *masc. sing* भुगतान
payment, calculation *masc. sing* हिसाब
pea *pulao*/ rice *masc. sing* मटर पुलाव
peanuts *fem. sing.* मूँगफली
peas *fem. sing.* मटर
peeled *adj. masc./fem./pl.* छिला, छिली, छिले
picture *fem. sing.* तस्वीर
piece *masc. sing* टुकड़ा
pink *adj.* गुलाबी
pistachio *masc. sing.* पिस्ता
plain *adj.* सादा
plain *naan masc. sing.* सादा नान
plain rice *masc. pl.* सादे चावल
police station *masc. sing.* थाना
pond *masc. sing.* तालाब
potato *masc. sing.* आलू
prescription *fem. sing.* पर्ची
problem *fem. sing.* तक़लीफ़, परेशानी
pulse, legume *fem. sing.* दाल
put more, add more *phrase* और डालो!

Q

quarter kilo *masc. sing.* पाव भर
quarter of a rupee, 75 *paise masc. pl.* पिचहत्तर पैसे

R

raddish, *daikon fem. sing.* मूली
rain *fem. sing.* बारिश
raisin *fem. sing.* किशमिश
rather small *adj. masc./fem./pl.* छोटा सा, सी, से
rather strange *adj. masc./fem./pl.* अजीब सा, सी, से
red *adj.* लाल

red chilli powder *fem. sing.* पिसी लाल मिर्च

reduce a little bit *phrase* थोड़ा कम करो!

remainder *adj.* बकाया

rent *masc. sing.* किराया, भाड़ा

reservation *masc. sing.* आरक्षण

residence *masc. sing.* निवास

rest *masc. sing.* आराम

return *fem. sing.* वापसी

return from somewhere *v.i.* से लौटना, से वापस आना

rice *masc. sing.* चावल

rickshaw driver *masc. sing.* रिक्शे वाला

ride *fem. sing.* सवारी

right away *phrase* उसी समय

right behind *cpp.* के पीछे ही

right now *adv.* अभी

river *fem. sing.* नदी

road *masc. sing.* सड़क, रास्ता, मार्ग

roasted *adj. masc./fem./pl.* भुना, भुनी, भुने

roof *fem. sing.* छत

room *masc. sing* कमरा

rotten *adj. masc./fem./pl.* सड़ा हुआ, सड़ी हुयी, सड़े हुये

round trip *cpp.* दोनों तरफ का, की

rupee *masc. sing.* रुपया

S

salt *masc. sing.* नमक

sari *fem. sing.* साड़ी

savings *fem. sing.* बचत

Say the right price *phrase* ठीक दाम लगाओ!

sea *masc. sing.* सागर

season *fem. sing.* ऋतु

second *adj.* दूसरा, दूसरी, दूसरे

selection *masc. sing.* चयन

service *fem. sing.* सेवा

seven *adj.* सात

signature *masc. sing.* हस्ताक्षर, दस्तख़त

silken *adj.* रेशमी

since *adv.* तब से

sir *masc. sing. (honorific)* बाबूजी

sister *fem. sing.* बहन

six *adj.* छह:

sixty *adj.* साठ

small *adj. masc./fem./pl.* छोटा, छोटी, छोटे

smaller than *adj. masc./fem./pl.* से छोटा, छोटी, छोटे

smallest of all *adj. masc./fem./pl.* सबसे छोटा, छोटी, छोटे

smoke *masc. sing.* धुआँ

so *conj./interj.* तो

so little *adj. masc./fem./pl.* इतना सा, सी, से

soap bar *fem. sing.* साबुन की बट्टी

some *indef. pron.* कुछ

someone *indef. pron.* कोई

someone (to) *oblique indef. pron.* किसी को

someone's *adj. masc./fem./pl.* किसी की, का, के

son *masc. sing.* बेटा

south *adj.* दक्षिण

space *fem. sing* जगह

spiced *pulao*/rice *masc. sing* मसाला पुलाव

spinach *masc. sing* पालक

square (in a city) *masc. sing* चौक

stair *fem. sing.* सीढ़ी

staircase *fem. pl.* सीढ़ियाँ

stale *adj.* बासी

starch *masc. sing* कलफ़

state *masc. sing* राज्य, प्रदेश

steamed *adj.* दम

storied *adj. masc./fem./pl.* मंज़िला, मंज़िली, मंज़िले

story of a building *fem. sing* मंज़िल

student *masc./fem. sing.* विद्यार्थी

study room *masc. sing* पढ़ने का कमरा

stuff, luggage, things *masc. sing* सामान

stuffed or plain Indian bread *masc. sing* पराँठा

subcontinent *masc. sing.* उपमहाद्वीप

suddenly *adv.* अचानक

sugar *fem. sing.* चीनी

summer *fem. sing.* गर्मी

T

tasty *adj.* मज़ेदार, स्वादिष्ट

tea leaves *fem. sing.* चाय की पत्ती

ten *adj.* दस

tenth *adj. masc./fem./pl.* दसवाँ, दसवी, दसवे

test (medical examination) *fem. sing.* जाँच

than *pp.* से

the one who *conj./clause connector* जो

theft *fem. sing.* चोरी

then *cpp.* फिर, उसके बाद

thirty *adj.* तीस

thirty minutes after (time) *adj.* साढ़े

this much *adj.* इतना

throat *masc. sing.* गला

till *pp.* तक

time *masc. sing.* समय, वक़्त

to arrive *v.i.* आना, आ जाना

to ask for *v.t.* माँगना

to bathe *v.i.* नहाना

to be anxious, worried *v.i.* घबराना

to be doubtful *v.i.* शक होना

to be stolen *v.i.* चोरी हो जाना, चोरी चले जाना

to be unaware of *v.i.* मालूम नही होना

to become aware about *v.i.* पता लगना

to become, to be *v.i.* होना

to become, to happen *v.i.* हो जाना

to begin *v.t.* शुरू करना

to break down *v.i.* ख़राब हो जाना

to bring and drop *v.t.* लाकर छोड़ना

to brush (teeth) *masc. v.t.* मंजन करना

to bring back *v.t.* ले आना

to cause to write *v.t.* लिखवाना

to charge money *v.t.* पैसे लेना

to clean (dish) *v.t.* माँजना

to come *v.i.* आना

to come back *v.i.* वापस आना

to come down *v.i.* उतरना

to continue to take *v.i.* लेते रहना

to cook *v.t.* पकाना

to cost money *v.i.* पैसे लगना

to count *v.t.* गिनना

to depart *v.i.* जाना, निकलना

to deposit *v.t.* जमा कराना

to disappear *v.i.* ग़ायब हो जाना

to do *v.t.* करना, कर लेना

to drink *v.t.* पीना

to drive *v.t.* चलाना

to eat *v.t.* खाना

to end, to finish *v.i.* ख़त्म हो जाना

to exchange *v.t.* बदलना

to exercise *masc./fem. v.t.* व्यायाम/कसरत करना

to feel, to seem *v.i.* लगना

to file a report *v.t.* रिपोर्ट करना

to fill in spomething *v.t.* भरना

to fill out, to fill up *v.t.* भरना

to find out *v.t.* पता लगाना

to finish up *v.t.* ख़त्म कर देना

to get, to obtain *v.i.* मिलना

to get off *v.i.* उतरना

to give *v.t.* देना

to give away *v.t.* दे देना

to give opportunity *v.t.* मौक़ा देना

to go *v.t.* जाना

to go to sleep *comp. v.i.* सो जाना

to halt *v.i.* रुकना

to hand over *v.t.* दे देना

to have applied (starch on clothes) *v.t.* लगवाना

to have check cashed *v.t.* चैक भुनवाना

to have done *v.t.* करवाना

to have exchanged *v.t.* बदलवाना

to have made *v.t.* बनवाना

to have opened *v.t.* खुलवाना

to have problems *v.i.* ख़राबी आ जाना

to have washed *v.t.* धुलवाना

to have withdrawn *v.t.* निकलवाना

to help *fem. v.t.* की मदद करना

to know *v.t.* जानना

to leave, to depart *v.i.* निकलना, जाना निकलना

to like *v.i.* अच्छा लगना, पसंद होना

to like *v.t.* पसंद करना

to listen *v.t.* सुनना

to live *v.i.* रहना

to look at *v.t.* देख लेना

to look for *v.t.* को ढूंढना

to make *v.t.* बना देना, बनाना

to make noise (engine, car) *v.t.* आवाज़ करना

to move *v.i.* चलना

to open *v.t.* खोलना

to operate *v.t.* चलाना

to order *v.t.* मंगाना

to park *v.i.* खड़ी होना

to price *v.t.* दाम लगाना, भाव लगाना

to put *v.t.* डालना

to put/pour *v.t.* डाल देना

to reach *v.i.* पहुँचना

to receive a report *v.i.* रिपोर्ट मिलना

to reduce *v.i.* कम करना

to say, to tell, to speak *v.t.* बोलना

to see, to watch *v.t.* देखना

to seem, to appear like *v.i.* लगना

to send *v.t.* भेजना

to show *v.t.* दिखाना

to sleep *v.i.* सोना

to sit *v.i.* बैठना

to someone *pron. oblique* किसी को

to stay *v.i.* रुकना, ठहरना

to stop *v.i.* ठहरना, रुकना

to stop (as a mechanism) *v.i.* बंद हो जाना

to suspect *v.t.* शक़ करना

to take action *v.t.* कार्रवाई करना

to take away *v.i.* ले जाना

to take out (from inside of X) *v.t.* निकाल देना

to take time *v.i.* समय लगना

to take, to charge *v.t.* लेना

to tell *v.t.* बता देना, बताना

to understand *v.i.* समझना

to wake up *v.i.* उठना

to walk *v.i.* चलना, घूमना

to want *v.t.* चाहना

to wash *v.t.* धोना

to wash up *v.t.* धो देना

to weigh *v.t.* तोलना

today *adv.* आज

tomato *masc. sing.* टमाटर

tooth paste/powder *masc. sing.* मंजन

travel *masc. sing.* यात्रा, सफ़र

tunic *masc. sing.* कुर्ता

turmeric *fem. sing.* हल्दी

twenty *adj.* बीस

twenty years old *adj. masc./fem./pl.* बीस साल का, की, के

two *adj.* दो

two rupees and a half *masc. pl.* ढाई रुपये

U

union territory *masc. pl.* संघ राज्य

up till *pp.* तक

upper *adj. fem.* ऊपरी, ऊपर की

utensil *masc. sing.* बर्तन

V

vegetable *fem. sing.* भाजी, सब्ज़ी,

vegetarian शाकाहारी

ventilated *adj.* हवादार

very good *adj.* बहुत बढ़िया

very many *adj. masc./fem./pl.* बहुत सा, सी, से

very small *adj. masc./fem./pl.* छोटा सा, सी, से

W

wait *masc. sing.* इंतज़ार

washed (without husk) *adj. fem.* धुली हुयी

washerman *masc. sing.* धोबी

water *masc. sing.* पानी, जल

way *masc. sing.* रास्ता, पथ, मार्ग

weakness *fem. sing.* कमज़ोरी

week *masc. sing.* सप्ताह

weigh properly, correctly *phrase* ठीक से तोलो!

west *adj.* पश्चिम

what times *question word* किस-किस समय, कब-कब

wheat flour *masc. sing.* गेहूँ का आटा

when *question word* कब

where from *question word* कहाँ से

which one *adj. masc./fem./pl.* कौन सा, सी, से

white *adj.* सफ़ेद

who all *question word* कौन-कौन

whole *adj.* साबुत

why not *fem. sing.* क्यों नहीं

window *fem. sing.* खिड़की

winter *fem. sing.* सर्दी

with *cpp* के साथ

with husk *adj. fem.* छिलके वाली

with Lukhnawi work *adj. masc* लखनवी काम का

woman *fem. sing.* औरत, महिला

wooden bed *masc. sing.* तख़त

work *masc. sing.* काम

worship *fem. sing.* पूजा

wrinkled ankle tight pajama *masc. sing.* चूड़ीदार पजामा

written *adj. masc.* लिखा

Y

year *masc. sing.* साल

yellow *adj. masc./fem./pl.* पीला, पीली, पीले

yogurt shake *fem. sing.* लस्सी

you *pron.* आप, तुम ,तू

younger *adj. masc./fem./pl.* छोटा, छोटी, छोटे

your *adj. masc. sing.* आपका, तुम्हारा, तेरा

your *adj. fem.* आपकी, तुम्हारी, तेरी

your *adj. masc. pl.* आपके, तुम्हारे, तेरे

your, my, his, her *adj. masc. sing.* अपना

your, my, his, her *adj. fem.* अपनी

your, my, his, her *adj. masc. pl.* अपने

ANSWER KEY

Chapter 1.1 Personal Information
Practice 3 (p. 27)
1. मैं जॉन हूँ।
2. तुम कौन हो?
3. आप कहाँ से हैं?
4. आप कैसे हैं?
5. आप लोग कहाँ से हैं?
6. हम अमरीकन हैं / हम अमरीकी हैं।
7. यह मैट है।
8. वह सूज़न है।
9. ये पिताजी हैं
10. ये बच्चे हैं।
11. वे कौन हैं।

Practice 2 (p. 29)
1. इसकी बेटी
2. इसका बेटा
3. इसकी बेटी
4. इसका बेटा
5. इसके बच्चे
6. इसके बच्चे

Practice 3 (pp. 29–30)
1. उनकी बेटी
2. उनका बेटा
3. उनकी बेटी
4. उनका बेटा
5. उनके बच्चे
6. उनके बच्चे
7. उनके बच्चे
8. उनके बच्चे

Practice 4 (p. 30)
मेरी माँ / मेरी बहन / मेरे पिताजी /
मेरे भाई / मेरे पति

. . . .

Chapter 1.2 Introducing Oneself
Practice 2 Fill in the blanks (p. 35)
1. मेरा नाम
2. है
3. बीस साल की
4. एक विद्यार्थी
5. में
6. भारत से
7. मेरा घर
8. परिवार छोटा सा
9. परिवार में
10. पिताजी
11. माता जी
12. एक बड़ा भाई
13. छोटी बहन
14. शिक्षक
15. माँ गृहिणी
16. दसवीं कक्षा में

Practice 3 (p. 35)
(Own answers)

. . . .

Chapter 1.3 Greetings
Practice 3 Translation (pp. 38–39)
1. आपका नाम क्या है?
2. आप कहाँ से हैं?
3. ——— में कहाँ से?
4. आपके गृहिणी में कौन-कौन हैं?
5. क्या आप शादी-शुदा हैं?
6. आपके बच्चे कितने साल के हैं?
7. आपके पति क्या करते हैं?
8. आपकी पत्नी क्या करती हैं?
9. क्या आप भी काम करतीं हैं?

Practice 4 (p. 39)
(Own answers)

. . . .

Chapter 1.4 My Home

Practice 1 Matching (p. 45)

1. in the house
2. at home
3. above the house
4. below the house
5. in front of the house
6. behind the house
7. near the house
8. around the house

Practice 2 (p. 45)

1. in the room
2. at the room
3. above the room
4. below the room
5. in front of the room
6. behind the room
7. near the room
8. around the room
9. from the room

Practice 3 (p. 46)

1. बग़ीचे
2. दरवाज़े
3. रास्ते
4. कमरे
5. ग़ुसलख़ाने

Practice 4-1 Label the pictures (p. 46–47)

1. बग़ीचे में
2. दरवाज़े पर
3. रास्ते पर
4. कमरे में

Practice 4-2 Description (p. 47)

1. बग़ीचे में एक मेज़ है। मेज़ पर कप और पलेट हैं। मेज़ के आसपास दो कुर्सियाँ हैं।
2. दरवाज़े पर एक आदमी है।
3. रास्ते के आसपास पेड़ हैं।
4. कमरे में/के अन्दर एक लड़की है। लड़की के सामने एक पलंग, एक कालीन और एक मेज़ है।

Practice 5 Label the pictures (p. 47)

1. सीढ़ी पर
2. कमोड पर
3. पलंग पर
4. कम्प्यूटर के ऊपर
5. कुर्सियों के
6. प्लेट्स के पास

Practice 6 (p. 48)

(Own answers)

Practice 7 Identifying parts of speech (p. 49)

Postpositions: में के आगे के पास के पीछे के चारों तरफ़ की दोनों तरफ़ के सामने की तरफ़ पर

Nouns: घर फूल बग़ीचा जगह चारदीवारी दरवाज़ा गाड़ी पेड़ छत केलू काँच रास्ता खिड़की

Adjectives: सुन्दर हरी-हरी बहुत बड़ा छोटा सा सफ़ेद नीली भूरा मुख्य एक दो चार

Practices 8–10 (pp. 50–52)

(Own answers)

Practice 11 (p. 52)

1. के सामने
2. के सामने
3. के ऊपर
4. के ऊपर
5. के साथ
6. के साथ
7. पर
8. पर
9. सबसे ऊपर
10. सबसे ऊपर
11. से बड़ी
12. से छोटा

Comparatives

Practice 2 Translation (p. 55)

1. उसका कमरा, मेरे कमरे से बड़ा है।

2. पढ़ने का कमरा, सोने के कमरे से छोटा है।

3. बैठक, सोने के कमरे से सुन्दर है।

4. मेरे पिताजी का कमरा, मेरे कमरे से अच्छा है।

Practice 3 (p. 56)

1. हवादार

2. सुंदर

3. साफ़

4. लंबी

Practice 5 Comprehension Check (p. 58)

1. रोशन का घर दो मंज़िला है/ रोशन के घर में दो मंज़िलें हैं।

2. सबसे ऊपर छत है।

3. तीसरा कमरा, बच्चों के पढ़ने का कमरा है।

4. घर में दो गुसलख़ाने हैं।

5. घर के पीछे

6. घर में सीढ़ियाँ, रसोईघर की बगल में हैं।

Practice 6 Create Questions (p. 59)

1. आपका घर कितनी मंज़िला है?

2. खाने का कमरा कहाँ है?

3. घर के पीछे क्या है?

4. वह कमरा कैसा है?

5. सबसे ऊपर क्या है?

. . . .

Chapter 1.5 My Daily Routine

Practice 1 Verbs in the Habitual Tense (p. 63)

1. पीता   पीते   पीती   पीतीं

2. जाता   जाते   जाती   जातीं

3. घूमता   घूमते   घूमती   घूमतीं

4. आता   आते   आती   आतीं

5. करता   आते   आती   आतीं

6. बनाता   बनाते   बनाती   बनातीं

Practice 2 (p. 63)

1. करते

2. खाता

3. जाती

4. पकातीं

5. देखता

Practice 3 English to Hindi Translation (p. 64)

1. राम सुबह सात बजे स्कूल जाता है।

2. शीला रात को आठ बजे रात का खाना पकाती है।

3. वह रोज़ शाम को पाँच बजे लाइब्रेरी जाती है।

4. वह शाम को टी.वी देखता है।

5. रेनू रसोई में अपनी माँ की मदद करती है।

Practice 4 (p. 65)

1. नहा   कर / के   नहाकर / नहाके

2. जा   कर / के   जाकर / जाके

3. खा   कर / के   खाकर / खाके

4. सो   कर / के   सोकर / सोके

5. बना   कर / के   बनाकर / बनाके

Practice 5 Rewriting the sentences (p. 65)

1. लड़का स्कूल से आकर टी.वी देखता है।

2. पिताजी घर आकर अख़बार पढ़ते हैं।

3. वह घर पहुँचकर अपनी माँ की मदद करती है।

Practice 7 (p. 67)

(Own answers)

Practice 8 Fill in the blanks (pp. 68–69)

1. तुम करती हो?
2. जाती हूँ।
3. तुम रहती हो?
4. रुककर
5. पढ़ाई करके   योगा

6. करके सीधे
7. घर जाती
8. पहुँचकर
9. नहाती-धोती   थोड़ा आराम
10. रसोई में की मदद लगभग हम देखकर सो जाती

Practice 9 Comprehension Questions (p. 69)

1. मीरा स्कूल के बाद लाइब्रेरी जाती है।
2. लाइब्रेरी में रुककर मीरा पढ़ाई करती है।
3. नहा धोकर और थोड़ी देर आराम करके मीरा माँ की मदद करती है।
4. नहीं, मीरा व्यायाम करके सीधे घर जाती है।
5. घर पहुँचकर मीरा नहाती-धोती है, आराम करती है, माँ की मदद करती है और खाना खाकर थोड़ी देर टी.वी देखती है।

• • • • • • • • • • • • • •

Chapter 2.1 At a Train Station in India

Practice 1 Vocabulary-Building Exercise (p. 77)

1. to go from one place to another
2. the price for transportation
3. a pre-arrangement to secure space
4. a place where a person ends his/her journey
5. at an upper level
6. to come back from somewhere
7. a grade of seating arrangement in a plane or a train
8. to depart

9. a detailed description
10. to fill out
11. the act of inscribing your name
12. to desire
13. indicates need
14. to move
15. age
16. the date of a month

Practice 2 (pp. 78–79)

1. चाहिए
2. भरना
3. जानना
4. कब-कब
5. सुबह
6. पहली

7. निकलती
8. दूसरी
9. सवा
10. कौन
11. गाड़ियाँ
12. चलतीं

13. कितना समय लगता
14. दो घंटे
15. से
16. तक
17. जाती
18. किराया

19. लगता
20. छह बजे वाली
21. चार सौ साठ
22. दीजिए
23. लीजिए

Practice 4 Pre-Reading Exercise (p. 81)

Nouns: स्त्री गंतव्य पता यात्री हस्ताक्षर वापसी विवरण

Adjectives: निचली सही ऊपरी पहली

Verbs: भरना चलना चाहिए निकलना

Practice 5 (p. 81)
(Own answers)

. . . .

Chapter 2.2 Travel Arrangements

Practice 1 Grammar (p. 85)

1. मुझे जाना है।
2. मुझे टिकट ख़रीदने हैं।
3. मुझे शाकाहरी खाना मंगाना है।
4. हमें वहाँ जल्दी पहुँचना है।
5. उन्हें निकलना है।
6. इसे हवाई जहाज़ में सोना है।
7. उन्हें अपनी माँ को फ़ोन करना है।
8. मुझे किराया पता करना है।
9. मुझे नौ तारीख़ को वापस आना है।

Practice 3 (pp. 88–89)

First causative	Second causative	First causative	Second causative
1. बुलाना	से बुलवाना	7. बिकाना	से बिकवाना
2. खोलना	से खुलवाना	8. सिखाना	से सिखवाना
3. छुड़ाना	से छुड़वाना	9. खिंचाना	से खिंचवाना
4. खुलाना	से खुलवाना	10. जलाना	से जलवाना
5. रोकना	से रुकवाना	11. चलाना	से चलवाना
6. मिलाना	से मिलवाना		

Practice 4 (p. 89)
(Own answers)

Practice 5 (pp. 90–91)

1. टिकट बुक कराना
2. तारीख़ें
3. खाली जगह
4. विमान का किराया
5. टिकट
6. आने-जाने का
7. आगमन-प्रस्थान
8. शाकाहारी
9. सस्ता
10. महंगा
11. गंतव्य

Practice 6 Vocabulary-Building Exercise (p. 91)

1. जाना
2. हवाई जहाज़
3. महंगा
4. पहुँचने वाली जगह

Practice 8 Listening Exercise (p. 93)

1. To say
2. To do
3. To tell
4. To have done
5. To reach
6. To sleep
7. To eat
8. To come
9. To order
10. To take out
11. To ask for
12. To go
13. To give
14. To take
15. To complete the work

Practice 9 Post-Listening Exercise (pp. 93–94)

1. इस महीने की अट्ठारह तारीख को (18th of this month)
2. कॉलर को लंदन जाना है। (London)
3. दो हफ़्ते बाद तीन तारीख को (two weeks later, on the 3rd)
4. इकोनॉमी (economy)
5. चालीस हज़ार रुपये (40,000 Rs.)
6. रात दस बजे प्रस्थान और सुबह पौने सात बजे आगमन (Departing 10 p.m. at night and arriving in London at 6:45 a.m.)
7. माँसाहारी (non-vegetarian)

Travel Related Advice and Suggestions

Practice 1 Translation (p. 96)

1. Decide
    a. Travel date
    b. Destination
    c. To buy a one-way or round-trip ticket

2. Make a list and write.
    a. The number of children, adults and seniors going with you
    b. What are their names and ages

3. Tell the travel agent
    a. What else you would like to book along with the ticket
    b. You would like to book in a first class or in an economy class.
    c. Your reference for the seat—near the window, in the middle or the corner seat aisle.

4. Ask the travel agent …
    a. What type of food is served on baord.
    b. The amount of luggage you take.
    c. The weight allowance for the luggage.
    d. Details of the flight's arrival and departure times.

Practice 2 (p. 97)

(Own answers)

. . . .

Chapter 2.3 Hiring an Auto Rickshaw

Practice 1 (p. 101)

1. (to stop) रुकूँगा/रुकूँगी रुकोगे/रुकोगी रुकेगा/ रुकेगी रुकेंगे/रुकेंगी रुकेगा/ रुकेगी रुकेंगे/रुकेंगी
2. (to sit) बैठूँगा/बैठूँगी बैठोगे/बैठोगी बैठेगा/ बैठेगी बैठेंगे/बैठेंगी बैठेगा/ बैठेगी बैठेंगे/बैठेंगी
3. (to get off) उतरूँगा/उतरूँगी उतरोगे/उतरोगी उतरेगा/उतरेगी उतरेंगे/उतरेंगी उतरेगा/ उतरेगी उतरेंगे/उतरेंगी

Practice 2 Pre-Listening Exercise (p. 102)

1. यहाँ से	3. सवारी	5. अगर तुम जाना चाहते हो	7. चलना
2. दे देना	4. अरे	6. बैठना	8. पैसे लगना

Practice 4 (p. 103)

1. कितना लोगे
2. अरे ऑटोवाले रूकना!!!

Practice 5 (p. 103)

1. हम हमेशा अस्सी में जाते हैं।	2. हम सिर्फ़ अस्सी रुपये देंगे।	3. चलना है तो चलो।

Practice 6 (pp. 104–105)

1. रुकना	5. कितना	9. ठीक, बोलो, भई।	13. कम, दे देना
2. बैठो , जाना	6. कहाँ	10. ज़्यादा, नहीं, हैं	14. चलो, ठीक है
3. चलोगे	7. उतरना	11. लूँगा	15. बैठो
4. सवारियाँ	8. लगेंगे	12. जाते, चलो	

. . . .

Chapter 2.4 Hiring a Cycle Rickshaw

Practice 1 Translation (p. 107)

1. मुझे आज वापस आना है   क्या तुम्हें भी आज वापस आना है?
2. मुझे साइकिल रिक्शा में बैठना है   क्या तुम भी साइकिल रिक्शा में बैठोगे?

Imperatives

Practice 2 (p. 113)

1. मेरा काम कर देना	3. तुम मेरे दोस्त को बता देना कि कल आऊँगा
2. यह बैग वहाँ रख देना	4. तुम मुझे बाज़ार में उतार देना

Practice 3 Vocabulary-Building Exercise (p. 114)

1. दूर	3. भईया	5. कम	7. तुरंत
2. रुपये	4. चौक	6. चढ़ाई	

Practice 4 (pp. 114–115)

1. सुनो भैया	7. बहुत	13. तुरंत	19. आने-जाने
2. भैया	8. दूर	14. कितनी	20. बता दिया
3. बाबू जी	9. चढ़ाई	15. दुकान	21. दे दीजिएगा
4. चौक	10. थोड़ा कम	16. मिनट का	22. वापसी
5. लोगे	11. दे देना	17. वापस	23. दूँगा
6. तीस	12. लाकर छोड़	18. ले आऊँगा	24. आइये, बैठिये

Practice 5-1 (p. 117)

1. रुपये लगना	2. रुपये लेना	3. समय लगना

Practice 5-2 (p. 117)

1. मुझे वहाँ कुछ काम है फिर मुझे वापस आना है।

2. वहाँ आने जाने और का क्या लोगे?

Practice 5-3 (p. 117)

1. बाबू दो रुपया कम दे दीजियेगा।
    Sir you can give me two rupees less.
2. मैं आपको वापस भी ले आऊँगा।
    I can bring you back too.
3. बाबू अब हमने एक तरफ़ का बता दिया।
    Sir, I have told you the one-way fare.
4. जो समझियेगा दे दीजियेगा।
    Whatever you think is appropriate, just give me that.

Practice 6 Post-Listening Activity (pp. 117–118)

1. मुझे पास के बाज़ार जाना है।
2. उसका तुम क्या लोगे?
3. क्या तुम वापस भी आओगे?
4. बाबू जी, वह तो बहुत दूर है।
5. आपको वहाँ कितना समय लगेगा?
6. तीस रुपये तो बहुत ज़्यादा हैं।
7. क्या तुम दस-पन्द्रह मिनट ठहर सकते हो?
8. जो आप ठीक समझें, दे दीजिए।
9. आइये, बैठिये।

Practice 7 Comprehension Check (p. 119)

1. रमेश को चौक तक जाना है।
2. क्योंकि चौक बहुत दूर है और वहाँ चढ़ाई भी है।
3. रिक्शेवाला रमेश को पचपन रुपये में ले जाने को तैयार हुआ।
4. क्योंकि रमेश को बाज़ार में दुकान में कुछ काम है।
5. रमेश को बाज़ार में दस-पन्द्रह मिनट तक रुकना है।

. . . .

Chapter 3 Inquiring about Opening a Bank Account

Practice 1 Translation (p. 124)

1. Everyone has to fill out a form in the bank.   बैंक में सबको फ़ॉर्म भरना पड़ता है।
2. Often we have to wait a long time.   कई बार बैंक में बहुत इंतज़ार करना होता है।
3. Lots of documents have to be shown in order to open an account.   बैंक में खाता खोलने के लिए बहुत से काग़ज़ात दिखाने पड़ते हैं।
4. I will have to open an account.   मुझे/ मुझको खाता खोलना पड़ेगा।
5. My father had to go to the bank yesterday.   कल मेरे पिताजी को बैंक जाना पड़ा।
6. Sam had to show his identification card. सैम को अपना परिचय पत्र दिखाना पड़ा।
7. People will have to deposit the form.   लोगों को फ़ॉर्म जमा कराने होंगे।
8. Full information must be given to the bank.   बैंक में पूरी जानकारी देनी होगी।
9. We are having to open a bank account.   हमें/हमको खाता खोलना पड़ रहा है।
10. They have to go to the embassy.   उनको दूतावास जाना पड़ रहा है।

Practice 3 Vocabulary Building (p. 125)

1.	काम	6.	खुलवाना	11.	करना पड़ेगा	16.	दिखाना
2.	कब	7.	क़ाग़ज़ात	12.	सकना	17.	जमा कराना
3.	सप्ताह	8.	कोई	13.	भरना	18.	बंद होना
4.	ठहरना	9.	बात करना	14.	देना	19.	फिर
5.	ख़ाता	10.	बताना	15.	जानकारी	20.	आऊँगा

Practice 5 Comprehension Check (p. 127)

1. डेविड एक हफ़्ते पहले भारत आया।
2. डेविड को बैंक में खाता खुलवाना है।
3. सबसे पहले डेविड को बैंक मैनेजर से बात करनी होगी।
4. बैंक सुबह दस बजे खुलता है और पाँच बजे बंद होता है।

Practice 6 Translation (pp.127–128)

1. आपको बैंक में पाँच हज़ार रुपये जमा कराने पड़ेंगे।
2. मुझे बैंक में खाता खोलने के लिए क्या करना पड़ेगा।
3. तुम्हारे पास बैंक के बारे में कोई जानकारी है?
4. मुझे बचत खाता खोलना है।

. . . .

Chapter 3.2 Opening a Bank Account

Practice 1 Labeling (p. 129)

1.	जमा कराना	4.	दिखाना	7.	बदलना	10.	हस्ताक्षर
2.	निकालना	5.	फ़ॉर्म भरना	8.	प्रमाण	11.	इंतज़ार
3.	भुनाना	6.	मुद्रा	9.	राशि		

Practice 2 (p. 130)

1.	खाता	3.	इंतज़ार	5.	बचत
2.	परिचय	4.	भुनवाना	6.	राशि

Practice 3 (pp.130–131)

1.	बताइये	3.	खाता	5.	बचत	7.	निवास
2.	सेवा	4.	खुलवाना	6.	दूतावास	8.	कितने साल

Practice 4 (p. 133)

1.	अच्छा तो	4.	क़ाग़ज़ात	7.	प्रमाण पत्र	10.	क़ाग़ज़ात
2.	एक फ़ॉर्म भरना होगा	5.	फ़ोटो	8.	जमा कराने	11.	मुलाकात
3.	पूरी जानकारी	6.	परिचय पत्र निवास	9.	कम से कम		

Practice 5 Post-Listening Exercise (p. 134)

1. फ़ोटो पहचान पत्र   निवास का प्रमाण पत्र   नौकरी का प्रमाण पत्र
2. एक हज़ार रुपये
3. क्योंकि उसके पास पूरी राशि, क़ाग़ज़ात और भरा हुआ फ़ॉर्म नहीं है।

. . . .

Chapter 3.3 Cashing a Check

Practice 1 Matching (p. 135)

1. Signature
2. Service
3. To withdraw
4. To do
5. Should I do
6. Behind
7. Two thousand five hundred

Practice 2 (pp. 135–136)

(Own answers)

. . . .

Chapter 4.1 In the Marketplace

Practice 2 (p. 143)

1. Cauliflower
2. Carrot
3. Radish
4. Eggplant
5. Fresh
6. Cilantro
7. Cost
8. Pricey
9. Wholesale market
10. To price
11. To say
12. To put
13. Change
14. How much is it?

Practice 4 Post-Listening Exercise (p. 144)

1. (a) अरे सब्ज़ी वाले! (Listen, vegetable vendor)

   (b) बहनजी (Madam/sister)
2. Fresh cabbage, cauliflower, carrots, tomatoes, cilantro and bell pepper/capsicum
3. इतनी महंगी!! ठीक दाम बोलो| सब्ज़ीमंडी में तो यह बीस रुपये किलो है।
4. Familiar: लो बोलो दोगे चलो दे दो

   Neutral: रुकना देना दाम लगाना डाल देना
5. कुल कितने हुए?
6. क्या भाव दी कैसे दिए

Practice 5 (p. 145)

1. रुकना
2. आया
3. पास
4. चाहिए
5. भाव दी
6. महंगी
7. दोगे

Practice 6 (p. 145)

1. मुझे पाव भर गाजर चाहिए।
2. टमाटर क्या भाव दिए?
3. इन सबके कितने हुए?
4. बहुत दाम लगा रहे हो।
5. इतनी महंगी!! ठीक दाम बोलो।
6. मुझे धनिया का एक गुच्छा देना।
7. कुछ हरी मिर्चें और अदरक का एक टुकड़ा भी डाल देना।
8. तुम्हारे पास पाँच सौ के खुल्ले हैं?

. . . .

Chapter 4.2 At the Grocery Store

Practice 1 Verb Conjugation (p. 150)

1. धुलना धुल ेा, ेी, ेे धुला, धुली, धुले धुला हुआ, धुली हुआ, धुले हुये
2. छिलना छिल ेा, ेी, ेे छिला, छिली, छिले छिला हुआ, छिली हुयी, छिले हुये
3. पिसना पिस ेा, ेी, ेे पिसा, पिसी, पिसे पिसा हुआ, पिसी हुयी, पिसे हुये

Practice 2 (pp. 150–151)

1. झाड़ू	7. साबुत लाल मिर्च	13. राजमा	19. छोले
2. साबुन	8. लौंग	14. मैदा	20. काजू
3. मंजन	9. साबुत धनिया	15. आटा	21. पिस्ता
4. तेल	10. धनिया पाउडर	16. हल्दी	22. बादाम
5. नमक	11. साबुत दालचीनी	17. मूँगफली	23. किशिमश
6. चीनी	12. दालचीनी पाउडर	18. दालें	24. तेजपत्ता

Practice 3 (p. 152)

Group 1

1. Salt	3. Wheat flour	5. Turmeric
2. Sugar	4. All-purpose flour	

Group 2

1. Toothpaste	2. Broom	3. Soap

Group 3

1. Pulse	2. Rice	3. Chickpeas	4. Kidney bean

Group 4

1. Cumin	2. Black pepper	3. Cinnamon

Group 5

1. Peanut	3. Almond	5. Cashew
2. Cardamom	4. Pistachio	6. Raisin

Group 6

1. Oil	2. Olive oil	3. Peanut oil

Group 7

1. Bread	2. Butter	3. Biscuit

Practice 4 (p. 153)

Nouns

1. राशन	5. नमक	10. राजमा
2. सामान	6. डिब्बा	11. मूँगफली
3. चीनी	7. मिचर	12. दाम
4. चाय की पत्ती	8. हल्दी	13. रुपये
	9. पैकेट	14. तेल

Adjectives

1.	एक	4.	लाल	7.	छिली
2.	आधा	5.	ढाई सौ ग्राम	8.	एक सौ अस्सी
3.	पिसी	6.	डेढ़	9.	बड़ा वाला

Verbs

1.	आइये	3.	लेना	5.	निकाल देना
2.	दूँ	4.	है	6.	दे देना

Measurements and weights

1.	एक	3.	ढाई सौ ग्राम	5.	डेढ़	7.	बड़ा वाला
2.	आधा	4.	किलो	6.	एक सौ अस्सी		

Practice 5 Comprehension (p. 153)

1. (1) आइये (3) लेना (5) निकाल देना
    (2) दूँ (4) है (6) दे देना
2. (1) बहन जी (2) भइया

Practice 7 Comprehension Check (p. 156)

1. (1) जैतून का तेल तो नहीं है (2) बादाम तो अभी नहीं हैं, ख़त्म हो गये हैं।
2. (1) कितनी दे दूँ? (2) पेस्ट दूँ या पाउडर?
3. अच्छा अब मेरा बिल बना दो। कितने का बना?

Practice 8 Fill in the Blanks (p. 156)

1.	डबल रोटी	5.	बट्टियाँ	9.	बादाम	13.	चाहिए
2.	मक्खन	6.	मंजन	10.	डाल देना	14.	बना दीजिए
3.	झाड़ू	7.	भर	11.	ख़त्म हो गये हैं		
4.	साबुन	8.	किशमिश	12.	साबुत		

· · · · · · · · · · · · · ·

Chapter 4.3 Shopping for Clothes

Practice 1 (pp. 159–160)

1. Polite: मुझे सूती सलवार-कुर्ते दिखाइये।
    Extra-Polite: मुझे सूती सलवार-कुर्ते दिखाइयेगा।

2. Polite: एक पगड़ी भी निकाल दीजिए।
    Extra-Polite: एक पगड़ी भी निकाल दीजिएगा।

3. Polite: डिज़ाइन वाला नहीं, सादा निकालिए।
    Extra-Polite: डिज़ाइन वाला नहीं, सादा निकालिएगा।

4. Polite: आप कुर्ता ट्राई कर लीजिए।
    Extra-Polite: आप कुर्ता ट्राई कर लीजिएगा।

Practice 2 Translation (p. 160)

1.   आज आपको क्या दिखाऊँ?
2.   सूती में दिखाऊँ या रेशमी में?
3.   जी, आपको कुर्ता-पाजामा आपके नाप का दिखाऊँ?

Practice 3 Fill in the Blanks (pp. 160–161)

1.	लीजियेगा	4.	दिखाइयेगा	7.	देखिये
2.	दिखाइये	5.	देखिये	8.	निकाल दीजिये
3.	देखिये	6.	दिखाइये	9.	दिखाइये

At a Garment Store 1
Part 1 Fill in the Blanks (pp. 161–162)

1.	दिखाऊँ	6.	दिखाइये	11.	रंग	16.	चुन्री	21.	रुपये
2.	सलवार	7.	मिलेंगे	12.	फूलों	17.	कितने	22.	दे
3.	कुर्ते	8.	पसंद	13.	वाला	18.	का	23.	दूँ
4.	सूती	9.	सादे	14.	नीले	19.	पन्द्रह	24.	निकाल
5.	रेशमी	10.	हल्के	15.	पीले	20.	सौ	25.	दीजिए

At a Garment Store 2
Practice 6 (p. 165)

Nouns: कुर्ता, पाजामा, चुन्री, पगड़ी, चीज़, दाम

Cognates: सर, साइज़, पार्टी, बिल, सिल्क, आर्टीफ़ीशियल, कॉन्ट्रास्ट, ट्राई, फ़िक्सड

Adjectives: रेशमी, सूती, काला वाला, पार्टी लायक, मरून वाला, क्रीम वाला, साढ़े, चार, हज़ार, तीन, मैडम का, क्रीम रंग की

Adverbs: आज

Verbs: दिखाना, चाहिए, आना, कर लेना, निकाल देना, बना देना, होना, लगाना, लेना, ले

Practice 7 Comprehension Check (p. 166)

1.   आदमी को रेशमी कुर्ता-पाजामा चाहिए।
2.   दुकानदार आदमी को फ़िटिंग/ट्रायल रूम में ले गया
3.   कुर्ते-पजामे के साथ चुन्री भी आयेगी।
4.   दुकानदार आदमी को पगड़ी बेचने की कोशिश कर रहा है।
5.   आदमी को दुकानदार को चार हज़ार पाँच सौ रुपये देने हैं।

· · · · · · · · · · · · · ·

Chapter 4.4 At a Sari Emporium
Practice 2 Translation (p. 169)

1.   आज मैं आपको क्या दिखाऊँ?
2.   आपको किस तरह की/कैसी साड़ी दिखाऊँ?
3.   आपको किस रेंज की साड़ी दिखाऊँ?
4.   आज मैं आपकी क्या सेवा करूँ?

Practice 3 Translation (p. 173)

1. आपके पास सिल्क की साड़ियाँ हैं?/क्या आपके पास सिल्क की साड़ियाँ हैं?

2. हमारे पास सिल्क की साड़ियाँ नहीं हैं।

3. उसके पास कई **अच्छी** साड़ियाँ हैं।

4. उनके पास कुछ **अच्छी** साड़ियाँ हैं।

Practice 5 (p. 174)

1. I like Indian clothes.

2. He/she will like it.

3. I like this *sari*.

4. What did you like?

5. He did not like that shirt.

Practice 6 Pre-Listening Activity (pp. 174–175)

1. कुछ

2. पास

3. चाहेंगी

4. चाहिए

5. से लेकर

6. साथ

7. आजकल

8. **अच्छी** लग रही है

Practice 7 Post-Listening Exercise A (p. 176)

1. Hindi: मुझे ज़री बॉडर की, बढ़िया सिल्क की साड़ी चाहिए। (Need)
   English: I need a good silk *sari* with a *zari* border.

2. Hindi: मुझे कुछ साड़ियाँ लेनीं हैं। (Desire)
   English: I need to buy few/some *saris*.

3. Hindi: हमें तीन चार हज़ार से आठ हज़ार तक की साड़ियाँ दिखाइये। (Request)
   English: Please show us *saris* ranging from 3-4,000 to 8,000.

Post-Listening Exercise B (p. 176)

1. Hindi: हमारे पास तीन हज़ार से लेकर एक लाख तक की साड़ियाँ हैं।
   English: We have *saris* from 3,000 to 100,000 rupees.

2. Hindi: हमें तीन चार हज़ार से आठ हज़ार तक की साड़ियाँ दिखाइये। (Request)
   English: Please show us *saris* ranging from 3-4,000 to 8,000 Rps.

Post-Listening Exercise C (p. 176)

1. Hindi: हमारे पास सब तरह की साड़ियों की वैराइटी है।
   English: We have all kinds of *saris*.

2. Hindi: आपके पास किस रेंज की साड़ियाँ हैं।
   English: What is the price range of your *saris*?

Practice 9 Comprehension Check (p. 178)

1. दुकानदार के पास शायद हर रेंज की साड़ियाँ हैं।

2. भागलपुरी साड़ी बिहार राज्य की है।

3. दुकानदार के पास मैसूर जॉर्जेट में दो रंगों के कॉम्बीनेशन गुलाबी एवं स्लेटी और नारंगी रंग में हैं।

4. हाँ, साड़ी के साथ ब्लाउज़ भी आता है।

Practice 10 Diaglogue Creation (p. 179)

(Own answers)

Chapter 5.1 Eating at a Roadside Restaurant
Practice 1 Vocabulary-Building Exercise (p. 185)

1. बुरा
2. बाहर
3. बाद में
4. के बाद
5. बे स्वाद
6. ज्यादा
7. तला-भुना
8. वहाँ

Practice 2 Classify (p. 186)
Bread: चपाती; पराँठा, मिस्सी रोटी, पनीर पराँठा
Utensils: चम्मच, कटोरी, काँटा
Breakfast/Snacks: पकौड़ा, पाव-भाजी
Beverages: छाछ, पानी
Vegetables: ककड़ी, छोला, टमाटर, मटर, प्याज़
Adjectives/Verbs/Adverbs: दे देना, अन्दर, सादा, यहाँ, दम, बाहर, ले आना

Practice 3 Part 1 (pp. 186–187)
1. We will sit outside and eat.
2. Give me a plate of fritters first.
3. Wait for 5 minutes.
4. Can you also get me a glass of water?
5. Let me see and I will let you know.
6. How long is it going to take?
7. Get the bill. How much is the total?
8. Can you also give me a spoon and a fork?
9. That's all. I don't need anything else.
10. Please give me a bottle of mineral water.

Practice 4 Comprehension Check (p. 188)
1. ग्राहक, बाहर खाट पर बैठना चाहते हैं।
2. खाने का मैन्यू बोर्ड पर लिखा है।

Practice 5 Post-Listening Exercise (pp. 188–189)
1. आदमी को पीने के लिए लस्सी चाहिए।
2. आदमी ने सबसे पहले एक प्लेट प्याज़ के पकौड़े मँगवाये।
3. खाने में आदमी ने दम आलू, गोभी, चपाती और ,मटर पुलाव मँगवाया।

Chapter 5.2 Seating in a Fine Restaurant
Practice 1 Pre-Listening Activity (pp. 190–192)
1. आइये
2. चार जने
3. बैठना
4. पसंद
5. करेंगे
6. खुले में
7. मेरे साथ आइये
8. ठीक
9. ताज़ी हवा
10. आप देख लिजिए

Practice 3 (pp. 192–193)
1. हम बाहर खुले में बैठना चाहेंगे।
2. हम चार जने हैं।
3. हाँ, यह जगह ठीक है| हम बाहर, खुले में बैठना चाहेंगे।

• • • • • • • • • • • • •

Ordering

Practice 2 (p. 194)

1. सर , आप ऑर्डर देने के लिए तैयार हैं? एपीटाइज़र में क्या लेंगे?

   Sir, Are you ready to place your order? What would you like to have for appetizer?

2. हाँ, पहले ये सब चीज़े ले आओ।

   Yes, get these things first.

3. a. ठीक है, तो दो जगह सिज़लर्स भी ले आना।

   Ok, then get me an order of sizzlers.

   b. साथ में बर्फ़ भी ले आना

   Also get the ice with it.

   These two sentences in terms of tone suggest that a customer is making a request.

. . . .

Chapter 5.3 Paying the Bill

Practice 1 Pre-Listening Activity (p. 195)

(Own answers)

Practice 3.1 (p. 197)

1. सर और कुछ लेंगे? आपको खाना पसंद आया? (hospitality)

   Sir, would you like to have something else? Did you enjoy the food?

2. थैंक्यू सर, फिर आइयेगा। (courtesy)

   Thank you sir, please come again.

Practice 3.2 (p. 197)

1. यह लीजिए सर, आपकी रसीद।   2. थैंक्यू सर, फिर आइयेगा।

Practice 3.3 (p. 197)

1. तुम हमारा बिल ले आओ   Just bring us the bill.

2. आप यहाँ साइन कर दीजिए।   Please sign here.

Practice 3.3 Hindi Sentences (p. 197)

1. बिल ले आओ!   3. क्या टिप बिल में शामिल है?

2. हमे खाना अच्छा लगा/ खाना अच्छा था।   4. क्या आप क्रैडिट कार्ड लेते हैं?

. . . .

Chapter 6.1 Hiring a Washerman

Practice 1 (p. 201)

(Own answers)

Practice 3 Post-Listening Exercise (p. 204)
1. के पीछे
2. भाई
3. घरों
4. करोगे
5. धुलवाने
6. ले जाना

Practice 4 Comprehension Check (p. 205)
1. रघुवीर एक धोबी है।
2. माधव भी एक धोबी है। वह लोगों के कपड़े धोता है।
3. शीला को माधव से कपड़े धुलवाने हैं और इस्त्री करवानी है।
4. शीला को साड़ियों पर कलफ़ लगवाना है।

Practice 5 Comprehension Check Part 2 (p. 206)
1. शीला को एक दिन बाद/परसों कपड़े चाहिएँ।
2. शीला को साड़ियाँ धुलवानी हैं, कलफ़ लगवाना है और उन पर **इस्त्री** करवानी है।
3. धोबी ने शीला से पिछले महीने का हिसाब माँगा।

Practice 6 (p. 206)
1. शीला
2. माधव धोबी
3. शीला
4. माधव धोबी
5. माधव धोबी
6. माधव धोबी
7. शीला
8. शीला

. . . .

Chapter 6.2 Reporting a Theft
Practice 1 Vocabulary-Building Exercise (p. 210)
1. खो जाना
2. लौटना
3. रहने की जगह की जानकारी
4. मालूम होना
5. रुकना
6. बताना

Practice 2 (p. 210)
1. आना
2. मिल जाना
3. आ जाना
4. स्वदेश
5. उधार
6. चलना

Practice 3 Comprehension Check (pp. 211–212)
1. ऑफ़िस कम्प्यूटर, सूटकेस, कपड़े, टिकट, पासपोर्ट, कुछ नक़द
2. चोरी की जानकारी चोरी के तुरंत बाद दी गई।
3. मोनिका को होटल के ही किसी आदमी पर शक़ है।
4. चोरी के समय मोनिका नहा रही थी।

Practice 4 Fill in the blanks (p. 212)
1. चोरी
2. लिखवानी
3. के ही
4. सब कुछ
5. सामान

Practice 5 Vocabulary-Building Exercise (p. 213)
1. कितने दिनों तक
2. लौटना
3. रुकना
4. संपर्क करवाना
5. किसी के बारे में बताना
6. जल्द ही
7. मालूम होना

. . . .

Chapter 6.2

Practice 6 Part 2 (p. 214)

1. Instructions:

   (1) Hindi: आप अपना पता और फ़ोन नंबर हमें लिखवा दें।

   English: Please give us your telephone number.

   (2) Hindi: आप अपने पासपोर्ट चोरी होने की जानकारी उन्हें दें।

   English: Please give them the information about your passport being stolen.

2. Causative Verbs

   (1) वहाँ हम आपके दूतावास से आपकी बात करवाएँगे।

   (2) आप अपना पता और फ़ोन नंबर लिखवा दें।

Practice 7 Comprehension Questions (p. 214)

1. Monica has to fly home the next day.
2. The police went to the hotel to investigate the theft.

Practice 7 (Hindi Sentences) (pp. 214–215)

1.	मुझे रिपोर्ट लिखवानी है।	4.	अब मैं क्या करूँ?
2.	मेरा सामान चोरी हो गया है।	5.	मुझे तो कल ही घर वापस जाना है।
3.	मैं नीचे रेस्तराँ में थी/था।	6.	क्या आप मेरा संपर्क मेरे दूतावास से करवा सकते हैं?

. . . .

Chapter 6.3 At the Doctor's

Practice 1 Vocabulary- Building (p. 220)

1.	ज़ुकाम	4.	खून	7.	तकलीफ़	10.	दवाई
2.	बुख़ार	5.	घबराहट	8.	कमज़ोरी	11.	बुख़ार उतरना
3.	मुँह खोलो	6.	जाँच करना	9.	खाँसी	12.	पर्ची

Practice 1 Part 2 (Creative Writing) (p. 221)

(Own answers)

Practice 3 Post-Listening Exercise (p. 222)

1.	मेरी तबियत ठीक नहीं है।	5.	मुझे ठंड लग गयी है।
2.	मुझे पिछले तीन दिन से बुख़ार हो रहा है।	6.	मुझे बहुत खाँसी हो रही है।
3.	मुझे ठंड लग रही है।	7.	कोई घबराने वाली बात तो नहीं है?
4.	मुझे बहुत कमज़ोरी लग रही है।		

Practice 4

(Own answers)

Practice 5 Comprehension Check (p. 223)

1. मोहन को तेज़ ज़ुकाम हो रहा है और खाँसी भी हो रही है।

2. हाँ, मोहन घबरा रहा है।

3. डॉक्टर को लगता है कि मोहन को ठंड लग गयी है और इनफैक्शन हो गया है।

4. मोहन को दवा, डॉक्टर की दुकान के नीचे बनी फ़र्मेसी से मिलेगी।

5. डॉक्टर ने मोहन को खाने के साथ एक गोली सुबह और एक गोली शाम को लेने के कहा है।

Follow up appointment

Practice 7 Post-Listening Exercise (p. 225)

1. मेरे सिर और गले में अभी भी बहुत दर्द है।

    Translation: My head and throat are still hurting a lot.

2. क्या निगलने में तक़लीफ़ हो रही है?

    Translation: Are you having problem swallowing?

3. खाने-पीने में बहुत दर्द होता है।

    Translation: I am having problem swallowing food.

Practice 8 Doctor's questions (p. 226)

1. तो, अब तबियत कैसी है तुम्हारी?

    Translation: So, how are you feeling now?

2. क्या दवा से बुखार उतरा?

    Translation: Did the medication help with the fever?

3. क्या निगलने में तक़लीफ़ हो रही है?

    Translation: Do you have trouble swallowing?

4. बुखार कब उतरा?

    Translation: How long has it been since the fever went away?

Practice 9 Doctor's instructions (p. 226)

1. नीचे लैब में जाकर टैस्ट करवा लेना।

    Translation: Go get the tests done downstairs.

2. अपनी दवाइयाँ लेते रहना।

    Translation: Keep taking the medication.

3. यह रही खून के जाँच की पर्ची, आज ही जाकर करवा लेना।

    Translation: Here's a referral. Go and get it done today.

4. दो दिन बाद मुझसे आकर मिलना।

    Translation: Come back to see me in two days.

• • • • • • • • • • • • •

Chapter 6.4 Hiring a Maid

Practice 1 Verb Conjugation (pp. 228–229)

Main verb	Habitual Present	Perfect	Future
कर लेना (example)	कर लेता/लेती/कर लेतीं/कर लेते	कर लिया/कर ली/ कर लिये/कर लीं	कर लेगा/कर लेगी/ कर लेंगी/कर लेंगे
ले लेना (to take away)	ले लेता/ ले लेती/ ले लेतीं/ले लेते	ले लिया/लेली/ले लिये/ले लीं	ले लेगा/ले लेगी/ले लेंगी/ले लेंगे
आ जाना (to come back)	आ जाता/आ जाती/आ जातीं/ आ जाते	आ गया/आ गयी/आ गये/आ गयीं	आ जायेगा/ आ जायेगी/आ जायेंगी/ आ जायेंगे
बना देना (to make ready)	बना देता/बना देती/बना देतीं/बना देते	बना दिया/बना दी/बना दिये/बना दीं	बना देगा/बना देगी/बना देंगी/बना देंगे
पका देना (to cook)	पका देता/पका देती/ पका देतीं/ पका देते	पका दिया/पका दी/पका दिये/पका दीं	पका देगा/पका देगी/पका देंगी/पका देंगे
चले जाना (to go back)	चला जाता/चली जाती/चली जातीं/ चले जाते	चला गया/चली गयी/चले गये/चली गयीं	चला जायेगा/चली जायेगी/चली जायेंगी/चले जायेंगे
बैठ जाना (to sit down)	बैठ जाता/बैठ जाती/बैठ जातीं/बैठ जाते	बैठ गया/बैठ गयी/बैठ गये/ बैठ गयीं	बैठ जायेगा/बैठ जायेगी/ बैठ जायेंगी/ बैठ जायेंगे
कर लेना (to complete work)	कर लेता/लेती/कर लेतीं/कर लेते	कर लिया/कर ली/कर लिये/कर लीं	कर लेगा/कर लेगी/कर लेंगी/कर लेंगे
माँज लेना (to wash up dishes)	माँज लेता/माँज लेती/ माँज लेतीं/माँज लेते	माँज लिया/माँज ली/माँज लिये/माँज लीं	माँज लेगा/माँज लेगी/माँज लेंगी/माँज लेंगे
कर जाना (to finish up and go)	कर जाता/कर जाती/कर जातीं/कर जाते	कर गया/कर गयी/कर गये/कर गयीं	कर जाएगा/कर जाएगी/ कर जाएंगी/कर जायेंगे

Practice 2 (p. 229)

1. मेरे घर आने से पहले पूरा काम ख़त्म कर लेना।
2. कामवाली ने खाना बना लिया है।
3. मेरे घर आने से पहले सारे बर्तन माँज देना।
4. घर साफ़ कर दो।
5. आप जाइये। मैं सारा काम कर लूँगी।
6. सुनो ! मेरे घर आने से पहले उससे खाना बनवा लेना।

Practice 3 Fill in the blanks (p. 230)

1. तुम्हारा
2. मेरा
3. काम करती हो।
4. बर्तन माँजती, पकाती
5. कितने घरों में
6. पाँच घरों में, दो घरों में
7. सुबह, करना शुरू करती हो
8. से, तक
9. शाम को

Practice 4 Post-Listening Exercise (p. 231)

1. Meaning: <u>Afternoon</u>
    Translation: <u>Come tomorrow in the afternoon.</u>
2. Meaning: <u>Place</u>
    Translation: <u>I also need a place to live.</u>
3. Meaning: <u>to cook</u>
    Translation: <u>Do you also know how to cook?</u>
4. Meaning: <u>wash dishes</u>
    Translation: <u>How much will you charge to wash dishes?</u>
5. Meaning: <u>to start from</u>
    Translation: <u>When do I have to start?</u>

Comprehension Questions (p. 232)

1. मीना बर्तन माँजती है और खाना पकाती है।
2. वह सुबह छह: बजे से दिन में दो बजे तक काम करती है।
3. शाम को, वह एक घर में खाना पकाती है।

Practice 5 Vocabulary Building Exercise (p. 232)

1. (1) दोनों समय   (3) बर्तन   (5) बनवाना   (7) काम
    (2) रहने की जगह   (4) तारीख़   (6) शुरु करना   (8) बर्तन माँजना
2. (Own answers)

Practice 6 (p. 233)

(Own answers)

Practice 7 (p. 234)

1. I have to have the dishes washed. (employer)
2. Do you have to have the food cooked? (maid)
3. Do you have a place for me to live? (maid)
4. I will cook at your house. (maid)
5. I don't have time. (maid)
6. I am going to talk to my husband and will let you know. (employer)
7. How much will you give per month? (maid)

Practice 9 Post-Listening Activity (p. 235)

1. आपको क्या-क्या काम करवाना है?
    Translation: <u>What is the work you want done?</u>
2. मुझे दोनों समय का खाना बनवाना है।
    Translation: <u>I need to have food prepared for both times.</u>
3. बरतन भी करवाने हैं।
    Translation: <u>I also need to have the dishes washed.</u>
4. मैं अपने पति से बात करके कल तुम्हें बताऊँगी।

5. Sentences with compound verbs
   (1) आपके घर काम भी कर दूँगी

   Translation: <u>I can also do your household work.</u>

   (2) खाना भी बना दूँगी।

   Translation: <u>I can also prepare food.</u>

· · · · · · · · · · · · ·

Chapter 6.5 Car Trouble

Practice 2 (p. 242)

(Own answers)

Practice 3 Vocabulary Building (p. 242)

1. ख़राब	4. बिल्कुल नहीं	7. किनारे पर	10. चले जाना
2. नौकर	5. क्यों	8. अपने आप	
3. चलना	6. दूर के	9. पास	

Practice 4 (p. 244)

1. ख़राब	4. इंतज़ार	7. बंद	10. मालिक
2. ख़राबी	5. किसी को	8. कोई	11. पास के
3. धुआँ	6. आवाज़	9. के किनारे	

Practice 5A (p. 244)

1. मेरी गाड़ी ख़राब हो गई है।

   Translation: <u>My car broke down.</u>
2. अचानक गाड़ी से धुआँ निकलने लगा।

   Translation: <u>Suddenly smoke started to come out from the car.</u>
3. इंजन से जलने की बदबू सी आ रही थी।

   Translation: <u>There was a strange smell coming out of the car.</u>
4. गाड़ी अजीब सी आवाज़ कर रही थी

   Translation: <u>The car was making strange noises.</u>

Practice 5B (p. 245)

1. एक मैकेनिक किसी की गाड़ी ठीक करने के लिए पास के गाँव गया है।

   Translation: <u>One of the mechanics has gone to the nearby village to repair a car.</u>
2. कोई बात नहीं, मैं उसका इंतज़ार कर लेता हूँ।

   Translation: <u>No problem, I can wait for him.</u>

Practice 5C (p. 245)

1. वह कब तक आ जायेगा?

   Translation: <u>What time is he expected to be back?</u>
2. कोई बात नहीं, मैं उसका इंतज़ार कर लेता हूँ।

   Translation: <u>No problem, I can wait for him.</u>

3. जी अच्छा, आप यहाँ तख़्त पर बैठ जाइये।

    Translation: <u>Ok sir, please have a seat on this wooden bench.</u>

Practice 6 Comprehension Check (pp. 245–246)

1. यात्री कार ठीक करने की दुकान के मालिक से मिला क्योंकि उसे अपनी गाड़ी ठीक करवानी थी।

2. यात्री की गाड़ी से अचानक गाड़ी से धुआँ निकलने लगा था| इंजन से जलने की बदबू सी आ रही थी| गाड़ी अजीब सी आवाज़ कर रही थी.

3. दुकानदार ने कहा कि मैकैनिक पास के गाँव में एक गाड़ी ठीक करने के लिए गया है।

· · · · · · · · · · · · ·

Appendix

Practice 1 (pp. 248–249)

Rivers: Ganga, Yamuna, Krishna, Kaveri, Godavari, Narmada, Brahmputra

Mountains: Aravali, Satpuda, Himalaya, Nilgiri

Desert: Thaar

Sea: Arabian

Practice 2 (p. 251)

1. है   3. हैं   5. है

2. हैं   4. है

Practice 3 (p. 252)

1. आमतौर पर चार ऋतुएँ होती हैं।   4. जून में, भारत में बहुत गर्मी होती है।

2. ऐमेज़ॉन के जंगलों में बहुत बारिश होती है।   5. हिमालय पर बहुत बर्फ़ होती है।

3. उत्तरी क्षेत्रों में आमतौर पर बहुत ठंड होती है।

Practice 4 (p. 252)

Words for directions: दक्षिण-पूर्व, उत्तर-पश्चिम, उत्तर, दक्षिण, पूरब, दक्षिण

Words for Terrain: पर्वत माला, खाड़ी, रेगिस्तान, महासागर, द्वीप समूह, नदियाँ

Country Names: अफ़ग़ानिस्तान, पाकिस्तान, भूटान, म्यांमार, बाँग्लादेश, श्री लंका

Practice 5 Post-Listening Exercise (p. 253)

1. महासागर   4. दुनिया   7. समुद्र तट

2. पर्वत माला   5. द्वीप   8. सर्दी का मौसम

3. रेगिस्तान   6. खाड़ी   9. बारिश का मौसम

Creative Writing (p. 254)

(Own answers)

· · · · · · · · · · · · ·

Audio Listing

Chapter 6 Interacting with Locals

06.01 Vocabulary Hiring a Washerman

06.02 Practice 2 Part 1 Hiring a Washerman

06.03 Practice 5 Part 2 Hiring a Washerman

06.04 Vocabulary Reporting a Theft

06.05 Practice 3 Part 1 Reporting a Theft

06.06 Practice 6 Part 2 Reporting a Theft

06.07 Vocabulary At the Doctor's

06.08 Practice 2 Part 1 At the Doctor's

06.09 Practice 5 Part 1 At the Doctor's

06.10 Practice 6 Part 2 Follow-up
Appointment

06.11 Vocabulary Hiring a Maid

06.12 Practice 4 Part 1 Hiring a Maid

06-13 Part 1 Hiring a Maid

06.14 Practice 7

06.15 Practice 8 Part 2 Hiring a Maid

06.16 Vocabulary Car Trouble

06-17 Practice 4 Part 1 Car Trouble

06-18 Part 2 Car Trouble

Appendix Geography of India

A0-01